1500 color mixing recipes

FOR OIL • ACRYLIC • WATERCOLOR

Achieve precise color when painting
landscapes, portraits, still lifes, and more

WILLIAM F. POWELL

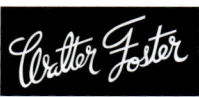

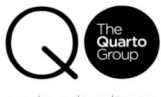

Brimming with creative inspiration, how-to projects, and useful information to enrich your everyday life, quarto.com is a favorite destination for those pursuing their interests and passions.

First published in 2021 by Walter Foster Publishing, an imprint of The Quarto Group. 100 Cummings Center, Suite 265D, Beverly, MA 01915, USA.
T (978) 282-9590 **F** (978) 283-2742 **www.quarto.com • www.walterfoster.com**

Walter Foster Publishing titles are also available at discount for retail, wholesale, promotional, and bulk purchase. For details, contact the Special Sales Manager by email at specialsales@quarto.com or by mail at The Quarto Group, Attn: Special Sales Manager, 100 Cummings Center, Suite 265D, Beverly, MA 01915, USA.

ISBN: 978-1-60058-896-9

Printed in Guangdong, China TT082025
10 9 8 7 6

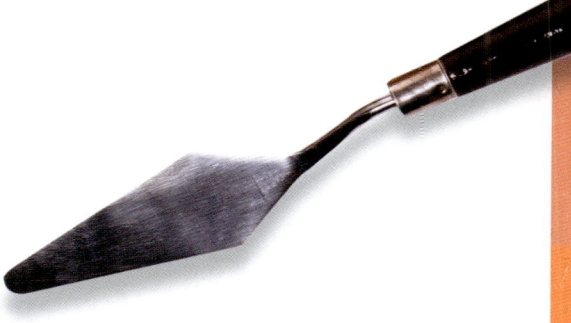

Contents

BEFOREYOUBEGIN

In this helpful guide, you will learn how to mix more than 1,500 paint colors across a variety of media and subject matter. For the best results, please read through the next four pages of information and instructions carefully.

This book is divided into four Color Mixing Recipes sections for

Oil & Acrylic (page 12)

Watercolor (page 42)

Portraits (page 72)

Landscapes (page 116)

Following these four sections are three subject-specific Color Indexes for

Oil, Acrylic & Watercolor (page 154)

Portraits (page 163)

Landscapes (page 164)

This book also includes two reusable acetate Color Mixing Grids: one for mixing oil & acrylic paint; the other for mixing watercolor. These are located in the envelope inside the back cover. See Instructions on page 6 for detailed information about how to use the grids.

Before you start experimenting with any of the recipes, familiarize yourself with some basic Color Theory concepts (page 8), which will help guide you to attaining successful mixes.

HOW TO USE THIS BOOK

The paint colors needed to complete the recipes in this book are listed at the beginning of each color mixing section. Additionally, the colors used to create the mixes shown on any given page are listed at the top of each page. While most oil and acrylic paint colors share the same names, there are exceptions. The Oil/Acrylic Conversion Chart on page 174 features a list of paint names for each medium, noting any differences.

Please note that paint manufacturers may change color names from time to time and/or discontinue some colors altogether. If you are unable to locate the precise color name that is listed in a recipe, we recommend an Internet search to identify the color in question, followed by a review of color palettes from your preferred paint manufacturer to find a suitable alternative. In order to maintain the integrity of the author's original color mixing recipes, we have chosen not to edit or change any color names that may have been discontinued since publication of the original text.

Important Note About Color Variations: Paint colors can vary somewhat among brands; there can also be slight variations in color appearance due to the offset printing process. Nevertheless, if you use the color samples as a general guide, follow the recipes, and use accurate paint and water measurements, you will achieve great success in mixing the beautiful colors featured in this book.

1500 COLOR MIXING RECIPES: A STEP-BY-STEP GUIDE

Step One Determine the media (oil, acrylic, or watercolor) and/or subjects (landscapes, portraits) for which you'd like to mix a color. We chose acrylic for demonstration purposes.

Step Two Turn to the relevant Color Index in the back of the book. In this case, it is the Color Index for Oil, Acrylic & Watercolor on page 154.

Step Three Locate the color and/or subject within the chosen Color Index. For example, in the Color Index for Oil, Acrylic & Watercolor, the subject "Broccoli" is located on page 155. Next, select the shade associated with the subject. For "Broccoli," there are two shades to choose from: "Brown 81" and "Green 71." Select the numbered recipe that you want to paint. Let's choose "71."

Step Four Next, turn to the section on Color Mixing Recipes for Oil & Acrylic and find recipe "71." You'll note a color swatch and the recipe mix, which is "1 cerulean blue," "3 Naples yellow," and "1 speck cadmium orange."

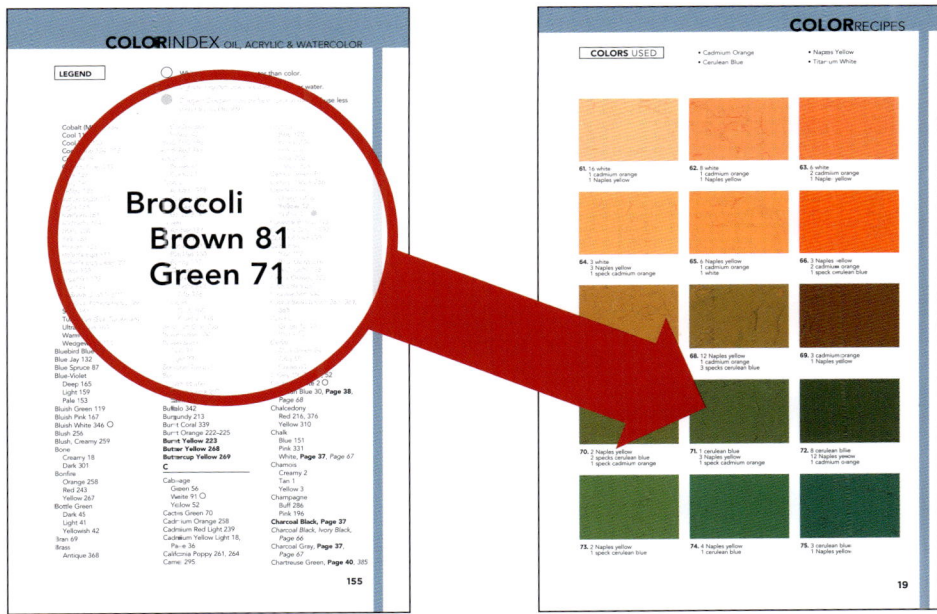

Step Five Select the appropriate acetate Color Mixing Grid for your media. Measure each of the recipe's colors on the grid according to the Instructions on page 6 and mix.

ADDITIONAL NOTES ABOUT THE COLOR INDEXES
- Unless otherwise noted, the recipe numbers are the same for both the Oil & Acrylic and Watercolor sections.
- Some index entries list page numbers instead of, or in addition to, recipe numbers; these are clearly indicated. Review the Legend at the top of the first page of each Index for more details.
- The Color Index for Portraits (page 163) includes the recipes for the Color Mixing for Portraits section. This is the only index that references only page numbers for the recipes.
- The Color Index for Landscapes (page 164) includes recipes for the Color Mixing for Landscapes section.

INSTRUCTIONS

HOW TO USE THE OIL & ACRYLIC MIXING GRID

Select the acetate Color Mixing Grid for Oil & Acrylic located in the envelope inside the back cover of this book. Use the Color Index to locate the recipe that you wish to mix.

Each square on the Color Mixing Grid represents one paint part. Recipes that call for a "speck" are measured at about the size of a large pinhead. These recipes are indicated with a dot • and are usually reserved for colors with more intensity.

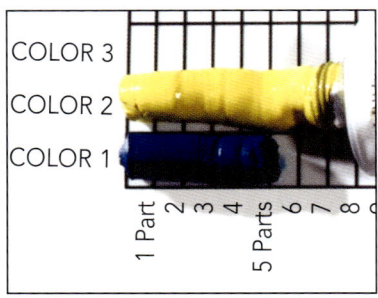

For example, Color Recipe #132 in the Landscape Color Recipes section calls for

2 white
2• cadmium yellow medium

Therefore, this recipe is 2 parts white, measured using two squares on the grid, and 2 specks (pinhead dots) measured in two squares on the grid.

Use your palette knife to transfer the mix to your mixing surface. Be sure to thoroughly clean your grid after every use.

Tip: When measuring using the grid, squeeze out paint in uniform widths and lengths, as much as possible, according to the recipe.

HOW TO USE THE WATERCOLOR MIXING GRID

Each watercolor recipe in this book indicates a specific Water Dilution Level, which increases or decreases a color's intensity. Level 1 is the thinnest, lightest intensity and requires the greatest amount of water. Level 2 is thin and light but calls for slightly less water than Level 1. Level 3 is medium intensity, requiring less water than Level 2. Level 4 is strong intensity, using just a small amount of water. Level 5 is the strongest intensity and needs little or no water. See the key at right for Water Level samples. Make sure to dilute your paint to the indicated level before using the grid to mix the color.

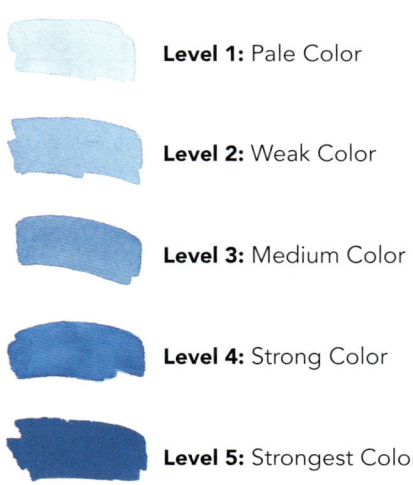

Level 1: Pale Color

Level 2: Weak Color

Level 3: Medium Color

Level 4: Strong Color

Level 5: Strongest Color

MEASURING THE COLORS

Select the acetate Color Mixing Grid for Watercolor located in the envelope inside the back cover of this book. The grid is divided into two sections. To mix larger amounts of paint, use the top section composed of ten rectangles. To mix smaller amounts of paint, use the bottom section composed of ten squares.

Each rectangle and each square represents 10% of the total mix. When the recipe calls for less than 10% of a color, use the smaller spaces on the grid (shown in the first rectangle in the top section and the first square in the bottom section). Each of these smaller spaces represents 1% of a color.

A recipe that calls for a "drop of paint" means that it is less than 1% of the mix. A drop of paint is about the size of a small bead of water. When using the top section of rectangles, a drop of paint should always be Water Level 5 (strongest color); when using the bottom section of squares, a drop always should be Water Level 4 (strong color).

MIXING THE PAINT ON THE GRID

Use the Color Index to locate the recipe that you wish to mix. For this demonstration, mix a large amount of color using the rectangles. Our Color Recipe is #45 in the Watercolor Recipes section (page 47).

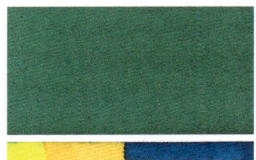

20% lemon yellow
30% cadmium yellow light
50% phthalo blue
Water Level 4

Dilute each of the paints to the stated Water Level before transferring the paint to the grid.

To create this, you'll mix 2 rectangles of lemon yellow (20%), 3 rectangles of cadmium yellow light (30%), and 5 rectangles of phthalo blue (50%). Next use a wet paintbrush to pull the diluted colors onto the grid in the suggested ratios; then mix the colors on the grid to achieve the desired color. Rinse and wipe the grid clean after every use.

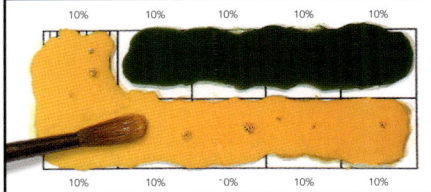

Filling the squares As you're measuring the paint on the grid (in this case, 60% cadmium yellow and 40% sap green), leave a bit of room between the colors to keep them from running into one another.

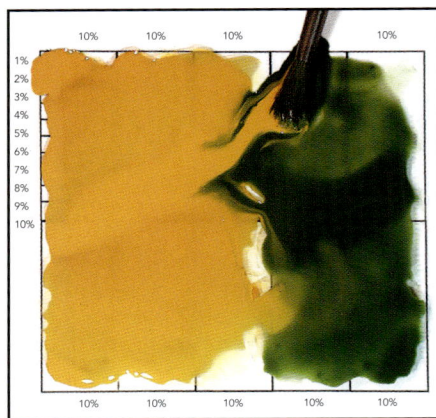

Using the grid as a palette Once you've finished measuring the paints on the grid, simply pull the colors together and mix them with your brush.

MIXES THAT CALL FOR OTHER RECIPE MIXES

Some of the color recipes in the book are made up of other color recipes. For example, Color Recipe #143 in the Oil & Acrylic section calls for 5 white, 4 recipe #138, and 1 recipe #150. This means you will first mix recipes #138 and #150 as instructed; then use each of them in the quantities indicated to create the new recipe #143.

COLORTHEORY

There are three things to consider when mixing colors: hue, value, and intensity (also known as **chroma**). **Hue** refers to the name of a pure color; **value** refers to the lightness or darkness of color; and **intensity** refers to the brightness or dullness of a color.

MIXING HUES

There are three **primary** colors (hues): yellow, red, and blue. All other colors are derived from these three hues.

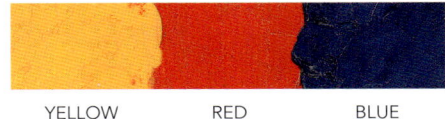

YELLOW   RED   BLUE

Mixing primary colors together results in a **secondary** color, as shown below.

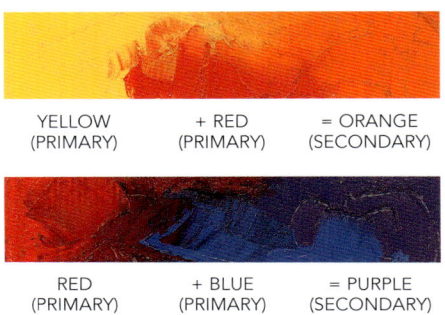

| YELLOW (PRIMARY) | + RED (PRIMARY) | = ORANGE (SECONDARY) |

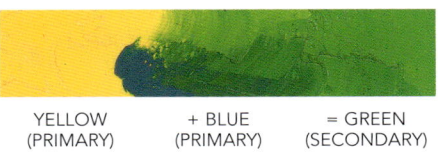

| YELLOW (PRIMARY) | + BLUE (PRIMARY) | = GREEN (SECONDARY) |

| RED (PRIMARY) | + BLUE (PRIMARY) | = PURPLE (SECONDARY) |

The secondary colors—orange, green, and purple—can be mixed with each other or any of the primary colors to create other colors.

Mixing a primary color—yellow, red, or blue—with a secondary color—orange, green, or purple—results in a third group known as **tertiary** colors. After mixing these colors, you can make a basic **color wheel** containing 12 major color groups. This makes a convenient chart that can be used as a working tool and reference guide for mixing colors and creating color palettes.

MIXING VALUES

Value is the lightness or darkness of a color. On the color wheel, yellow has the lightest value and purple has the darkest. Notice that the colors change in value, becoming lighter as they move up the color wheel and darker as they move down the color wheel.

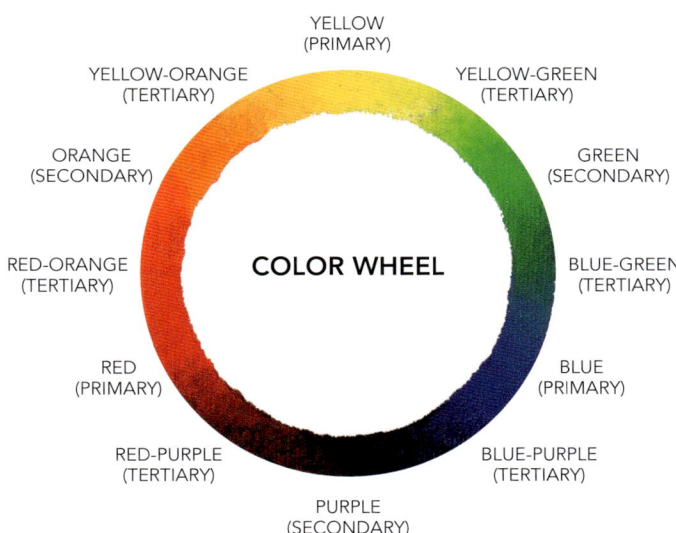

YELLOW (PRIMARY)
YELLOW-ORANGE (TERTIARY)
YELLOW-GREEN (TERTIARY)
ORANGE (SECONDARY)
GREEN (SECONDARY)
RED-ORANGE (TERTIARY)
BLUE-GREEN (TERTIARY)
COLOR WHEEL
RED (PRIMARY)
BLUE (PRIMARY)
RED-PURPLE (TERTIARY)
BLUE-PURPLE (TERTIARY)
PURPLE (SECONDARY)

MIXING TINTS, TONES, AND SHADES

Color is a phenomenon of light; without light there is no color. On the value scale of white to black, white is considered to be "light," and black is considered to be "dark." Dark is the absence of light and, therefore, the absence of color.

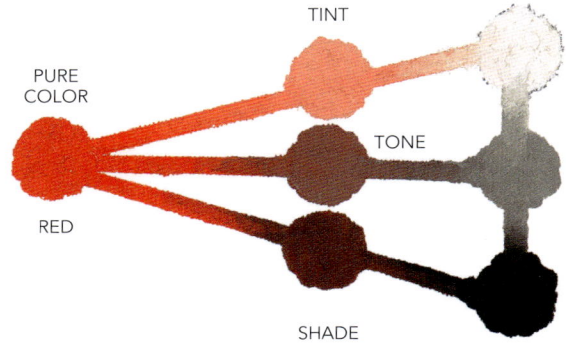

TINT

PURE COLOR

RED

TONE

SHADE

Adding white, or water for watercolors, to any color results in a **tint** of that color.

Adding gray to any color results in a **tone** of that color.

Adding black to any color results in a **shade** of that color.

Mixing white (or water) and black together in varying amounts creates a variety of grays known as the **value scale.** When a color is mixed with black, it is a **cool value** mix. A **warm value** mix can be made by using a dark warm color, such as burnt umber or a mix of burnt umber and ultramarine blue.

A painting done solely in white, black, and different values of gray is known as an **achromatic** painting. A painting done with tints, tones, and shades (along with various intensities) of a single color is known as a **monochromatic** painting.

KEEPING COLOR MIXES FRESH AND LIVELY

Color mixes can be kept "fresh" and less dull by following the two simple rules shown below.

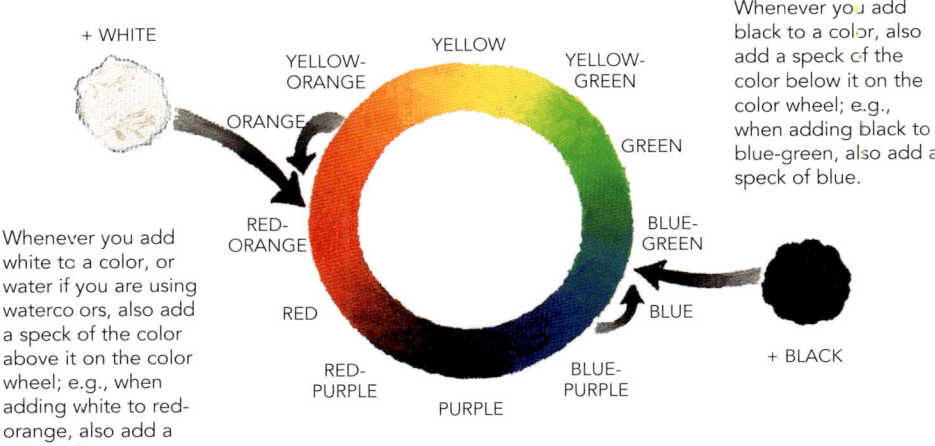

+ WHITE

YELLOW-ORANGE

YELLOW

YELLOW-GREEN

ORANGE

GREEN

RED-ORANGE

BLUE-GREEN

RED

BLUE

RED-PURPLE

BLUE-PURPLE

PURPLE

+ BLACK

Whenever you add black to a color, also add a speck of the color below it on the color wheel; e.g., when adding black to blue-green, also add a speck of blue.

Whenever you add white to a color, or water if you are using watercolors, also add a speck of the color above it on the color wheel; e.g., when adding white to red-orange, also add a speck of orange.

Whenever you add white (or water) or black to a color, the extra color selected from either above or below the color should be close to the color on the wheel. If you choose a color too far away, you will make a new color. The two colors should be analogous. (Colors that resemble one another but are slightly different and are close to each other on the color wheel are called **analogous** colors.)

COLORTHEORY

INTENSITY OR CHROMA

Bright colors, such as cadmium orange, are considered more **chromatic** than dull colors, such as burnt umber. The brighter, more chromatic colors are on the outer edge of the color wheel; the duller, less chromatic colors are on the inner circles. Notice that burnt umber (a less chromatic color) is a member of the yellow-orange family and that it is a complement to blue. It is important to know where each color fits on the color wheel.

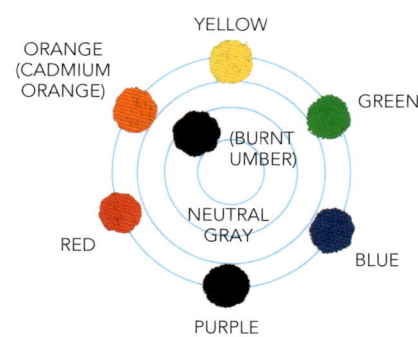

GRAYING COLORS NATURALLY

As explained on page 9, adding black, white, water, or values in between to a color results in shades, tints, and tones, respectively. This does not, however, produce a "natural" graying of colors. To obtain beautiful, **natural grays** of colors, you can use the color wheel and the following rules regarding **complements.**

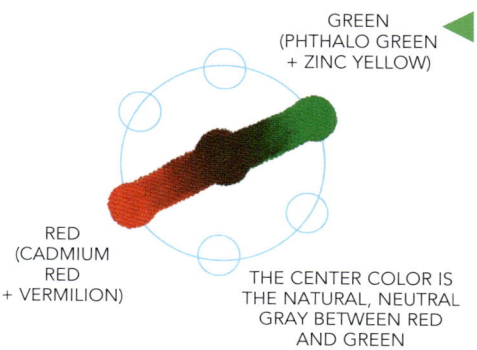

THE CENTER COLOR IS THE NATURAL, NEUTRAL GRAY BETWEEN RED AND GREEN

◀ MIXING DIRECT COMPLEMENTS

As shown at left, two colors that are directly across from each other on the color wheel are called **direct complements.** Direct complements can neutralize (gray) one another better than any other colors on the wheel. Mixing varying amounts of each color creates a natural graying of each color.

MIXING SPLIT COMPLEMENTS ◀

As shown at right, using the colors on each side of a color's direct complement provides a wider range of color mixes and a variety of neutral grays. This is known as a **split complement** mixture.

ORANGE
(CADMIUM
ORANGE)

CENTER COLOR IS THE
NATURAL, NEUTRAL
GRAY

BLUE-GREEN
(MANGANESE
BLUE)

BLUE-PURPLE
(ULTRAMARINE BLUE
+ SPECK PURPLE)

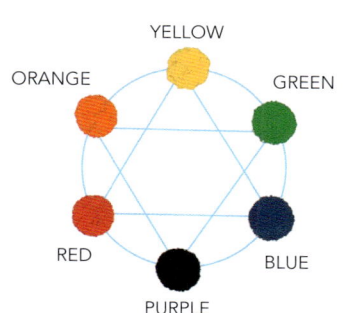

◀ MIXING TRIADS

As shown at left, a combination of any three colors equally distant from one another on the color wheel is known as a **triad.** A triad allows for a broader range of color mixes, yet maintains a true color harmony. Move the triad clockwise to the next three colors to produce a different combination of colors.

WARM AND COOL COLORS

Generally colors on the left side of the wheel (with the red family of colors) are considered **warm** colors, and colors on the right side of the wheel (with the blue family of colors) are considered **cool** colors.

Within all families of colors, however, there are both warm and cool colors. For instance, a blue that contains more red (purplish blue) is warmer than a blue that contains yellow (greenish blue). On the other side of the wheel, a red that contains more blue (purplish red) is cooler than a red that contains yellow (orangish red).

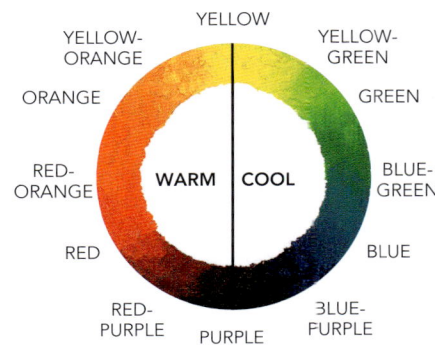

KEY COLOR HARMONY

The **key color** is the dominant color in a painting or in several different color mixtures. The key color is sometimes referred to as the "mother color" because a bit of the color is added to all of the mixtures to create color unity and harmony.

COLOR PSYCHOLOGY

Color psychology is a rather complex subject. Color affects our reactions, emotions, and feelings. Different people, however, may react differently to the same color or colors. For example, red may be a favorite color for some, blue or green for others. A few simple points on color psychology and the typical reactions to certain colors are illustrated below.

Dark colors, such as purples and deep blues, are considered moody or sometimes even threatening.

When bright, raw colors are placed next to one another, they appear loud, gaudy, and harsh. This is demonstrated here with the combination of blue, red, and green.

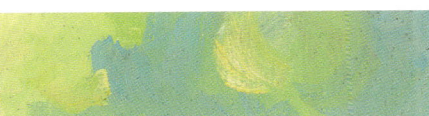

Light, bright colors are usually considered pleasant colors. If they aren't too bright, they are comfortable to view.

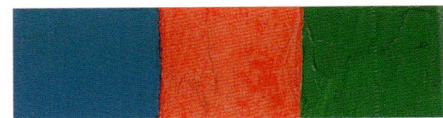

HIGH KEY AND LOW KEY USE OF COLOR

A painting that contains a lot of white and can be compared to the lighter end of the value scale is called a **high key** painting. A painting that contains a lot of black and darks and can be compared to the darker end of the value scale is called a **low key** painting.

Color Mixing for
Oil & Acrylic

PAINT COLORS NEEDED

You will need all of the following colors for the recipes in this section. Note: Some acrylic color names will vary depending on the manufacturer; also, some of these colors are not available in acrylic and must be mixed. Please refer to the Oil/Acrylic Conversion Chart (page 174).

Alizarin crimson

Burnt sienna

Burnt umber

Cadmium orange

Cadmium red light

Cadmium vermilion

Cadmium yellow medium

Cadmium yellow light

Cerulean blue

Chrome oxide green

Cobalt blue

Cobalt violet

Ivory black

Magenta

Mauve

Naples yellow

Permanent blue

Permanent green light

Phthalo blue

Phthalo green

Phthalo red rose

Phthalo yellow-green

Raw sienna

Titanium white

Ultramarine blue

Venetian red

Vermilion

Viridian green

Yellow ochre

Zinc yellow

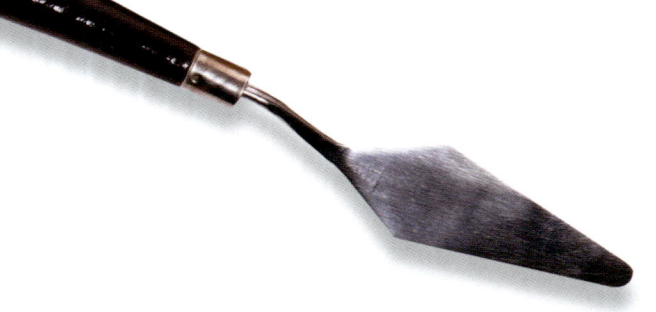

Contents

COLORS USED

- Cadmium Yellow Light
- Cadmium Yellow Medium
- Naples Yellow
- Titanium White

1. 6 white
1 Naples yellow
1 speck cadmium yellow light

2. 18 white
1 cadmium yellow medium

3. 9 white
1 cadmium yellow light

4. 4 white
1 Naples yellow
1 speck cadmium yellow light

5. 10 white
1 cadmium yellow medium

6. 6 white
1 cadmium yellow light

7. 4 white
2 Naples yellow
1 cadmium yellow light

8. 5 white
1 cadmium yellow medium

9. 4 white
1 cadmium yellow light

10. 4 white
4 Naples yellow
1 cadmium yellow light

11. 3 white
1 cadmium yellow medium

12. 2 white
1 cadmium yellow light

13. 8 Naples yellow
2 white
1 cadmium yellow light

14. 1 white
1 cadmium yellow medium

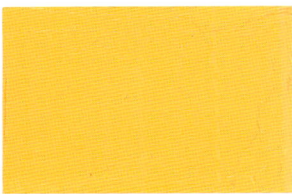

15. 1 white
1 cadmium yellow light

COLORS USED

- Cadmium Yellow Light
- Cerulean Blue
- Titanium White

16. 5 white
1 cadmium yellow light

17. 1 white
1 cadmium yellow light

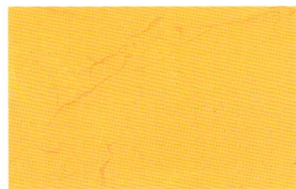

18. Cadmium yellow light (pure)

19. 5 white
1 cadmium yellow light
1 speck cerulean blue

20. 16 white
16 cadmium yellow light
1 cerulean blue

21. 16 cadmium yellow light
1 cerulean blue

22. 5 white
1 cadmium yellow light
2 specks cerulean blue

23. 8 white
8 cadmium yellow light
1 cerulean blue

24. 8 cadmium yellow light
1 cerulean blue

25. 10 white
2 cadmium yellow light
1 cerulean blue

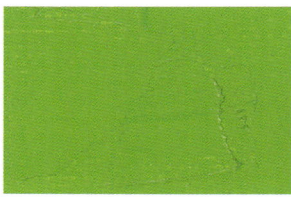

26. 16 white
16 cadmium yellow light
3 cerulean blue

27. 4 white
4 cadmium yellow light
1 cerulean blue

28. 15 white
4 cadmium yellow light
3 cerulean blue

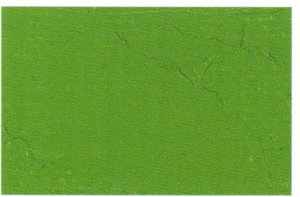

29. 4 white
4 cadmium yellow light
2 cerulean blue

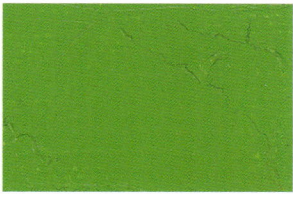

30. 3 white
3 cadmium yellow light
2 cerulean blue

- Phthalo Blue
- Titanium White
- Zinc Yellow

31. 5 white
1 zinc yellow

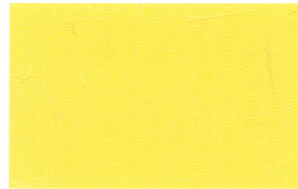

32. 1 white
1 zinc yellow

33. Zinc yellow (pure)

34. 5 white
1 zinc yellow
1 speck phthalo blue

35. 4 white
4 zinc yellow
1 speck phthalo blue

36. 5 zinc yellow
1 speck phthalo blue

37. 5 white
1 zinc yellow
2 specks phthalo blue

38. 4 white
4 zinc yellow
2 specks phthalo blue

39. 5 zinc yellow
2 specks phthalo blue

40. 5 white
1 zinc yellow
3 specks phthalo blue

41. 4 white
4 zinc yellow
3 specks phthalo blue

42. 16 zinc yellow
1 phthalo blue

43. 20 white
4 zinc yellow
1 phthalc blue

44. 16 white
16 zinc yellow
1 phthalo blue

45. 8 zinc yellow
1 phthalo blue

COLORRECIPES

COLORS USED

- Cadmium Yellow Medium
- Titanium White
- Viridian Green

46. 9 white
1 cadmium yellow medium

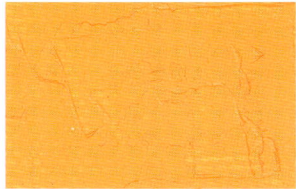

47. 2 white
1 cadmium yellow medium

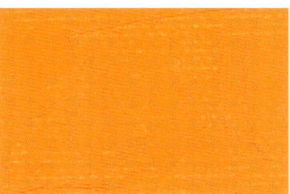

48. 1 white
4 cadmium yellow medium

49. 9 white
1 cadmium yellow medium
1 speck viridian green

50. 2 white
1 cadmium yellow medium
1 speck viridian green

51. 1 white
4 cadmium yellow medium
1 speck viridian green

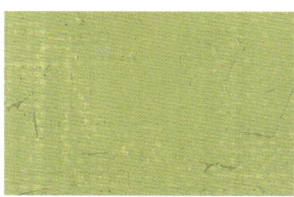

52. 18 white
2 cadmium yellow medium
1 viridian green

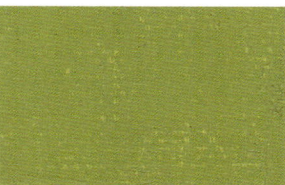

53. 8 white
4 cadmium yellow medium
1 viridian green

54. 2 white
8 cadmium yellow medium
1 viridian green

55. 9 white
1 cadmium yellow medium
1 viridian green

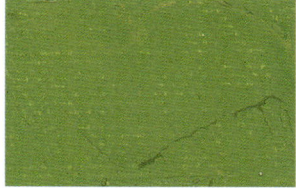

56. 4 white
2 cadmium yellow medium
1 viridian green

57. 1 white
4 cadmium yellow medium
1 viridian green

58. 9 white
1 cadmium yellow medium
2 viridian green

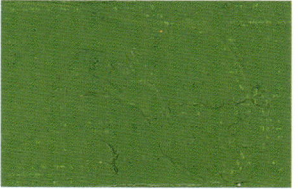

59. 2 white
1 cadmium yellow medium
1 viridian green

60. 1 white
4 cadmium yellow medium
2 viridian green

COLORS USED

- Cadmium Orange
- Cerulean Blue
- Naples Yellow
- Titanium White

61. 16 white
1 cadmium orange
1 Naples yellow

62. 8 white
1 cadmium orange
1 Naples yellow

63. 6 white
2 cadmium orange
1 Naples yellow

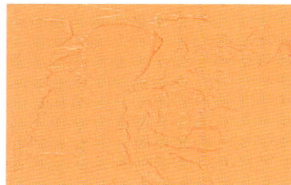

64. 3 white
3 Naples yellow
1 speck cadmium orange

65. 6 Naples yellow
1 cadmium orange
1 white

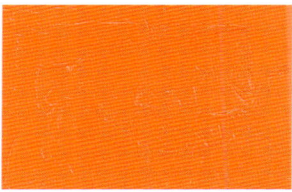

66. 3 Naples yellow
2 cadmium orange
1 speck cerulean blue

67. 3 Naples yellow
1 speck cadmium orange
1 speck cerulean blue

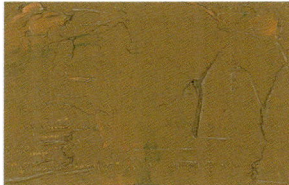

68. 12 Naples yellow
1 cadmium orange
3 specks cerulean blue

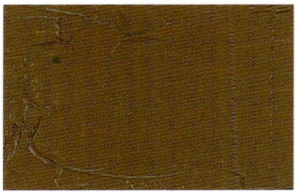

69. 3 cadmium orange
1 Naples yellow

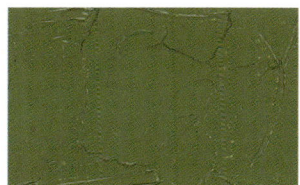

70. 2 Naples yellow
2 specks cerulean blue
1 speck cadmium orange

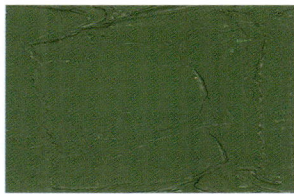

71. 1 cerulean blue
3 Naples yellow
1 speck cadmium orange

72. 8 cerulean blue
12 Naples yellow
1 cadmium orange

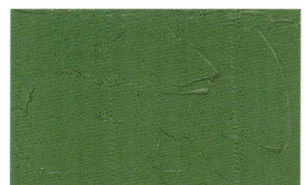

73. 2 Naples yellow
1 speck cerulean blue

74. 4 Naples yellow
1 cerulean blue

75. 3 cerulean blue
1 Naples yellow

COLORRECIPES

COLORS USED

- Phthalo Blue
- Raw Sienna
- Titanium White
- Zinc Yellow

76. 3 white
4 specks raw sienna
1 speck zinc yellow

77. 3 white
1 raw sienna
1 speck zinc yellow

78. 4 white
5 raw sienna

79. 8 white
4 zinc yellow
1 raw sienna

80. 6 recipe #77
1 recipe #90
5 specks zinc yellow

81. 2 recipe #78
1 speck recipe #90

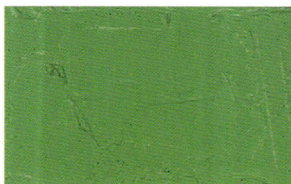

82. 5 white + 2 zinc yellow
1 speck recipe #90
1 speck raw sienna

83. 4 white + 8 recipe #90
2 raw sienna
1 zinc yellow

84. 2 recipe #78
1 recipe #90

85. 3 white
4 specks recipe #90
1 speck zinc yellow

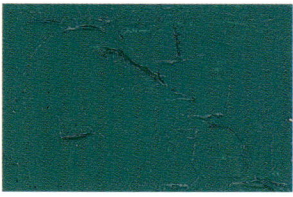

86. 1 white + 1 recipe #90
1 speck raw sienna
1 speck zinc yellow

87. 5 recipe #90
2 recipe #78

88. 8 white
1 recipe #90
4 specks zinc yellow

89. 1 recipe #90
2 white
1 speck raw sienna

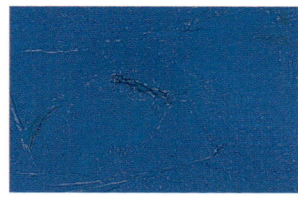

90. 1 white
1 phthalo blue

- Burnt Umber
- Naples Yellow
- Phthalo Blue
- Titanium White

91. 15 white
1 tiny speck recipe #105
1 tiny speck Naples yellow

92. 20 white
1 speck recipe #105
1 speck Naples yellow

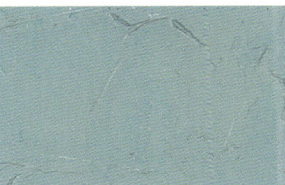

93. 15 white
1 speck recipe #105

94. 13 white
1 speck recipe #105
2 specks Naples yellow

95. 20 white
1 recipe #105
1 Naples yellow

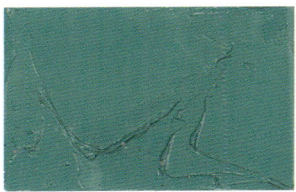

96. 14 white
1 recipe #105

97. 10 white
1 speck recipe #105
3 specks Naples yellow

98. 10 white
1 recipe #105
2 Naples yellow

99. 7 white
1 recipe #105

100. 17 white
1 recipe #105
3 Naples yellow

101. 5 white
1 recipe #105
3 Naples yellow

102. 3 white
1 recipe #105

103. 9 white
1 recipe #105
3 Naples yellow

104. 1 white
1 recipe #105
2 Naples yellow

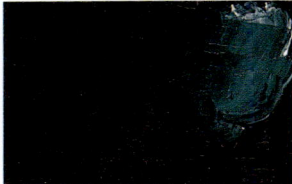

105. 2 burnt umber
1 phthalo blue

COLORRECIPES

COLORS USED

- Phthalo Blue
- Phthalo Green
- Titanium White

106. 14 white
1 speck phthalo green

107. 1 recipe #106
1 recipe #108

108. 14 white
1 speck phthalo blue

109. 12 white
2 specks phthalo green

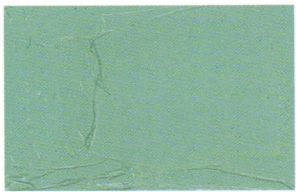

110. 1 recipe #109
1 recipe #111

111. 12 white
2 specks phthalo blue

112. 10 white
3 specks phthalo green

113. 1 recipe #112
1 recipe #114

114. 10 white
3 specks phthalo blue

115. 15 white
1 phthalo green

116. 1 recipe #115
1 recipe #117

117. 15 white
1 phthalo blue

118. 6 white
1 phthalo green

119. 1 recipe #118
1 recipe #120

120. 6 white
1 phthalo blue

COLORS USED

- Alizarin Crimson
- Cerulean Blue
- Permanent Blue
- Titanium White

121. 8 white
1 speck cerulean blue

122. 3 white
1 recipe #134

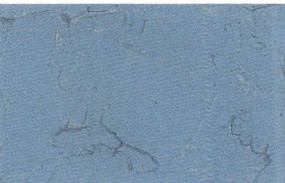

123. 18 white
1 permanent blue

124. 3 white
1 cerulean blue

125. 2 white
1 recipe #134

126. 2 white
1 permanent blue
1 speck alizarin crimson

127. 2 white
1 cerulean blue

128. 1 white
1 recipe #134
1 speck alizarin crimson

129. 3 white
2 permanent blue
1 speck alizarin crimson

130. 2 cerulean blue
1 white

131. 2 white
3 recipe #134
2 specks alizarin crimson

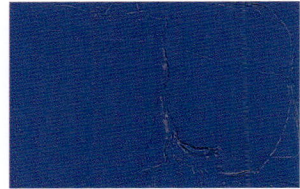

132. 2 permanent blue
1 white
1 speck alizarin crimson

133. 4 cerulean blue
1 speck white
1 speck alizarin crimson

134. 1 permanent blue
1 cerulean blue
1 speck white

135. 3 permanent blue
1 white
1 speck alizarin crimson

COLORS USED

- Alizarin Crimson
- Burnt Umber
- Permanent Blue
- Titanium White

136. 5 white
3 specks recipe #138

137. 2 white
2 recipe #138
1 recipe #150

138. 1 white
5 permanent blue

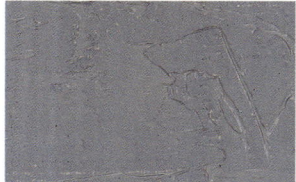

139. 4 white
1 speck recipe #138
1 speck recipe #150

140. 2 white
3 recipe #138
4 specks recipe #150

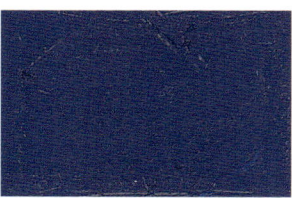

141. 3 white
6 recipe #138
1 recipe #150

142. 6 white
4 recipe #138
1 recipe #150

143. 5 white
4 recipe #138
1 recipe #150

144. 1 white
6 recipe #138
2 recipe #150

145. 4 white
6 recipe #138
1 recipe #150

146. 5 white
4 recipe #138
2 recipe #150

147. 3 white
6 recipe #138
3 recipe #150

148. 3 white
4 recipe #138
2 recipe #150

149. 2 white
5 permanent blue
3 recipe #150

150. 8 burnt umber
8 alizarin crimson
3 white

- Phthalo Red Rose
- Titanium White
- Ultramarine Blue

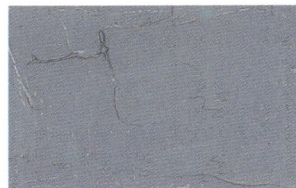
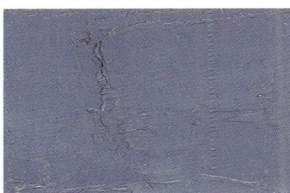

151. 6 white
1 speck ultramarine blue

152. 6 white
1 speck ultramarine blue
1 speck phthalo red rose

153. 6 white
1 speck ultramarine blue
2 specks phthalo red rose

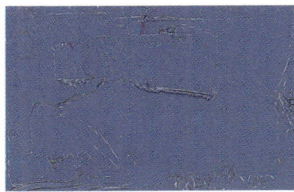

154. 4 white
1 ultramarine blue

155. 4 white
1 ultramarine blue
2 specks phthalo red rose

156. 4 white
1 ultramarine blue
1 phthalo red rose

157. 3 white
2 ultramarine blue

158. 6 white
4 ultramarine blue
1 phthalo red rose

159. 3 white
2 ultramarine blue
2 phthalo red rose

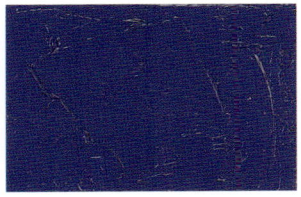

160. 2 white
3 ultramarine blue

161. 2 white
3 ultramarine blue
2 specks phthalo red rose

162. 2 white
3 ultramarine blue
1 phthalo red rose

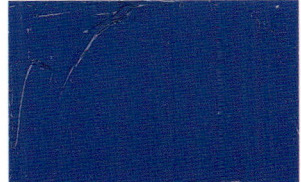

163. 1 white
3 ultramarine blue

164. 1 white
3 ultramarine blue
2 specks phthalo red rose

165. 1 white
3 ultramarine blue
1 phthalo red rose

COLORS USED

- Cobalt Violet
- Magenta
- Permanent Blue
- Titanium White

166. 10 white
1 cobalt violet
1 speck permanent blue

167. 10 white
1 cobalt violet

168. 20 white
1 magenta

169. 10 white
2 cobalt violet
1 permanent blue

170. 5 white
1 cobalt violet

171. 9 white
1 magenta

172. 6 white
2 cobalt violet
1 permanent blue

173. 3 white
1 cobalt violet

174. 4 white
1 magenta

175. 3 white
2 cobalt violet
1 permanent blue

176. 3 white
2 cobalt violet

177. 2 white
1 magenta

178. 1 white
2 cobalt violet
1 permanent blue

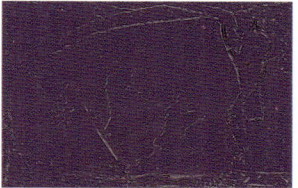

179. 1 white
2 cobalt violet

180. 1 white
2 magenta

COLORS USED

- Alizarin Crimson
- Cobalt Violet
- Phthalo Red Rose
- Titanium White

181. 5 white
1 speck phthalo red rose
1 speck cobalt violet

182. 5 white
1 speck phthalo red rose

183. 5 white
1 speck alizarin crimson

184. 8 white
2 phthalo red rose
1 cobalt violet

185. 4 white
1 phthalo red rose

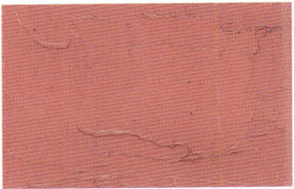

186. 14 white
1 alizarin crimson

187. 8 white
8 phthalo red rose
1 cobalt violet

188. 1 white
1 phthalo red rose

189. 12 white
2 alizarin crimson
1 phthalo red rose

190. 4 white
6 phthalo red rose
1 cobalt violet

191. 2 white
3 phthalo red rose

192. 12 white
6 alizarin crimson
1 phthalo red rose

193. 1 white
4 phthalo red rose
1 cobalt violet

194. 1 white
4 phthalo red rose

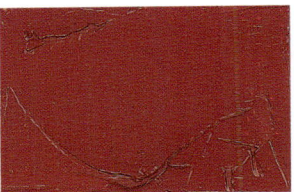

195. 12 white
10 alizarin crimson
1 phthalo red rose

- Burnt Sienna
- Burnt Umber
- Titanium White
- Venetian Red

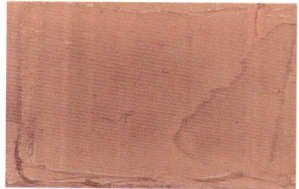

196. 5 white
1 speck Venetian red

197. 5 white
1 speck burnt umber

198. 6 white
1 burnt sienna

199. 5 white
2 specks Venetian red

200. 10 white
1 burnt umber

201. 4 white
1 burnt sienna

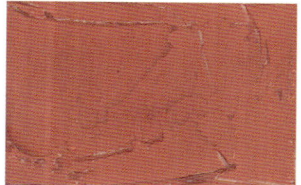

202. 5 white
3 specks Venetian red

203. 6 white
1 burnt umber

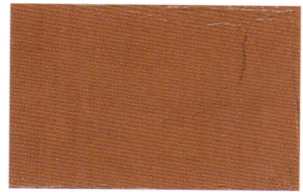

204. 2 white
1 burnt sienna

205. 12 white
1 Venetian red

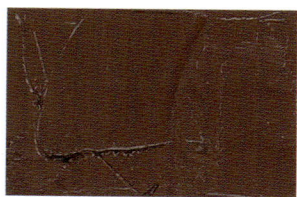

206. 4 white
1 burnt umber

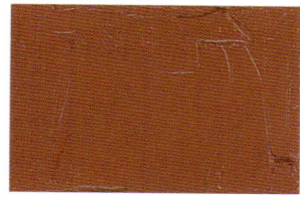

207. 1 white
1 burnt sienna

208. 3 white
1 Venetian red

209. 2 white
1 burnt umber

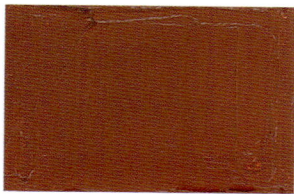

210. 1 white
2 burnt sienna

COLORS USED

- Alizarin Crimson
- Cadmium Yellow Light
- Titanium White

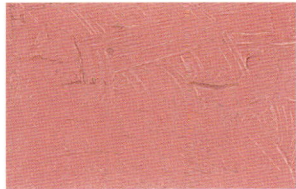

211. 20 white
1 alizarin crimson

212. 9 white
2 alizarin crimson

213. 1 white
3 alizarin crimson

214. 20 white
1 alizarin crimson
1 cadmium yellow light

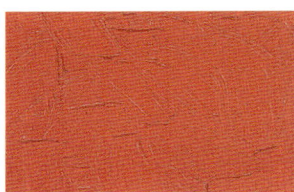

215. 11 white
3 alizarin crimson
5 cadmium yellow light

216. 1 white
3 alizarin crimson
2 cadmium yellow light

217. 20 white
1 alizarin crimson
3 cadmium yellow light

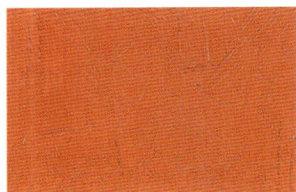

218. 9 white
2 alizarin crimson
5 cadmium yellow light

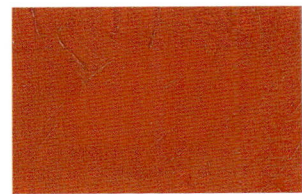

219. 1 white
3 alizarin crimson
9 cadmium yellow light

220. 20 white
1 alizarin crimson
7 cadmium yellow light

221. 4 white
1 alizarin crimson
5 cadmium yellow light

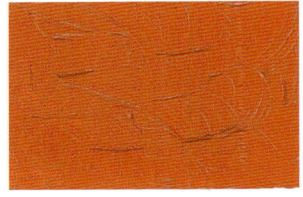

222. 1 white
3 alizarin crimson
11 cadmium yellow light

223. 20 white
1 alizarin crimson
20 cadmium yellow light

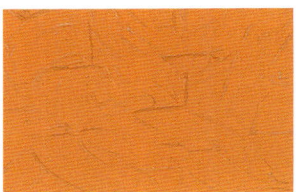

224. 4 white
1 alizarin crimson
12 cadmium yellow light

225. 1 white
3 alizarin crimson
18 cadmium yellow light

COLORS USED

- Cadmium Red Light
- Cadmium Vermilion
- Titanium White
- Yellow Ochre

226. 21 white
1 cadmium vermilion

227. 20 white
1 cadmium red light

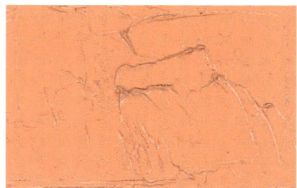
228. 6 white
1 recipe #240

229. 14 white
1 cadmium vermilion

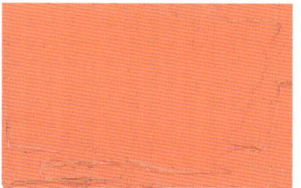
230. 7 white
1 cadmium red light

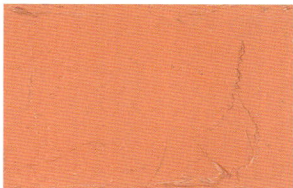
231. 4 white
1 recipe #240

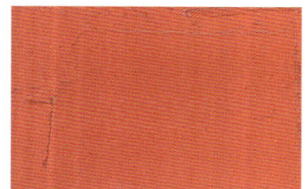
232. 3 white
1 cadmium vermilion

233. 2 white
1 cadmium red light

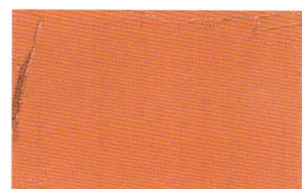
234. 2 white
1 recipe #240

235. 1 white
1 cadmium vermilion

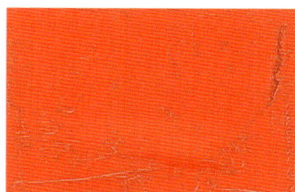
236. 1 white
2 cadmium red light

237. 1 white
1 recipe #240

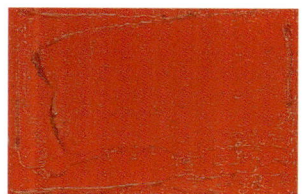
238. Cadmium vermilion (pure)

239. Cadmium red light (pure)

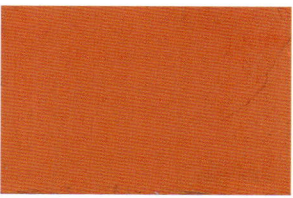
240. 1 yellow ochre
1 cadmium red light

COLORS USED

- Cadmium Red Light
- Titanium White
- Zinc Yellow

241. 18 white
1 cadmium red light

242. 8 white
2 cadmium red light

243. 2 white
4 cadmium red light

244. 18 white
1 cadmium red light
2 zinc yellow

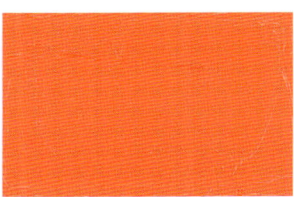

245. 16 white
4 cadmium red light
3 zinc yellow

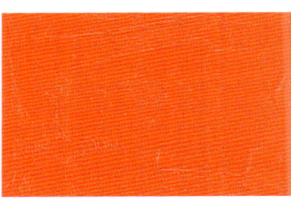

246. 2 white
4 cadmium red light
4 zinc yellow

247. 18 white
1 cadmium red light
4 zinc yellow

248. 8 white
2 cadmium red light
4 zinc yellow

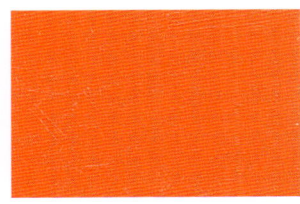

249. 2 white
4 cadmium red light
14 zinc yellow

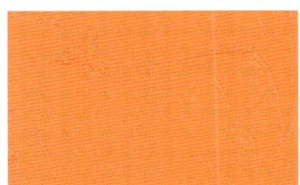

250. 18 white
1 cadmium red light
9 zinc yellow

251. 8 white
2 cadmium red light
7 zinc yellow

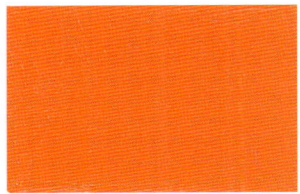

252. 1 white
2 cadmium red light
10 zinc yellow

253. 18 white
1 cadmium red light
18 zinc yellow

254. 4 white
1 cadmium red light
7 zinc yellow

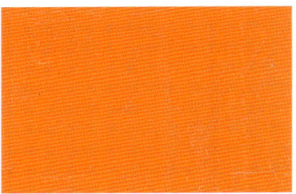

255. 1 white
2 cadmium red light
15 zinc yellow

COLORS USED

- Cadmium Orange
- Titanium White
- Zinc Yellow

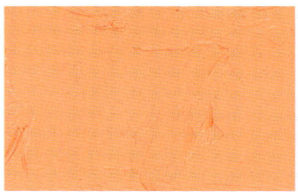

256. 10 white
1 cadmium orange

257. 4 white
1 cadmium orange

258. Cadmium orange (pure)

259. 10 white
1 cadmium orange
1 zinc yellow

260. 4 white
1 cadmium orange
1 zinc yellow

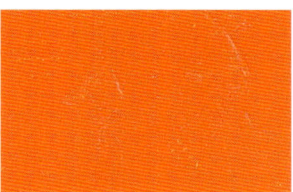

261. 2 zinc yellow
1 cadmium orange

262. 11 white
1 cadmium orange
3 zinc yellow

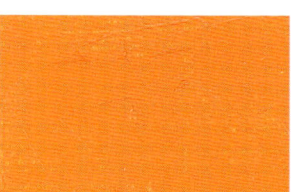

263. 8 white
2 cadmium orange
3 zinc yellow

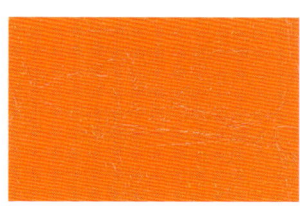

264. 7 zinc yellow
2 cadmium orange

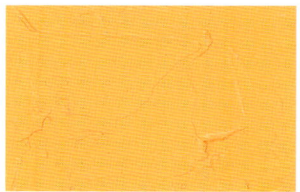

265. 8 white
1 cadmium orange
6 zinc yellow

266. 9 white
2 cadmium orange
3 zinc yellow

267. 5 zinc yellow
2 cadmium orange

268. 2 white
1 zinc yellow
1 speck cadmium orange

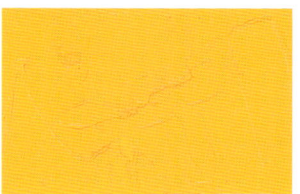

269. 9 white
2 cadmium orange
3 zinc yellow

270. 5 zinc yellow
3 specks cadmium orange

COLORS USED

- • Cadmium Orange
- • Permanent Green Light
- • Titanium White

271. 16 white
1 cadmium orange

272. 4 white
1 cadmium orange

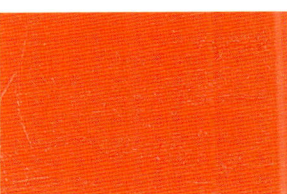

273. 2 white
2 cadmium orange

274. 32 white
2 cadmium orange
1 permanent green l ght

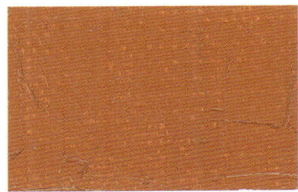

275. 8 white
2 cadmium orange
1 permanent green light

276. 2 white
2 cadmium orange
1 permanent green light

277. 16 white
1 cadmium orange
1 permanent green light

278. 8 white
2 cadmium orange
3 permanent green light

279. 2 white
2 cadmium orange
2 permanent green light

280. 32 wh te
2 cadmium orange
3 permanent green lig┐t

281. 8 white
2 cadmium orange
5 permanent green light

282. 2 white
2 cadmium orange
3 permanent green light

283. 32 whitə
2 cadmium orange
5 permanent green ligh┌

284. 4 white
1 cadmium orange
3 permanent green light

285. 4 white
4 cadmium orange
9 permanent green light

- Titanium White
- Ultramarine Blue
- Yellow Ochre

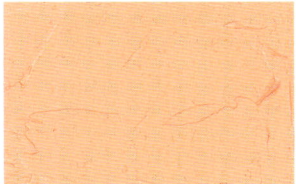

286. 8 white
1 yellow ochre

287. 8 white
1 yellow ochre
1 speck ultramarine blue

288. 8 white
1 yellow ochre
3 specks ultramarine blue

289. 5 white
2 yellow ochre

290. 5 white
2 yellow ochre
2 specks ultramarine blue

291. 5 white
3 yellow ochre
1 ultramarine blue

292. 6 white
3 yellow ochre

293. 6 white
3 yellow ochre
1 ultramarine blue

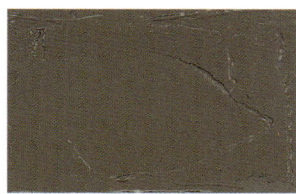

294. 6 white
4 yellow ochre
1 ultramarine blue

295. 1 white
2 yellow ochre

296. 4 white
8 yellow ochre
3 ultramarine blue

297. 2 white
5 yellow ochre
3 ultramarine blue

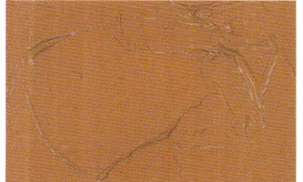

298. 1 white
5 yellow ochre

299. 5 yellow ochre
1 ultramarine blue

300. 2 yellow ochre
1 ultramarine blue

COLORS USED

- Burnt Sienna
- Cadmium Red Light
- Naples Yellow
- Titanium White

301. 3 white
1 Naples yellow

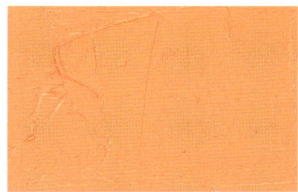

302. 2 white
2 Naples yellow
1 speck cadmium red light

303. 2 white + 2 Naples yellow
1 speck cadmium red light
1 speck burnt sienna

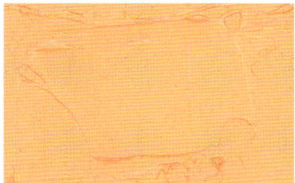

304. 5 white
5 Naples yellow

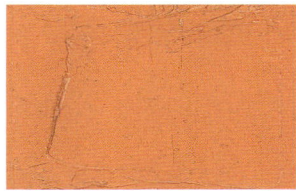

305. 1 white
4 Naples yellow
2 specks cadmium red light

306. 1 white + 5 Naples yellow
1 speck cadmium red light
2 specks burnt sienna

307. 5 Naples yellow
1 white

308. 4 white
24 Naples yellow
1 cadmium red light

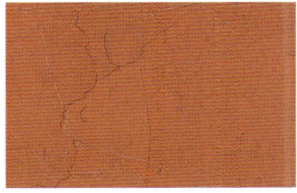

309. 1 white + 5 Naples yellow
1 burnt sienna
1 speck cadmium red light

310. 3 Naples yellow
1 speck burnt sienna

311. 4 white + 24 Naples yellow
1 cadmium red light
3 specks burnt sienna

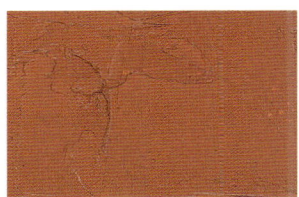

312. 2 white + 12 Naples yellow
1 cadmium red light
2 burnt sienna

313. 4 Naples yellow
1 burnt sienna

314. 2 Naples yellow
1 burnt sienna
1 speck cadmium red light

315. 2 Naples yellow
2 burnt sienna
1 speck cadmium red light

VALUERECIPES

COLORS USED

White has been added at the bottom of each color to show the tint of the color.

- Cadmium Yellow Light
- Ivory Black
- Titanium White

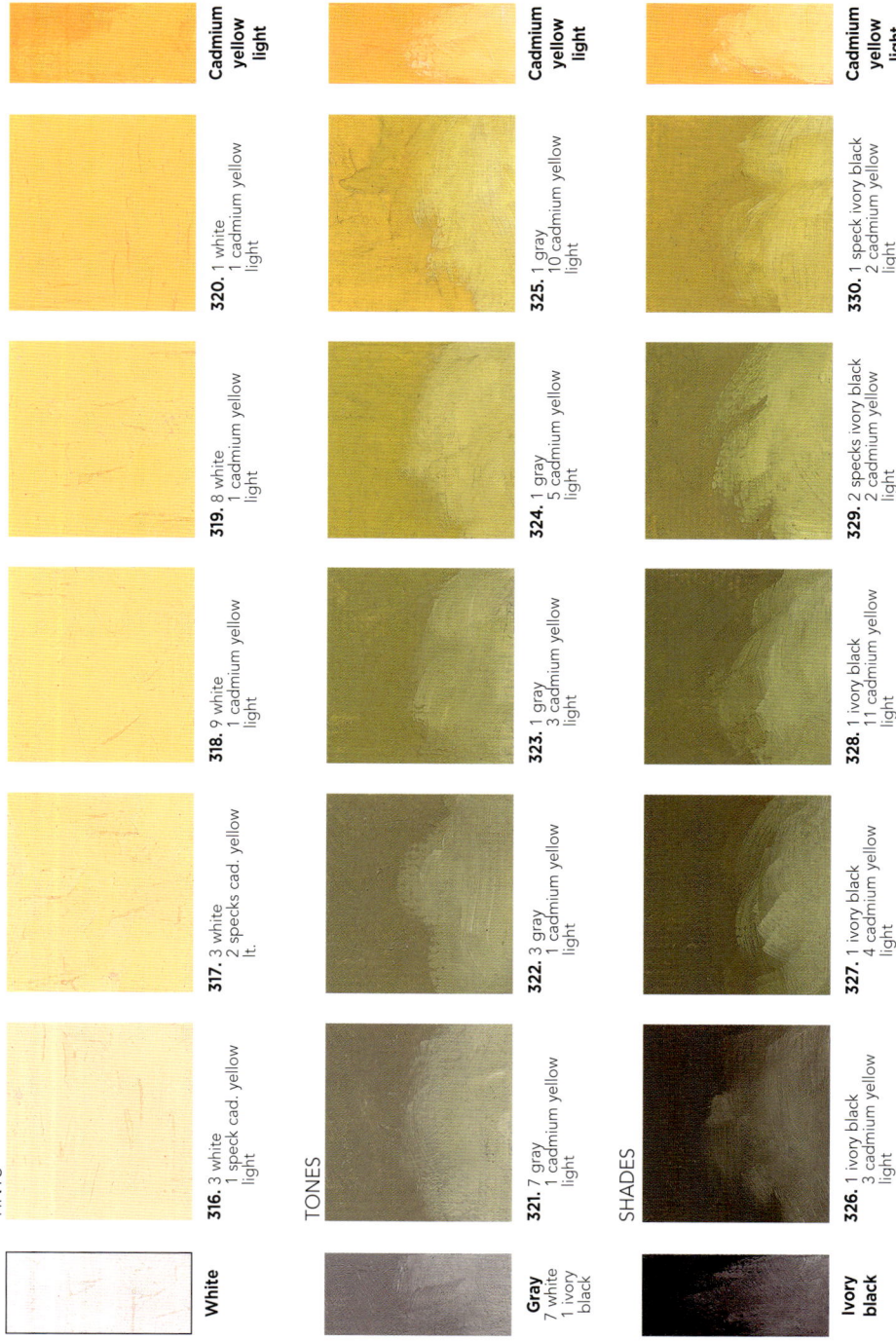

Cadmium yellow light

320. 1 white
1 cadmium yellow light

319. 8 white
1 cadmium yellow light

318. 9 white
1 cadmium yellow light

317. 3 white
2 specks cad. yellow lt.

316. 3 white
1 speck cad. yellow light

TINTS

White

Cadmium yellow light

325. 1 gray
10 cadmium yellow light

324. 1 gray
5 cadmium yellow light

323. 1 gray
3 cadmium yellow light

322. 3 gray
1 cadmium yellow light

321. 7 gray
1 cadmium yellow light

TONES

Gray
7 white
1 ivory black

Cadmium yellow light

330. 1 speck ivory black
2 cadmium yellow light

329. 2 specks ivory black
2 cadmium yellow light

328. 1 ivory black
11 cadmium yellow light

327. 1 ivory black
4 cadmium yellow light

326. 1 ivory black
3 cadmium yellow light

SHADES

Ivory black

COLORS USED

White has been added at the bottom of each color to show the tint of the color.

- Ivory Black
- Titanium White
- Vermilion

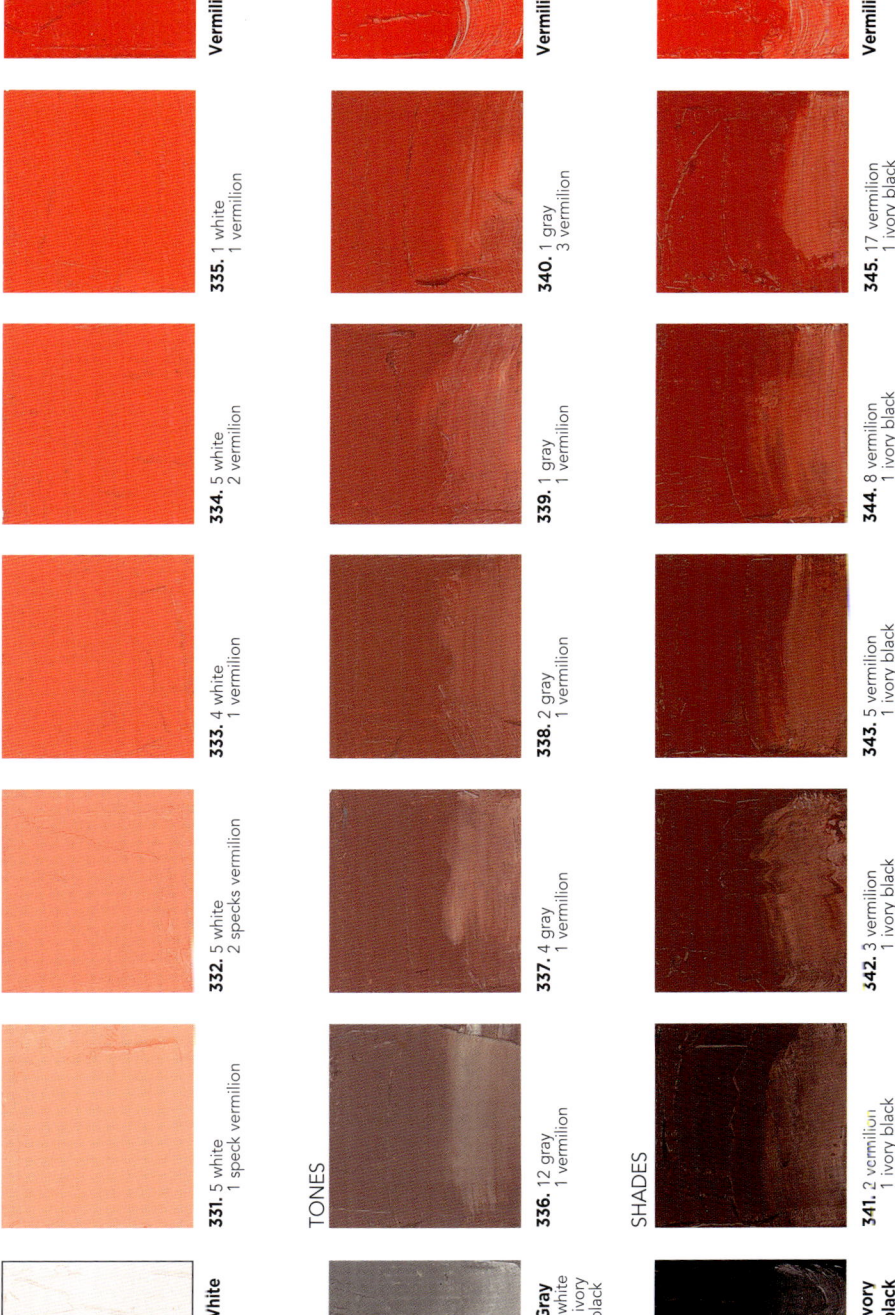

Vermilion

335. 1 white 1 vermilion

334. 5 white 2 vermilion

333. 4 white 1 vermilion

332. 5 white 2 specks vermilion

331. 5 white 1 speck vermilion

TINTS

White

Vermilion

340. 1 gray 3 vermilion

339. 1 gray 1 vermilion

338. 2 gray 1 vermilion

337. 4 gray 1 vermilion

336. 12 gray 1 vermilion

TONES

Gray 7 white 1 ivory black

Vermilion

345. 17 vermilion 1 ivory black

344. 8 vermilion 1 ivory black

343. 5 vermilion 1 ivory black

342. 3 vermilion 1 ivory black

341. 2 vermilion 1 ivory black

SHADES

Ivory black

COLORS USED

White has been added at the bottom of each color to show the tint of the color.

- Cerulean Blue
- Ivory Black
- Titanium White

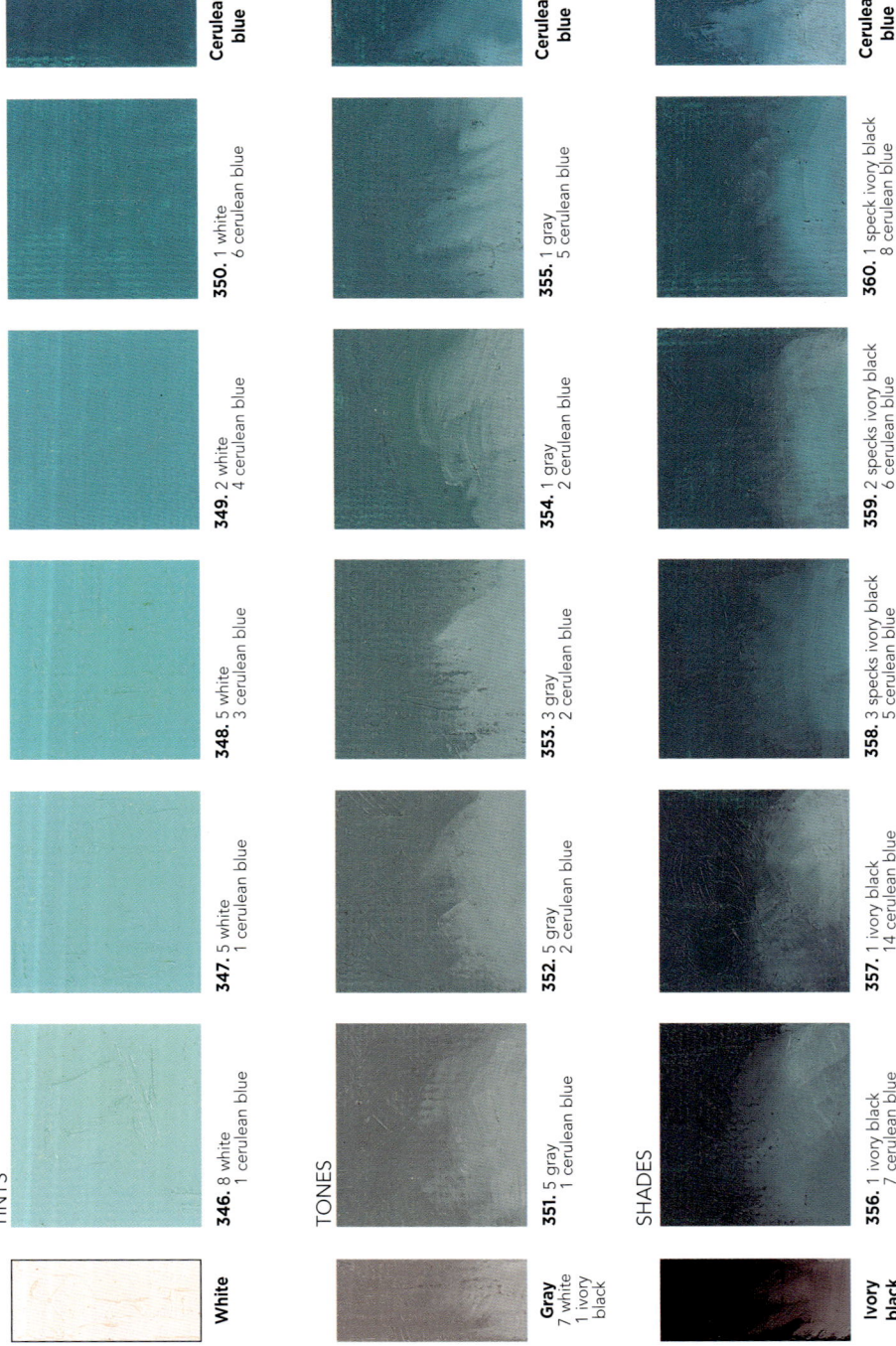

Cerulean blue

350. 1 white 6 cerulean blue

349. 2 white 4 cerulean blue

348. 5 white 3 cerulean blue

347. 5 white 1 cerulean blue

346. 8 white 1 cerulean blue

TINTS

White

Cerulean blue

355. 1 gray 5 cerulean blue

354. 1 gray 2 cerulean blue

353. 3 gray 2 cerulean blue

352. 5 gray 2 cerulean blue

351. 5 gray 1 cerulean blue

TONES

Gray 7 white 1 ivory black

Cerulean blue

360. 1 speck ivory black 8 cerulean blue

359. 2 specks ivory black 6 cerulean blue

358. 3 specks ivory black 5 cerulean blue

357. 1 ivory black 14 cerulean blue

356. 1 ivory black 7 cerulean blue

SHADES

Ivory black

GRAYING WITH COMPLEMENTS

COLORS USED

White has been added at the bottom of each color to show the tint of the color.

- Cadmium Orange
- Cadmium Yellow Medium
- Cadmium Yellow Pale

- Cerulean Blue
- Cobalt Violet
- Mauve

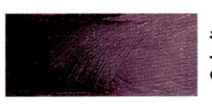
Cobalt violet

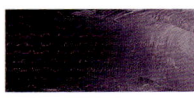
Mauve

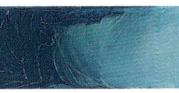
Cerulean blue

365. 1 cadmium yellow pale / 4 cobalt violet

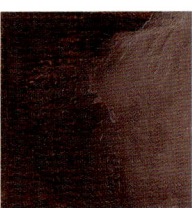
370. 1 cad. yellow medium / 2 mauve

375. 1 cadmium orange / 4 cerulean blue

364. 1 cadmium yellow pale / 1 cobalt violet

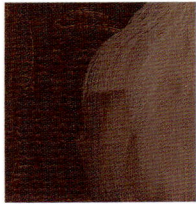
369. 1 cad. yellow medium / 1 mauve

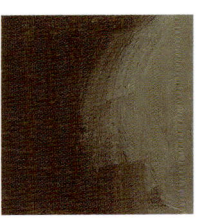
374. 1 cadmium orange / 2 cerulean blue

363. 4 cadmium yellow pale / 1 cobalt violet

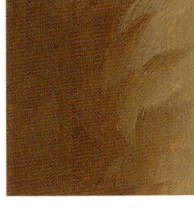

368. 4 cad. yellow medium / 1 mauve

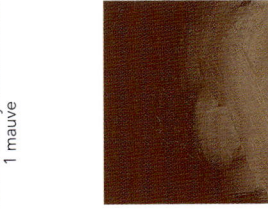
373. 1 cadmium orange / 1 cerulean blue

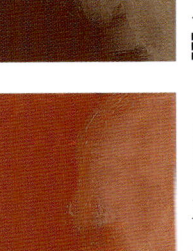
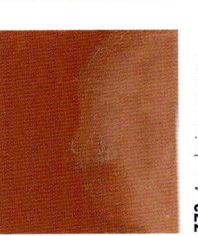

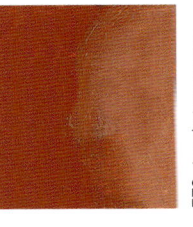
362. 7 cadmium yellow pale / 1 cobalt violet

367. 9 cad. yellow medium / 1 mauve

372. 4 cadmium orange / 1 cerulean blue

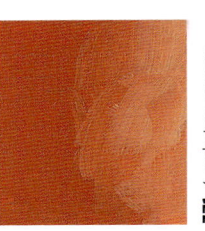
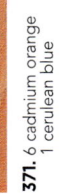
371. 6 cadmium orange / 1 cerulean blue

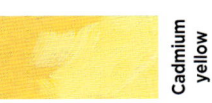
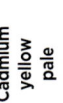
361. 1 cadmium yellow pale / 2 specks cobalt violet

Cadmium yellow pale

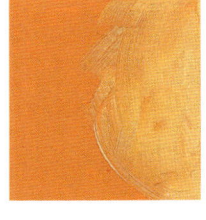
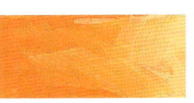
366. 2 cad. yellow medium / 1 speck mauve

Cadmium yellow medium

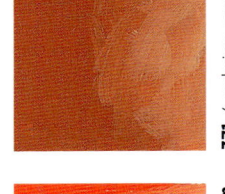
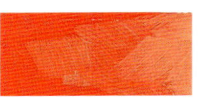
Cadmium orange

39

COLORS USED

White has been added at the bottom of each color to show the tint of the color.

- Alizarin Crimson
- Cadmium Red Light
- Cobalt Violet
- Permanent Green Light
- Phthalo Yellow-Green
- Zinc Yellow

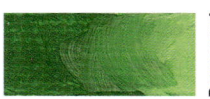
Permanent green light

Phthalo yellow-green

Zinc yellow

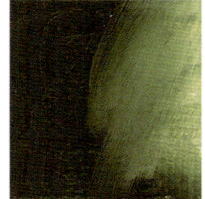
380. 1 speck cad. red light 1 permanent green light

385. 1 speck alizarin crimson 4 phthalo yellow-green

390. 1 speck cobalt violet 3 zinc yellow

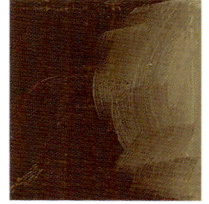
379. 1 speck cad. red light 3 permanent green light

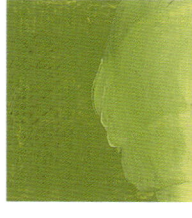
384. 1 speck alizarin crimson 3 phthalo yellow-green

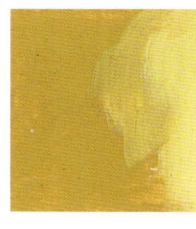
389. 1 speck cobalt violet 2 zinc yellow

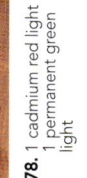
378. 1 cadmium red light 1 permanent green light

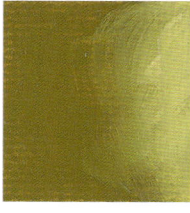
383. 2 specks aliz. crimson 1 phthalo yellow-green

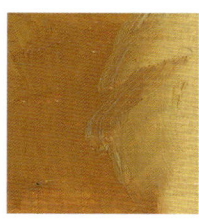
388. 2 cobalt violet 9 zinc yellow

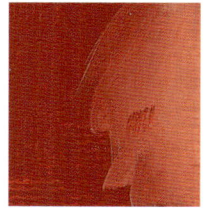
377. 2 cadmium red light 1 permanent green light

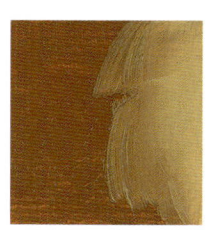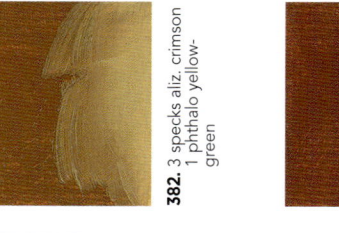
382. 3 specks aliz. crimson 1 phthalo yellow-green

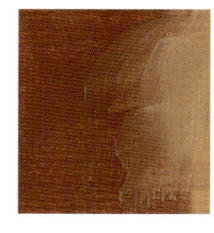
387. 1 cobalt violet 4 zinc yellow

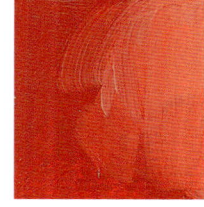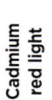
376. 1 cadmium red light 3 specks perm. green lt.

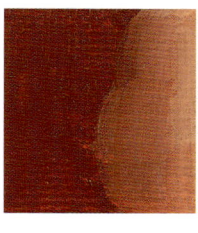
381. 1 alizarin crimson 4 phthalo yellow-green

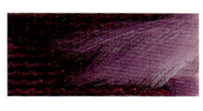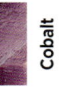
386. 2 cobalt violet 4 zinc yellow

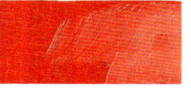
Cadmium red light

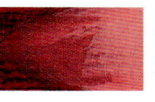
Alizarin crimson

Cobalt violet

Color Mixing for
Watercolor

PAINT COLORS NEEDED

Below you'll find all of the paint colors needed to create the color recipes in this section. Keep in mind that some color names will vary depending on the manufacturer. As you follow the recipes, you may also find that hues and strengths vary slightly from brand to brand, so you may need to adjust the recipes accordingly.

Burnt sienna

Burnt umber

Cadmium orange

Cadmium red light

Cadmium yellow

Cadmium yellow deep

Cadmium yellow light

Cadmium yellow medium

Cadmium yellow pale

Cerulean blue

Cobalt blue

Dioxazine violet

Gamboge

Hooker's green

Indian red

Ivory black

Lemon yellow

Mauve

Naples yellow

Permanent alizarin crimson

Permanent rose

Phthalo blue

Raw sienna

Sap green

Ultramarine blue

Vermilion

Viridian green

Yellow ochre

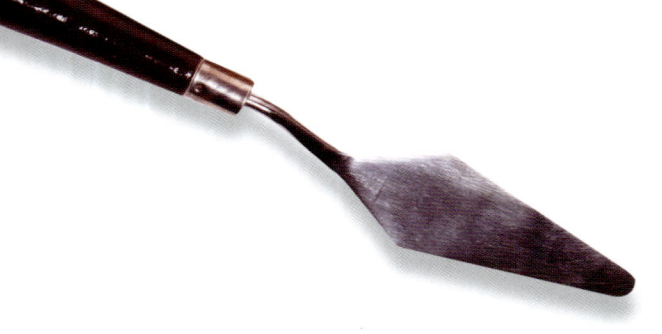

Contents

COLORS USED

- Cadmium Yellow Light
- Cadmium Yellow Medium
- Naples Yellow

1. 25% cadmium yellow light
75% Naples yellow
Water Level 1

2. 95% cadmium yellow medium
5% Naples yellow
Water Level 1

3. 100% cadmium yellow light
Water Level 1

4. 25% cadmium yellow light
75% Naples yellow
Water Level 1.5

5. 95% cadmium yellow medium
5% Naples yellow
Water Level 1.5

6. 100% cadmium yellow light
Water Level 1.5

7. 25% cadmium yellow light
75% Naples yellow
Water Level 2

8. 95% cadmium yellow medium
5% Naples yellow
Water Level 1.75

9. 100% cadmium yellow light
Water Level 1.75

10. 25% cadmium yellow light
75% Naples yellow
Water Level 2.5

11. 95% cadmium yellow medium
5% Naples yellow
Water Level 2

12. 100% cadmium yellow light
Water Level 2.5

13. 25% cadmium yellow light
75% Naples yellow
Water Level 3

14. 95% cadmium yellow medium
5% Naples yellow
Water Level 3

15. 100% cadmium yellow light
Water Level 3

COLORS USED

- Cadmium Yellow Light
- Cerulean Blue
- Lemon Yellow

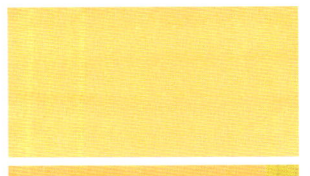

16. 90% cadmium yellow light
10% lemon yellow
Water Level 2.5

17. 100% cadmium yellow light
Water Level 3.5

18. 100% cadmium yellow light
Water Level 5

19. 30% cadmium yellow light
65% lemon yellow
5% cerulean blue
Water Level 2

20. 70% cadmium yellow light
15% lemon yellow
15% cerulean blue
Water Level 3

21. 70% cadmium yellow light
20% lemon yellow
10% cerulean blue
Water Level 2.5

22. 10% cadmium yellow light
65% lemon yellow
25% cerulean blue
Water Level 2.5

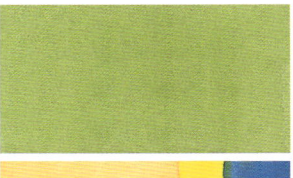

23. 60% cadmium yellow light
15% lemon yellow
25% cerulean blue
Water Level 3

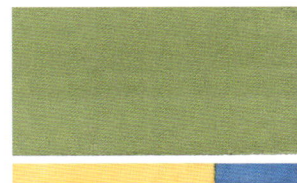

24. 65% cadmium yellow light
5% lemon yellow
30% cerulean blue
Water Level 3

25. 5% cadmium yellow light
70% lemon yellow
25% cerulean blue
Water Level 3

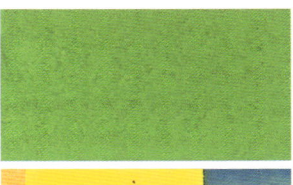

26. 10% cadmium yellow light
60% lemon yellow
30% cerulean blue
Water Level 3

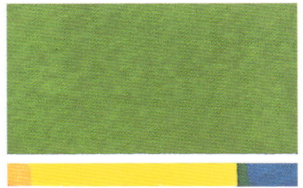

27. 10% cadmium yellow light
70% lemon yellow
20% cerulean blue
Water Level 3.5

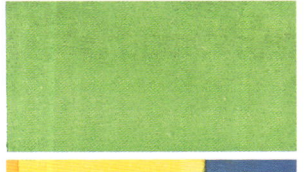

28. 5% cadmium yellow light
65% lemon yellow
30% cerulean blue
Water Level 3.5

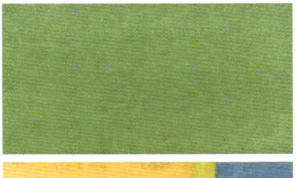

29. 60% cadmium yellow light
5% lemon yellow
35% cerulean blue
Water Level 3

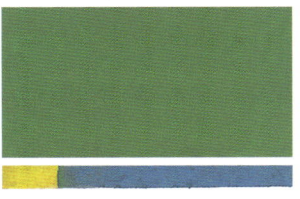

30. 20% lemon yellow
80% cerulean blue
Water Level 4

COLORS USED

- Cadmium Yellow Light
- Lemon Yellow
- Phthalo Blue

31. 65% lemon yellow
35% cadmium yellow light
Water Level 1

32. 65% lemon yellow
35% cadmium yellow light
Water Level 2

33. 65% lemon yellow
35% cadmium yellow light
Water Level 3.5

34. 88% lemon yellow
10% cadmium yellow light
2% phthalo blue
Water Level 2

35. 75% lemon yellow
20% cadmium yellow light
5% phthalo blue
Water Level 2

36. 75% lemon yellow
20% cadmium yellow ight
5% phthalo blue
Water Level 2.5

37. 85% lemon yellow
10% cadmium yellow light
5% phthalo blue
Water Level 2.5

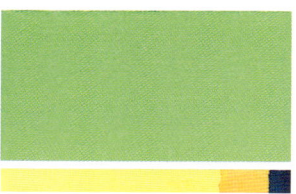

38. 80% lemon yellow
15% cadmium yellow light
5% phthalo blue
Water Level 2.5

39. 80% lemon yellow
15% cadmium yellow light
5% phthalo blue
Water Level 3

40. 85% lemon yellow
10% cadmium yellow light
5% phthalo blue
Water Level 3

41. 80% lemon yellow
10% cadmium yellow light
10% phthalo blue
Water Level 3

42. 50% lemon yellow
35% cadmium yellow light
15% phthalo blue
Water Level 3

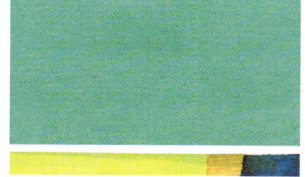

43. 70% lemon yellow
10% cadmium yellow light
20% phthalo blue
Water Level 3.5

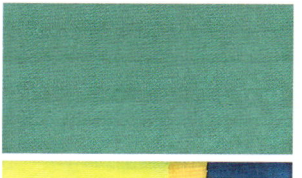

44. 60% lemon yellow
10% cadmium yellow light
30% phthalo blue
Water Level 4

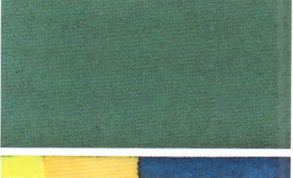

45. 20% lemon yellow
30% cadmium yellow light
50% phthalo blue
Water Level 4

COLORRECIPES

COLORS USED

- Cadmium Yellow Deep
- Cadmium Red Light
- Cobalt Blue
- Gamboge
- Permanent Rose
- Raw Sienna
- Viridian Green

46. 80% gamboge
20% raw sienna
Water Level 1

47. 80% gamboge
20% raw sienna
Water Level 2

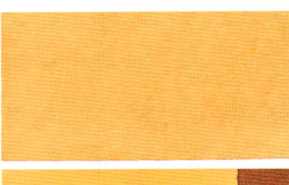

48. 80% gamboge
20% raw sienna
Water Level 3

49. 80% gamboge
19% raw sienna
1% viridian green
Water Level 1

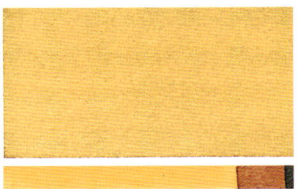

50. 80% gamboge
19% raw sienna
1% viridian green
Water Level 2

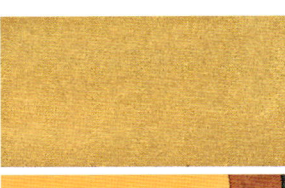

51. 80% gamboge
19% raw sienna
1% viridian green
Water Level 3

52. 98% gamboge
2% viridian green
Water Level 1

53. 95% gamboge
5% viridian green
Water Level 2

54. 90% gamboge
5% raw sienna
5% viridian green
Water Level 3

55. 30% gamboge
68% viridian green
2% permanent rose
Water Level 2.5

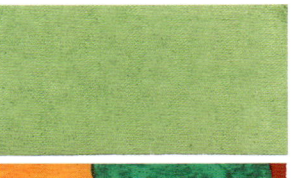

56. 35% cadmium yellow deep
60% viridian green
5% cadmium red light
Water Level 3

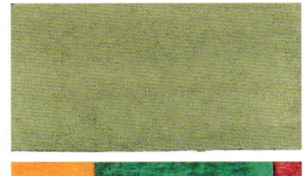

57. 30% cadmium yellow deep
60% viridian green
10% permanent rose
Water Level 3

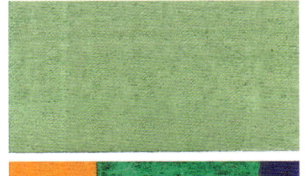

58. 20% cadmium yellow deep
60% viridian green
20% cobalt blue
Water Level 3

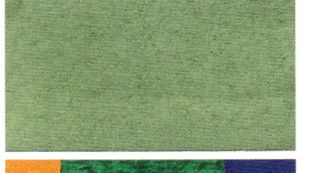

59. 20% cadmium yellow deep
55% viridian green
25% cobalt blue
Water Level 3

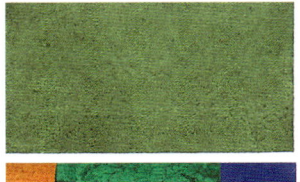

60. 20% cadmium yellow deep
55% viridian green
25% cobalt blue
Water Level 4

COLORS USED

- Burnt Umber
- Cadmium Orange
- Cadmium Red Light
- Cadmium Yellow Deep
- Cerulean Blue
- Naples Yellow
- Phthalo Blue
- Ultramarine Blue

61. 50% cadmium orange
50% cadmium red light
Water Level 1

62. 50% cadmium orange
50% cadmium red light
Water Level 2

63. 50% cadmium orange
50% cadmium red light
Water Level 3

64. 40% cadmium orange
60% cadmium red light
Water Level 1

65. 40% cadmium orange
60% cadmium red light
Water Level 2

66. 30% cadmium orange
70% cadmium red light
Water Level 2.5

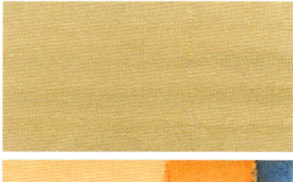

67. 60% Naples yellow
30% cadmium orange
10% cerulean blue
Water Level 2

68. 60% Naples yellow
25% cadmium orange
15% cerulean blue
Water Level 3

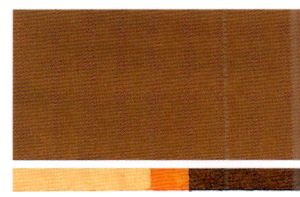

69. 50% Naples yellow
10% cadmium orange
40% burnt umber
Water Level 3

70. 30% cerulean blue
60% Naples yellow
10% cadmium orange
Water Level 3

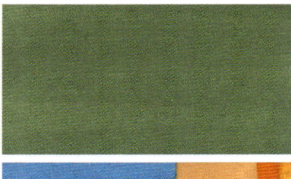

71. 60% cerulean blue
30% Naples yellow
7% cadmium orange
3% cadmium yellow deep
Water Level 3

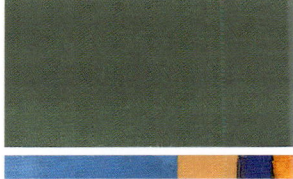

72. 60% cerulean blue
20% Naples yellow
10% ultramarine blue
10% cadmium yellow deep
Water Level 3.5

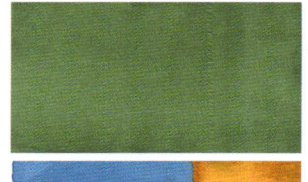

73. 60% cerulean blue
40% cadmium yellow deep
Water Level 3

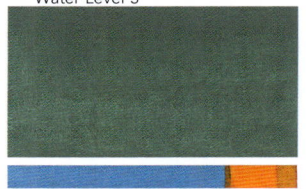

74. 80% cerulean blue
15% cadmium orange
5% cadmium yellow deep
Water Level 3

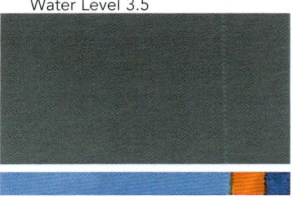

75. 80% cerulean blue
10% cadmium orange
10% phthalo blue
Water Level 3

COLORS USED

- Burnt Sienna
- Burnt Umber
- Gamboge
- Lemon Yellow
- Phthalo Blue
- Raw Sienna

76. 85% gamboge
15% raw sienna
Water Level 1

77. 80% raw sienna
20% burnt umber
Water Level 2

78. 75% raw sienna
25% burnt umber
Water Level 3

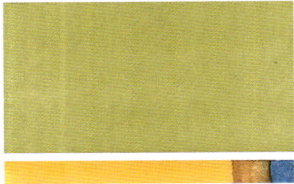

79. 80% gamboge
10% raw sienna
10% phthalo blue
Water Level 1

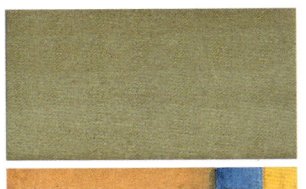

80. 75% raw sienna
15% phthalo blue
10% gamboge
Water Level 2

81. 65% raw sienna
15% burnt sienna
20% phthalo blue
Water Level 3

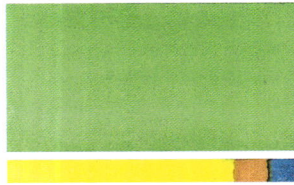

82. 80% lemon yellow
10% raw sienna
10% phthalo blue
Water Level 2

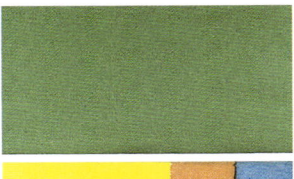

83. 60% lemon yellow
20% raw sienna
20% phthalo blue
Water Level 3

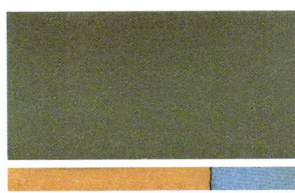

84. 70% raw sienna
30% phthalo blue
Water Level 3

85. 95% phthalo blue
5% lemon yellow
Water Level 2

86. 90% phthalo blue
5% raw sienna
5% lemon yellow
Water Level 3

87. 95% phthalo blue
5% raw sienna
Water Level 4

88. 100% phthalo blue
2 drops lemon yellow
Water Level 2

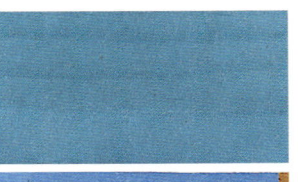

89. 100% phthalo blue
3 drops raw sienna
Water Level 3

90. 100% phthalo blue
Water Level 4

- Burnt Sienna
- Burnt Umber
- Lemon Yellow
- Naples Yellow
- Phthalo Blue
- Yellow Ochre

91. 1 drop recipe #105
1 drop lemon yellow
Water Level 1

92. 100% phthalo blue
1 drop yellow ochre
Water Level 1

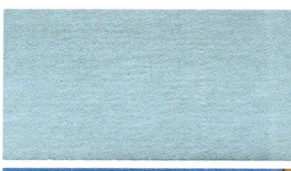

93. 98% phthalo blue
2% yellow ochre
Water Level 1

94. 60% lemon yellow
40% recipe #105
Water Level 1

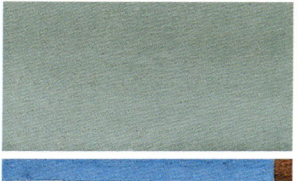

95. 90% phthalo blue
10% burnt sienna
Water Level 2

96. 95% phthalo blue
5% burnt umber
Water Level 2

97. 70% lemon yellow
30% recipe #105
Water Level 2

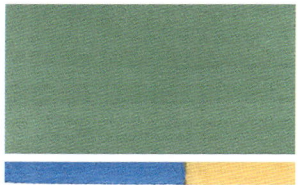

98. 60% phthalo blue
40% Naples yellow
Water Level 2

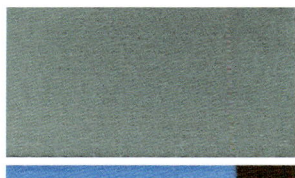

99. 80% phthalo blue
20% burnt umber
Water Level 3

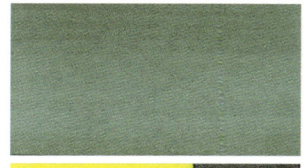

100. 65% lemon yellow
35% recipe #105
Water Level 2

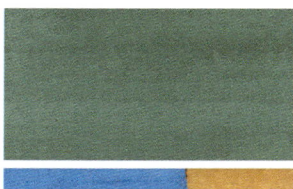

101. 65% phthalo blue
35% yellow ochre
Water Level 3

102. 70% phthalo blue
30% burnt umber
Water Level 3

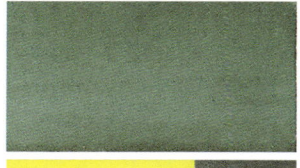

103. 65% lemon yellow
35% recipe #105
Water Level 3

104. 80% phthalo blue
20% yellow ochre
Water Level 4

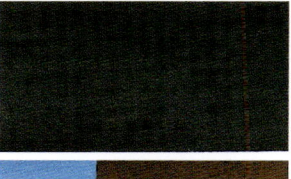

105. 40% phthalo blue
60% burnt umber
Water Level 4.5

COLORRECIPES

COLORS USED

- Phthalo Blue
- Viridian Green

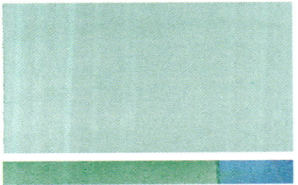

106. 75% viridian green
25% phthalo blue
Water Level 1

107. 50% viridian green
50% phthalo blue
Water Level 1

108. 100% phthalo blue
Water Level 1

109. 80% viridian green
20% phthalo blue
Water Level 2

110. 50% viridian green
50% phthalo blue
Water Level 2

111. 100% phthalo blue
Water Level 2

112. 85% viridian green
15% phthalo blue
Water Level 2.5

113. 50% viridian green
50% phthalo blue
Water Level 2.5

114. 100% phthalo blue
Water Level 2.5

115. 85% viridian green
15% phthalo blue
Water Level 3

116. 50% viridian green
50% phthalo blue
Water Level 3

117. 100% phthalo blue
Water Level 3

118. 90% viridian green
10% phthalo blue
Water Level 3.5

119. 50% viridian green
50% phthalo blue
Water Level 3.5

120. 100% phthalo blue
Water Level 3.5

- Cerulean Blue
- Permanent Rose
- Ultramarine Blue
- Viridian Green

121. 100% cerulean blue
Water Level 1

122. 60% cerulean blue
40% ultramarine blue
Water Level 1

123. 100% ultramarine blue
Water Level 1

124. 100% cerulean blue
Water Level 2

125. 60% cerulean blue
40% ultramarine blue
Water Level 2

126. 95% ultramarine blue
5% permanent rose
Water Level 2

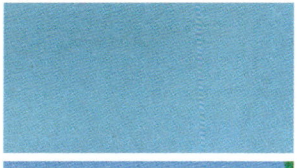

127. 98% cerulean blue
2% viridian green
Water Level 2.5

128. 60% cerulean blue
40% ultramarine blue
Water Level 3

129. 95% ultramarine blue
5% permanent rose
Water Level 3

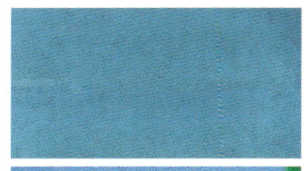

130. 95% cerulean blue
5% viridian green
Water Level 3

131. 60% cerulean blue
40% ultramarine blue
Water Level 3.5

132. 95% ultramarine blue
5% permanent rose
Water Level 4

133. 90% cerulean blue
5% viridian green
5% ultramarine blue
Water Level 4

134. 50% cerulean blue
50% ultramarine blue
Water Level 4

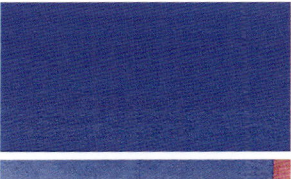

135. 95% ultramarine blue
5% permanent rose
Water Level 5

- Burnt Umber
- Permanent Alizarin Crimson
- Ultramarine Blue

136. 100% ultramarine blue
Water Level 1

137. 96% ultramarine blue
2% permanent alizarin crimson
2% burnt umber
Water Level 2

138. 98% ultramarine blue
2% permanent alizarin crimson
Water Level 3.5

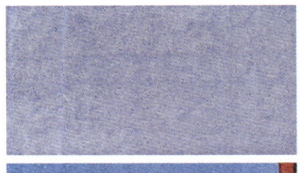

139. 95% ultramarine blue
4% permanent alizarin crimson
1% burnt umber
Water Level 1

140. 85% ultramarine blue
10% permanent alizarin crimson
5% burnt umber
Water Level 2.5

141. 95% ultramarine blue
4% permanent alizarin crimson
1% burnt umber
Water Level 2.5

142. 95% ultramarine blue
2% permanent alizarin crimson
3% burnt umber
Water Level 2.5

143. 80% ultramarine blue
20% permanent alizarin crimson
Water Level 2.5

144. 90% ultramarine blue
7% permanent alizarin crimson
3% burnt umber
Water Level 2.5

145. 95% ultramarine blue
3% permanent alizarin crimson
2% burnt umber
Water Level 3

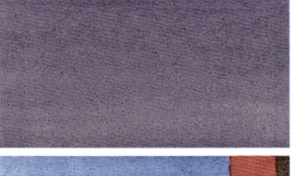

146. 80% ultramarine blue
15% permanent alizarin crimson
5% burnt umber
Water Level 3.5

147. 45% ultramarine blue
20% permanent alizarin crimson
35% burnt umber
Water Level 4

148. 95% ultramarine blue
4% permanent alizarin crimson
1% burnt umber
Water Level 4

149. 85% ultramarine blue
10% permanent alizarin crimson
5% burnt umber
Water Level 4

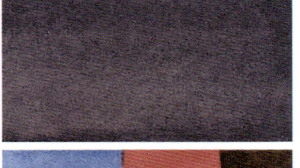

150. 45% ultramarine blue
30% permanent alizarin crimson
25% burnt umber
Water Level 5

- Cerulean Blue
- Permanent Rose
- Ultramarine Blue

151. 80% ultramarine blue
20% cerulean blue
Water Level 1

152. 60% ultramarine blue
30% cerulean blue
10% permanent rose
Water Level 1

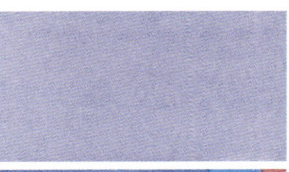

153. 75% ultramarine blue
15% cerulean blue
10% permanent rose
Water Level 1

154. 80% ultramarine blue
20% cerulean blue
Water Level 2

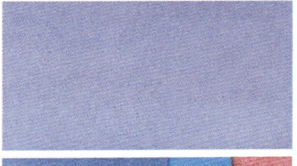

155. 60% ultramarine blue
20% cerulean blue
20% permanent rose
Water Level 2

156. 50% ultramarine blue
20% cerulean blue
30% permanent rose
Water Level 2

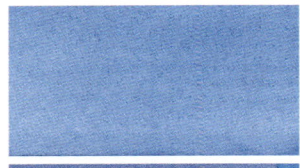

157. 90% ultramarine blue
10% cerulean blue
Water Level 2.5

158. 70% ultramarine blue
25% cerulean blue
5% permanent rose
Water Level 2.5

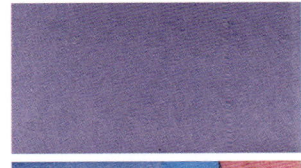

159. 55% ultramarine blue
20% cerulean blue
25% permanent rose
Water Level 2.5

160. 90% ultramarine blue
10% cerulean blue
Water Level 3

161. 75% ultramarine blue
20% cerulean blue
5% permanent rose
Water Level 3

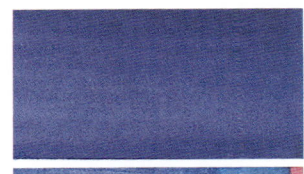

162. 70% ultramarine blue
25% cerulean blue
5% permanent rose
Water Level 3

163. 100% ultramarine blue
Water Level 4

164. 75% ultramarine blue
20% cerulean blue
5% permanent rose
Water Level 3

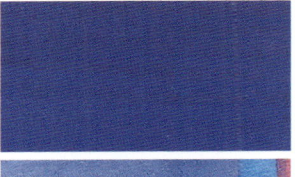

165. 80% ultramarine blue
15% cerulean blue
5% permanent rose
Water Level 4

- Cobalt Blue
- Permanent Alizarin Crimson
- Permanent Rose
- Ultramarine Blue

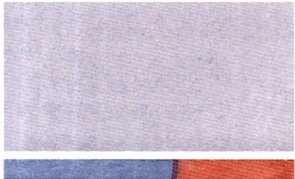

166. 60% cobalt blue
40% permanent alizarin crimson
Water Level 1

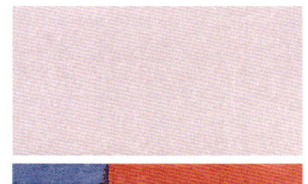

167. 35% cobalt blue
65% permanent alizarin crimson
Water Level 1

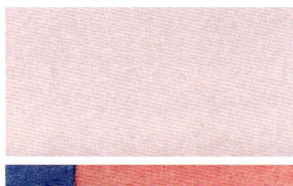

168. 25% ultramarine blue
75% permanent rose
Water Level 1

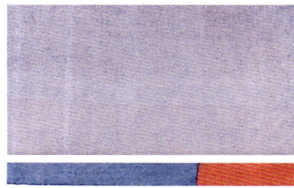

169. 65% cobalt blue
35% permanent alizarin crimson
Water Level 2

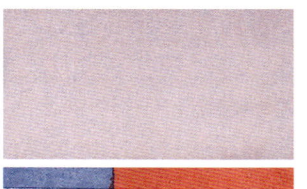

170. 40% cobalt blue
60% permanent alizarin crimson
Water Level 2

171. 25% ultramarine blue
75% permanent rose
Water Level 2

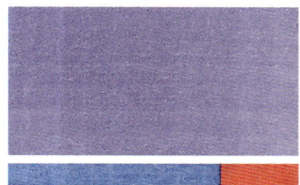

172. 75% cobalt blue
25% permanent alizarin crimson
Water Level 2.5

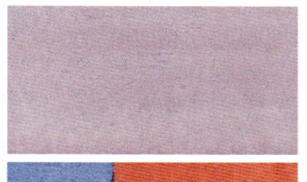

173. 40% cobalt blue
60% permanent alizarin crimson
Water Level 3

174. 25% ultramarine blue
75% permanent rose
Water Level 2.5

175. 75% cobalt blue
25% permanent alizarin crimson
Water Level 3

176. 45% cobalt blue
55% permanent alizarin crimson
Water Level 3

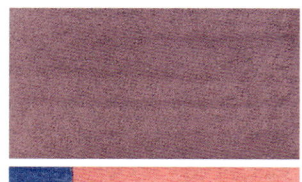

177. 25% ultramarine blue
75% permanent rose
Water Level 3

178. 80% cobalt blue
20% permanent alizarin crimson
Water Level 3.5

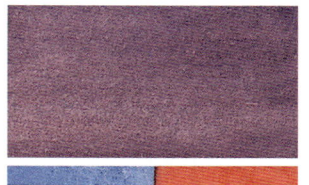

179. 50% cobalt blue
50% permanent alizarin crimson
Water Level 3.5

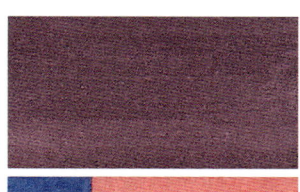

180. 30% ultramarine blue
70% permanent rose
Water Level 3.5

COLORS USED

- Cobalt Blue
- Permanent Alizarin Crimson
- Permanent Rose

181. 100% permanent rose
2 drops cobalt blue
Water Level 2

182. 100% permanent rose
Water Level 1

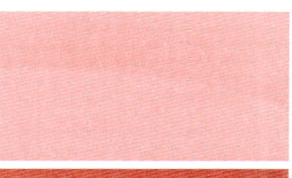

183. 99% permanent alizarin crimson
1% permanent rose
Water Level 1

184. 100% permanent rose
2 drops cobalt blue
Water Level 2.5

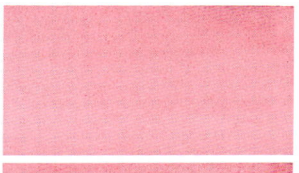

185. 100% permanent rose
Water Level 2

186. 65% permanent alizarin crimson
35% permanent rose
Water Level 2

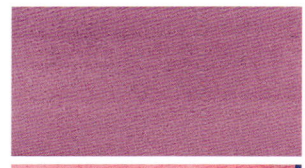

187. 100% permanent rose
3 drops cobalt blue
Water Level 3

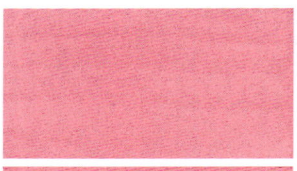

188. 100% permanent rose
Water Level 3

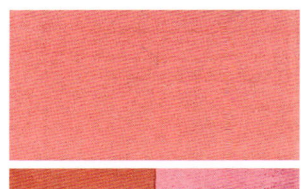

189. 55% permanent alizarin crimson
45% permanent rose
Water Level 3

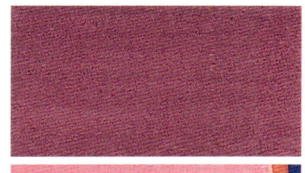

190. 90% permanent rose
6% permanent alizarin crimson
4% cobalt blue
Water Level 2

191. 100% permanent rose
Water Level 3.5

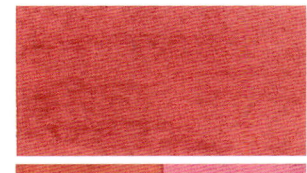

192. 50% permanent alizarin crimson
50% permanent rose
Water Level 3.5

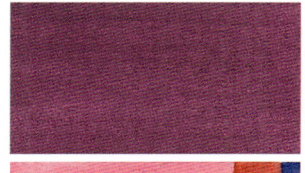

193. 80% permanent rose
15% permanent alizarin crimson
5% cobalt blue
Water Level 4

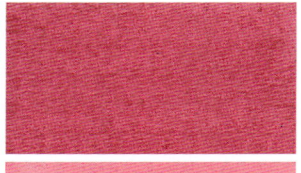

194. 100% permanent rose
Water Level 4

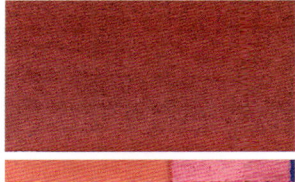

195. 60% permanent alizarin crimson
40% permanent rose
1 drop cobalt blue
Water Level 4

COLORRECIPES

COLORS USED

- Burnt Umber
- Burnt Sienna
- Indian Red

196. 100% Indian red
Water Level 1

197. 100% burnt umber
Water Level 1

198. 100% burnt sienna
Water Level 1

199. 100% Indian red
Water Level 2

200. 100% burnt umber
Water Level 2

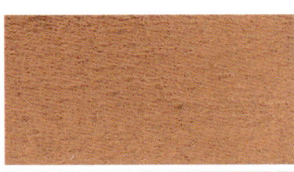

201. 100% burnt sienna
Water Level 2

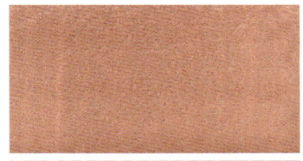

202. 100% Indian red
Water Level 3

203. 100% burnt umber
Water Level 3

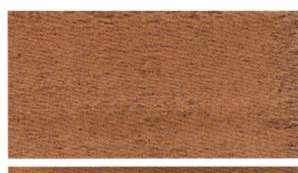

204. 100% burnt sienna
Water Level 3

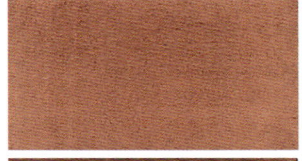

205. 100% Indian red
Water Level 4

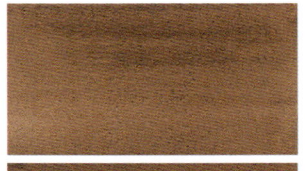

206. 100% burnt umber
Water Level 4

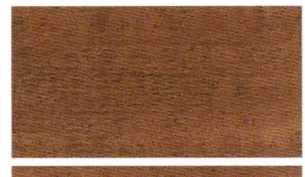

207. 100% burnt sienna
Water Level 4

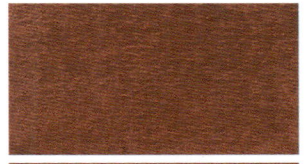

208. 100% Indian red
Water Level 5

209. 100% burnt umber
Water Level 5

210. 100% burnt sienna
Water Level 5

COLORS USED

- Cadmium Yellow
- Permanent Alizarin Crimson

211. 100% permanent alizarin crimson
Water Level 1

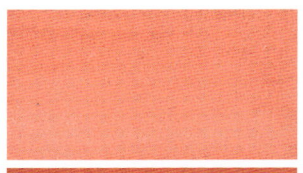

212. 100% permanent alizarin crimson
Water Level 3

213. 100% permanent alizarin crimson
Water Level 5

214. 80% permanent alizarin crimson
20% cadmium yellow
Water Level 2

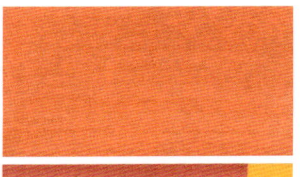

215. 85% permanent alizarin crimson
15% cadmium yellow
Water Level 3

216. 85% permanent alizarin crimson
15% cadmium yellow
Water Level 5

217. 40% permanent alizarin crimson
60% cadmium yellow
Water Level 2.5

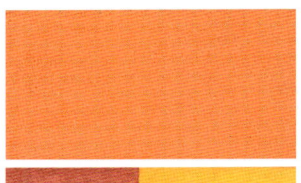

218. 45% permanent alizarin crimson
55% cadmium yellow
Water Level 3

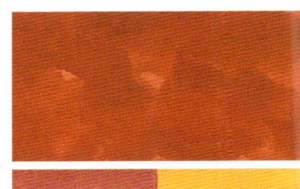

219. 50% permanent alizarin crimson
50% cadmium yellow
Water Level 5

220. 15% permanent alizarin crimson
85% cadmium yellow
Water Level 2.5

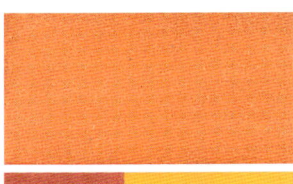

221. 40% permanent alizarin crimson
60% cadmium yellow
Water Level 3

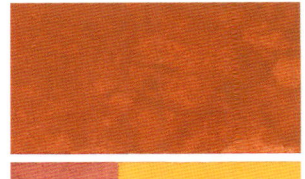

222. 35% permanent alizarin crimson
65% cadmium yellow
Water Level 5

223. 3% permanent alizarin crimson
97% cadmium yellow
Water Level 3

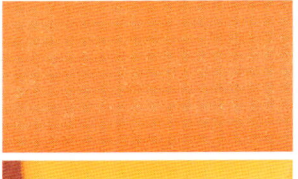

224. 5% permanent alizarin crimson
95% cadmium yellow
Water Level 3

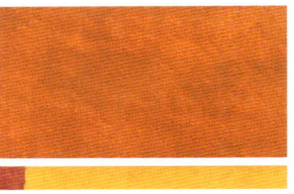

225. 10% permanent alizarin crimson
90% cadmium yellow
Water Level 5

COLOR RECIPES

COLORS USED

- Cadmium Red Light
- Vermilion
- Yellow Ochre

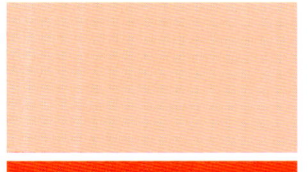

226. 100% vermilion
Water Level 1

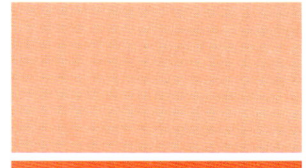

227. 100% cadmium red light
Water Level 1

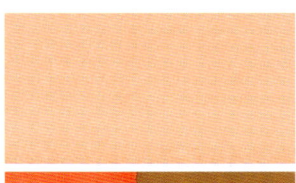

228. 65% cadmium red light
35% yellow ochre
Water Level 1

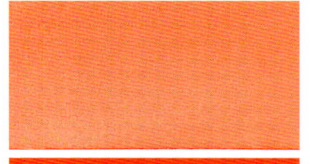

229. 100% vermilion
Water Level 2

230. 100% cadmium red light
Water Level 2

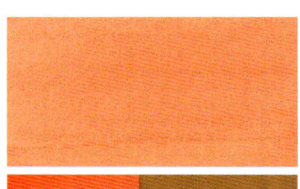

231. 65% cadmium red light
35% yellow ochre
Water Level 2

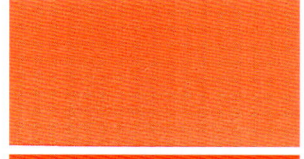

232. 100% vermilion
Water Level 3

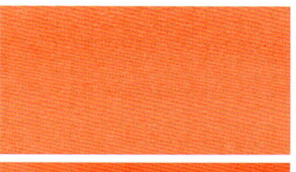

233. 100% cadmium red light
Water Level 3

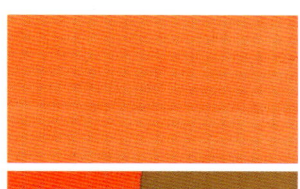

234. 65% cadmium red light
35% yellow ochre
Water Level 3

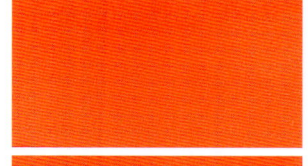

235. 100% vermilion
Water Level 4

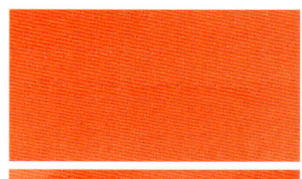

236. 100% cadmium red light
Water Level 4

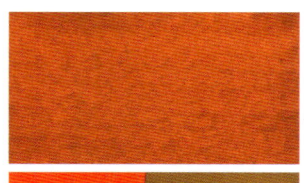

237. 65% cadmium red light
35% yellow ochre
Water Level 4

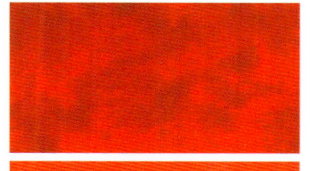

238. 100% vermilion
Water Level 5

239. 100% cadmium red light
Water Level 5

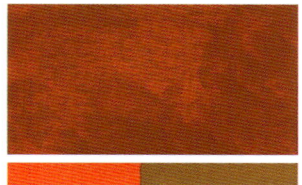

240. 65% cadmium red light
35% yellow ochre
Water Level 5

COLORS USED

- Cadmium Red Light
- Lemon Yellow

241. 100% cadmium red light
Water Level 1

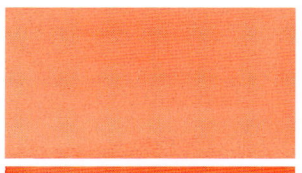

242. 100% cadmium red light
Water Level 3

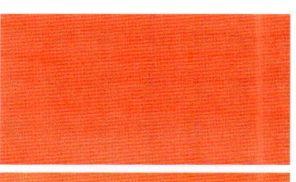

243. 100% cadmium red light
Water Level 4

244. 70% cadmium red light
30% lemon yellow
Water Level 2

245. 80% cadmium red light
20% lemon yellow
Water Level 3

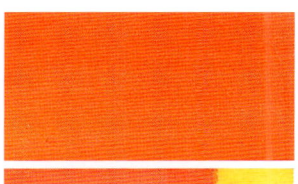

246. 75% cadmium red light
25% lemon yellow
Water Level 3.5

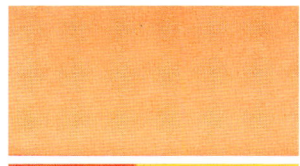

247. 45% cadmium red light
55% lemon yellow
Water Level 2

248. 60% cadmium red light
40% lemon yellow
Water Level 3

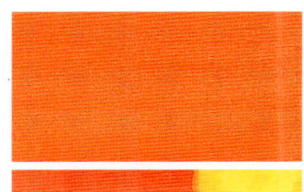

249. 65% cadmium red light
35% lemon yellow
Water Level 3.5

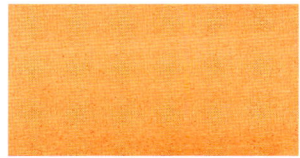

250. 25% cadmium red light
75% lemon yellow
Water Level 2

251. 35% cadmium red light
65% lemon yellow
Water Level 3

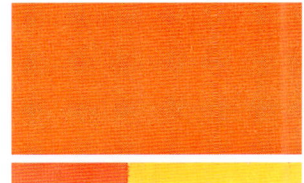

252. 40% cadmium red light
60% lemon yellow
Water Level 3.5

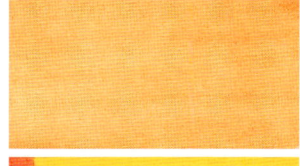

253. 10% cadmium red light
90% lemon yellow
Water Level 2

254. 15% cadmium red light
85% lemon yellow
Water Level 3

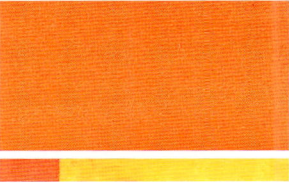

255. 20% cadmium red light
80% lemon yellow
Water Level 3.5

COLORS USED

- Cadmium Orange
- Lemon Yellow
- Naples Yellow

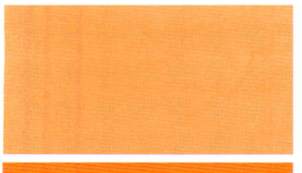

256. 100% cadmium orange
Water Level 2

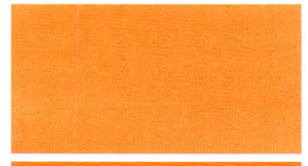

257. 100% cadmium orange
Water Level 3

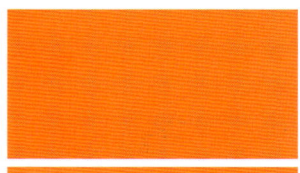

258. 100% cadmium orange
Water Level 5

259. 60% lemon yellow
40% cadmium orange
Water Level 2

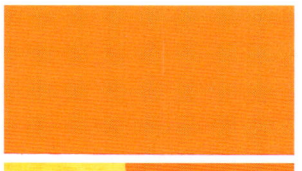

260. 45% lemon yellow
55% cadmium orange
Water Level 3

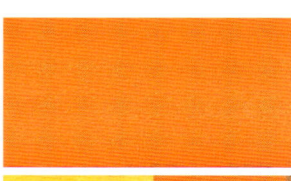

261. 55% lemon yellow
45% cadmium orange
1 drop Naples yellow
Water Level 4

262. 80% lemon yellow
20% cadmium orange
Water Level 2

263. 90% lemon yellow
10% cadmium orange
Water Level 3

264. 75% lemon yellow
25% cadmium orange
1 drop Naples yellow
Water Level 4

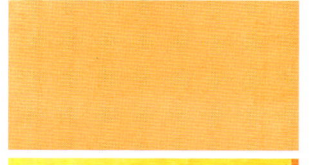

265. 100% lemon yellow
2 drops cadmium orange
Water Level 2

266. 100% lemon yellow
3 drops cadmium orange
Water Level 3

267. 85% lemon yellow
15% cadmium orange
1 drop Naples yellow
Water Level 3.5

268. 100% lemon yellow
1 drop cadmium orange
Water Level 2

269. 100% lemon yellow
2 drops cadmium orange
Water Level 3

270. 95% lemon yellow
5% cadmium orange
1 drop Naples yellow
Water Level 3

COLORS USED

- Cadmium Orange
- Cadmium Red Light
- Sap Green
- Viridian Green

271. 75% cadmium orange
25% cadmium red light
Water Level 2

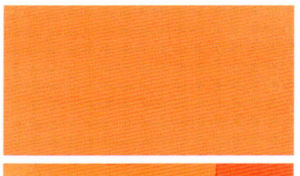

272. 75% cadmium orange
25% cadmium red light
Water Level 3

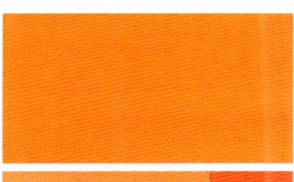

273. 75% cadmium orange
25% cadmium red light
Water Level 4

274. 100% recipe #271
1 drop viridian green
Water Level 2

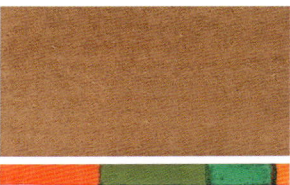

275. 40% cadmium red light
35% sap green
20% viridian green
5% cadmium orange
Water Level 2.5

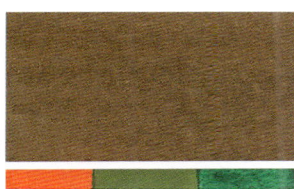

276. 35% cadmium red light
35% sap green
30% viridian green
Water Level 3

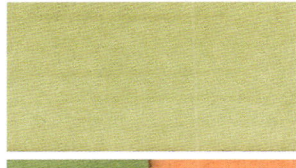

277. 50% sap green
50% recipe #274
Water Level 2

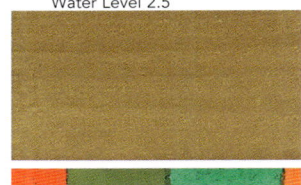

278. 20% cadmium red light
35% sap green
35% viridian green
10% cadmium orange
Water Level 3

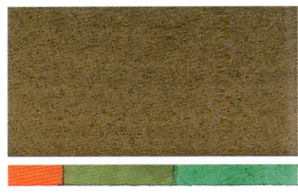

279. 25% cadmium red light
35% sap green
40% viridian green
Water Level 3

280. 70% sap green
10% viridian green
20% cadmium orange
Water Level 2

281. 15% cadmium red light
40% sap green
25% viridian green
20% cadmium orange
Water Level 3

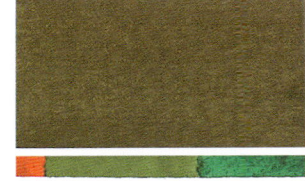

282. 15% cadmium red light
50% sap green
35% viridian green
Water Level 3.5

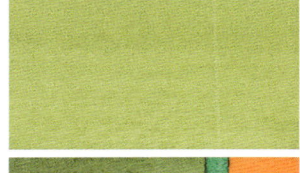

283. 70% sap green
5% viridian green
25% cadmium orange
Water Level 2

284. 90% recipe #280
10% viridian green
Water Level 3

285. 85% recipe #282
10% viridian green
5% cadmium orange
Water Level 4

63

COLORS USED

- Phthalo Blue
- Ultramarine Blue
- Yellow Ochre

286. 100% yellow ochre
Water Level 1

287. 100% yellow ochre
1 drop ultramarine blue
Water Level 1

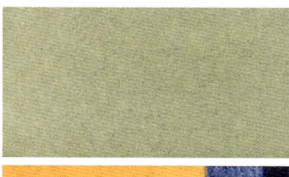

288. 70% yellow ochre
20% ultramarine blue
10% phthalo blue
Water Level 1

289. 100% yellow ochre
Water Level 2

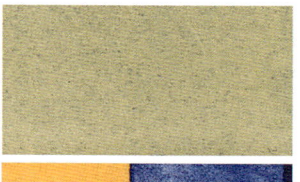

290. 50% yellow ochre
50% ultramarine blue
1 drop phthalo blue
Water Level 2

291. 70% yellow ochre
25% ultramarine blue
5% phthalo blue
Water Level 2

292. 100% yellow ochre
Water Level 2.5

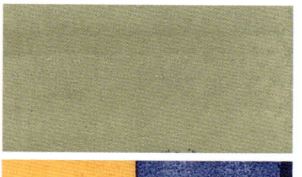

293. 50% yellow ochre
50% ultramarine blue
2 drops phthalo blue
Water Level 2.5

294. 70% yellow ochre
25% ultramarine blue
5% phthalo blue
Water Level 3

295. 100% yellow ochre
Water Level 3

296. 65% yellow ochre
35% ultramarine blue
Water Level 3

297. 75% yellow ochre
23% ultramarine blue
2% phthalo blue
Water Level 3

298. 100% yellow ochre
Water Level 4

299. 65% yellow ochre
35% ultramarine blue
Water Level 4

300. 70% yellow ochre
30% ultramarine blue
Water Level 4

COLORS USED

- Burnt Sienna
- Cadmium Red Light
- Naples Yellow
- Yellow Ochre

301. 100% Naples yellow
Water Level 1

302. 100% Naples yellow
1 drop cadmium red light
Water Level 1

303. 100% Naples yellow
1 drop cadmium red light
1 drop burnt sienna
Water Level 1

304. 100% Naples yellow
Water Level 2

305. 100% Naples yellow
2 drops cadmium red light
Water Level 2

306. 100% Naples yellow
2 drops cadmium red light
2 drops burnt sienna
Water Level 2.5

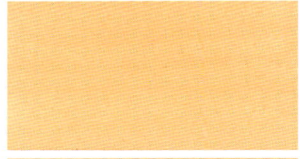

307. 100% Naples yellow
Water Level 2.5

308. 95% Naples yellow
5% cadmium red light
1 drop burnt sienna
Water Level 2.5

309. 90% Naples yellow
5% burnt sienna
5% yellow ochre
Water Level 3

310. 100% Naples yellow
1 drop burnt sienna
Water Level 3

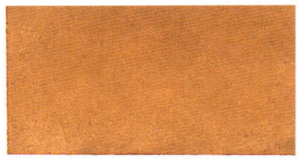

311. 90% Naples yellow
5% cadmium red light
5% yellow ochre
1 drop burnt sienna
Water Level 3.5

312. 80% Naples yellow
10% burnt sienna
10% yellow ochre
Water Level 4

313. 98% Naples yellow
2% burnt sienna
Water Level 3.5

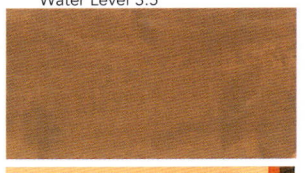

314. 95% Naples yellow
2% cadmium red light
3% burnt sienna
Water Level 4

315. 60% Naples yellow
30% burnt sienna
10% yellow ochre
Water Level 4

COLORS USED

- Ivory Black
- Lemon Yellow

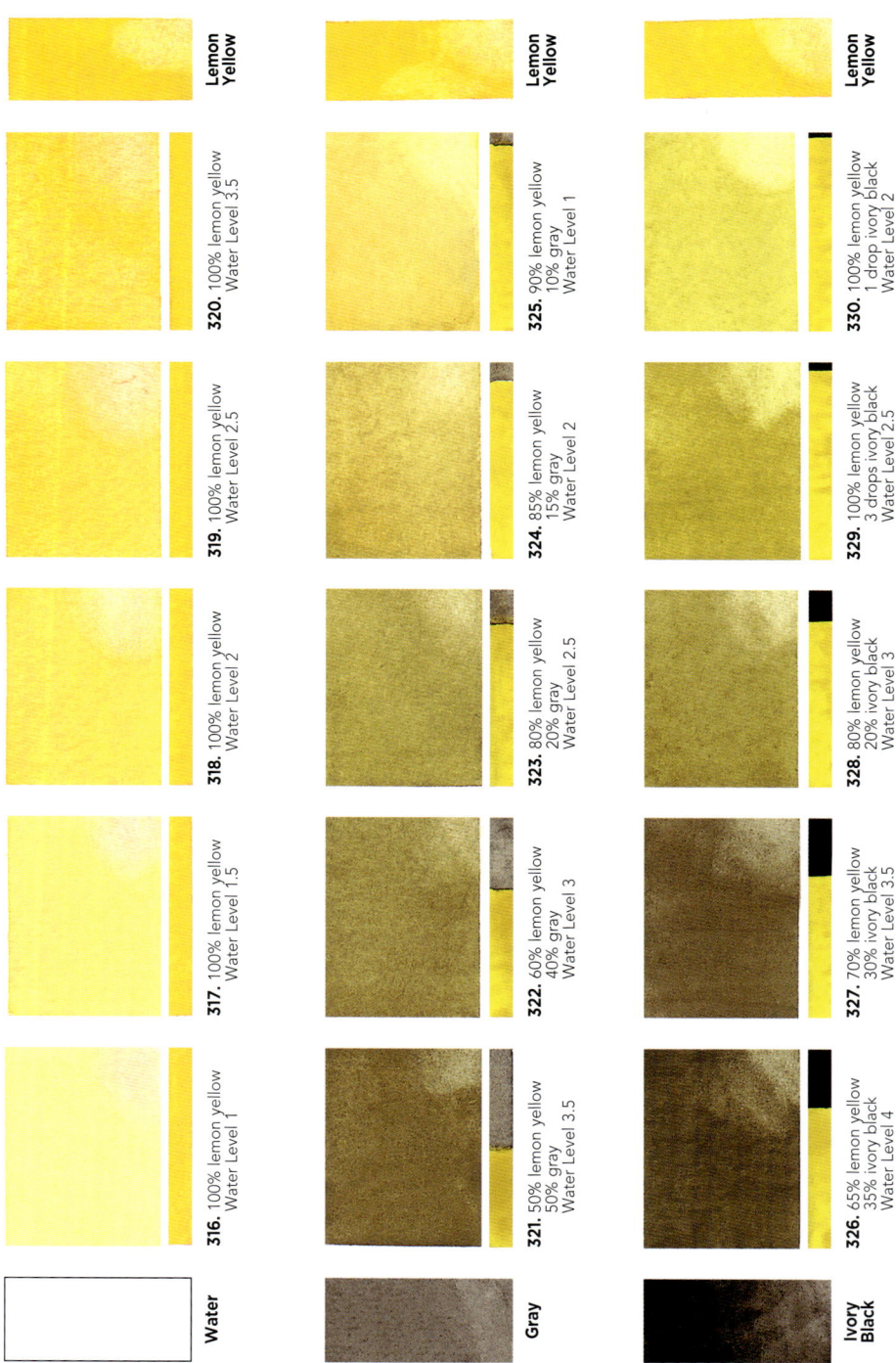

Lemon Yellow

320. 100% lemon yellow
Water Level 3.5

319. 100% lemon yellow
Water Level 2.5

318. 100% lemon yellow
Water Level 2

317. 100% lemon yellow
Water Level 1.5

316. 100% lemon yellow
Water Level 1

Water

Lemon Yellow

325. 90% lemon yellow
10% gray
Water Level 1

324. 85% lemon yellow
15% gray
Water Level 2

323. 80% lemon yellow
20% gray
Water Level 2.5

322. 60% lemon yellow
40% gray
Water Level 3

321. 50% lemon yellow
50% gray
Water Level 3.5

Gray

Lemon Yellow

330. 100% lemon yellow
1 drop ivory black
Water Level 2

329. 100% lemon yellow
3 drops ivory black
Water Level 2.5

328. 80% lemon yellow
20% ivory black
Water Level 3

327. 70% lemon yellow
30% ivory black
Water Level 3.5

326. 65% lemon yellow
35% ivory black
Water Level 4

Ivory Black

COLORS USED

- Cadmium Red Light
- Ivory Black

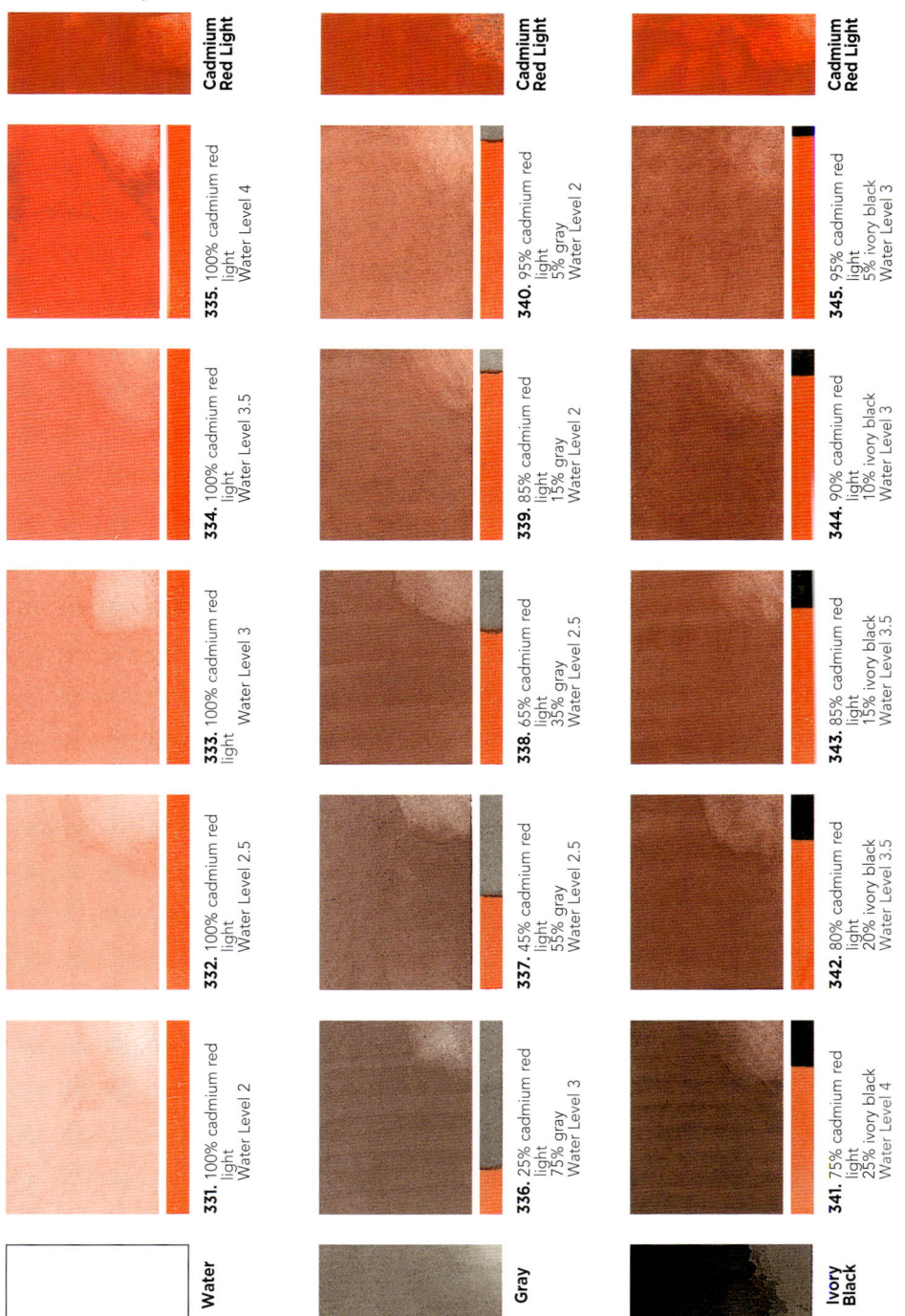

Cadmium Red Light

335. 100% cadmium red light
Water Level 4

334. 100% cadmium red light Water Level 3.5

333. 100% cadmium red light Water Level 3

332. 100% cadmium red light
Water Level 2.5

331. 100% cadmium red light
Water Level 2

Water

Cadmium Red Light

340. 95% cadmium red light
5% gray
Water Level 2

339. 85% cadmium red light
15% gray
Water Level 2

338. 65% cadmium red light
35% gray
Water Level 2.5

337. 45% cadmium red light
55% gray
Water Level 2.5

336. 25% cadmium red light
75% gray
Water Level 3

Gray

Cadmium Red Light

345. 95% cadmium red light
5% ivory black
Water Level 3

344. 90% cadmium red light
10% ivory black
Water Level 3

343. 85% cadmium red light
15% ivory black
Water Level 3.5

342. 80% cadmium red light
20% ivory black
Water Level 3.5

341. 75% cadmium red light
25% ivory black
Water Level 4

Ivory Black

VALUERECIPES

• Cerulean Blue
• Ivory Black

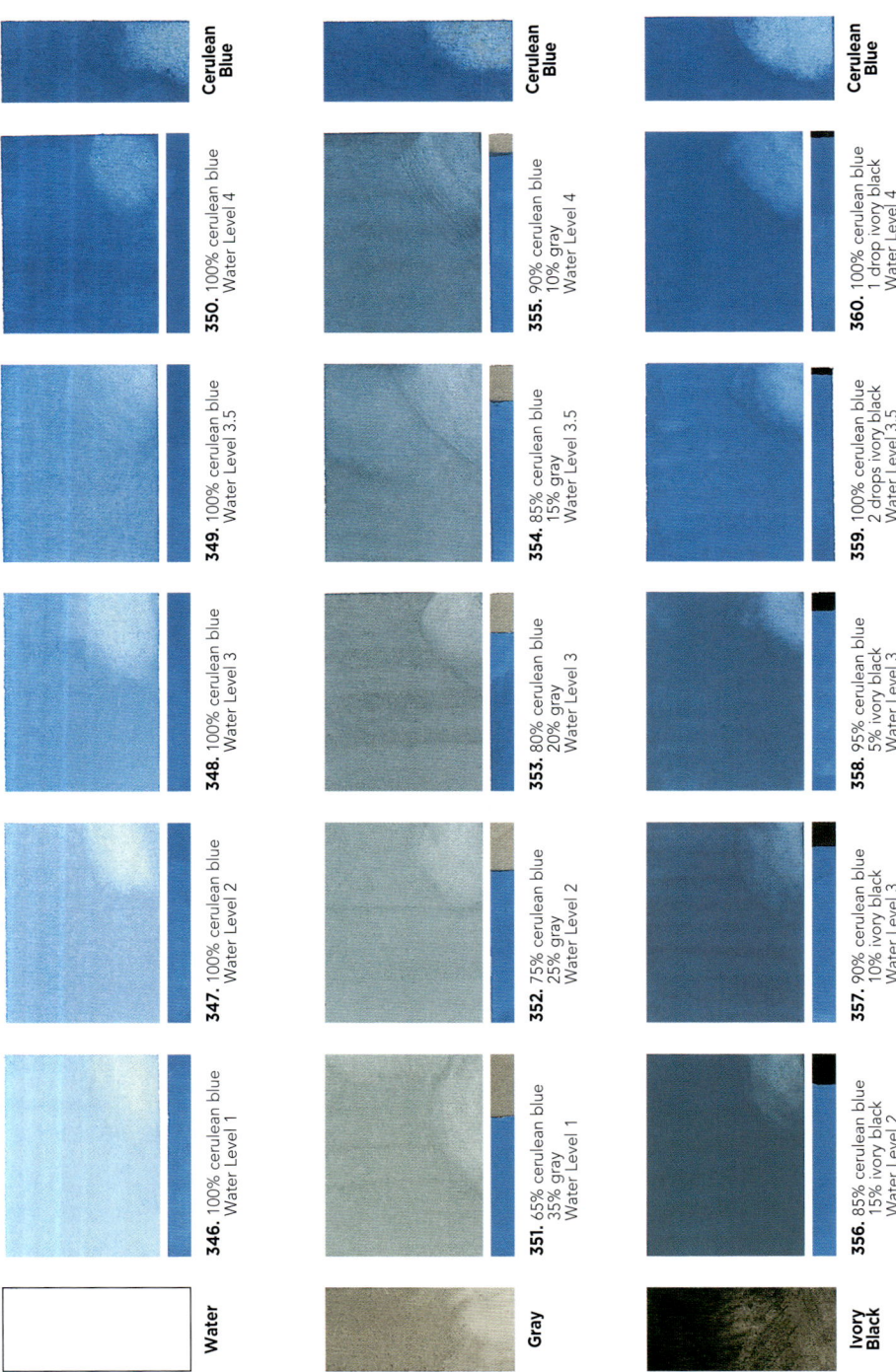

Cerulean Blue

350. 100% cerulean blue
Water Level 4

349. 100% cerulean blue
Water Level 3.5

348. 100% cerulean blue
Water Level 3

347. 100% cerulean blue
Water Level 2

346. 100% cerulean blue
Water Level 1

Water

Cerulean Blue

355. 90% cerulean blue
10% gray
Water Level 4

354. 85% cerulean blue
15% gray
Water Level 3.5

353. 80% cerulean blue
20% gray
Water Level 3

352. 75% cerulean blue
25% gray
Water Level 2

351. 65% cerulean blue
35% gray
Water Level 1

Gray

Cerulean Blue

360. 100% cerulean blue
1 drop ivory black
Water Level 4

359. 100% cerulean blue
2 drops ivory black
Water Level 3.5

358. 95% cerulean blue
5% ivory black
Water Level 3

357. 90% cerulean blue
10% ivory black
Water Level 3

356. 85% cerulean blue
15% ivory black
Water Level 2

Ivory Black

COLORS USED

- Cadmium Orange
- Cadmium Yellow
- Cadmium Yellow Deep
- Cerulean Blue
- Dioxazine Violet
- Mauve

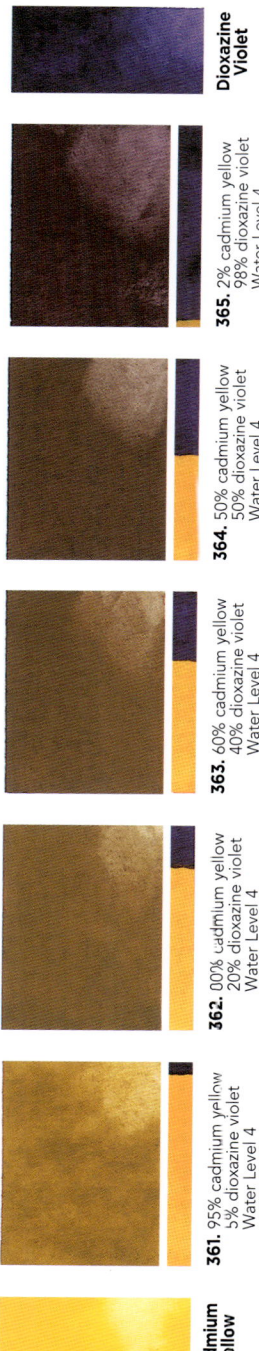

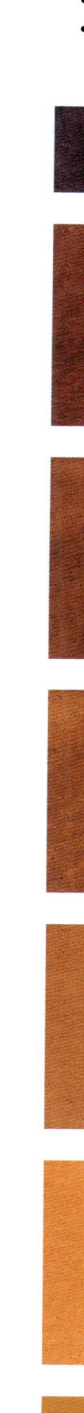

Dioxazine Violet

365. 2% cadmium yellow
98% dioxazine violet
Water Level 4

364. 50% cadmium yellow
50% dioxazine violet
Water Level 4

363. 60% cadmium yellow
40% dioxazine violet
Water Level 4

362. 80% cadmium yellow
20% dioxazine violet
Water Level 4

361. 95% cadmium yellow
5% dioxazine violet
Water Level 4

Cadmium Yellow

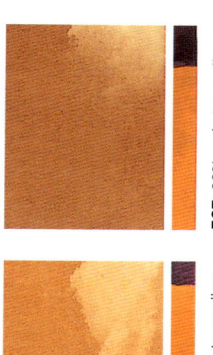

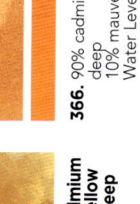

Mauve

370. 5% cadmium yellow
deep
95% mauve
Water Level 4

369. 30% cadmium yellow
deep
70% mauve
Water Level 3.5

368. 70% cadmium yellow
deep
30% mauve
Water Level 3

367. 80% cadmium yellow
deep
20% mauve
Water Level 3

366. 90% cadmium yellow
deep
10% mauve
Water Level 3

Cadmium Yellow Deep

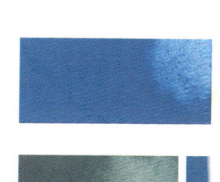

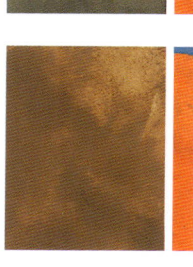
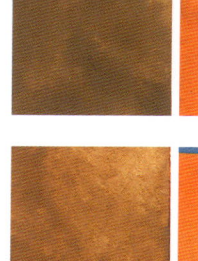
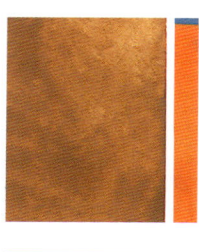
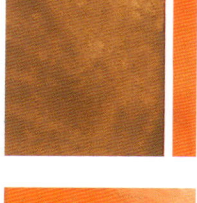
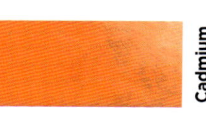

Cerulean Blue

375. 30% cadmium orange
70% cerulean blue
Water Level 4

374. 50% cadmium orange
50% cerulean blue
Water Level 4

373. 95% cadmium orange
5% cerulean blue
Water Level 4

372. 100% cadmium
orange
4 drops cerulean blue
Water Level 3.5

371. 100% cadmium
orange
2 drops cerulean blue
Water Level 3

Cadmium Orange

COLORS USED

- Cadmium Red Light
- Cadmium Yellow Pale
- Dioxazine Violet
- Hooker's Green
- Perm. Alizarin Crimson
- Sap Green

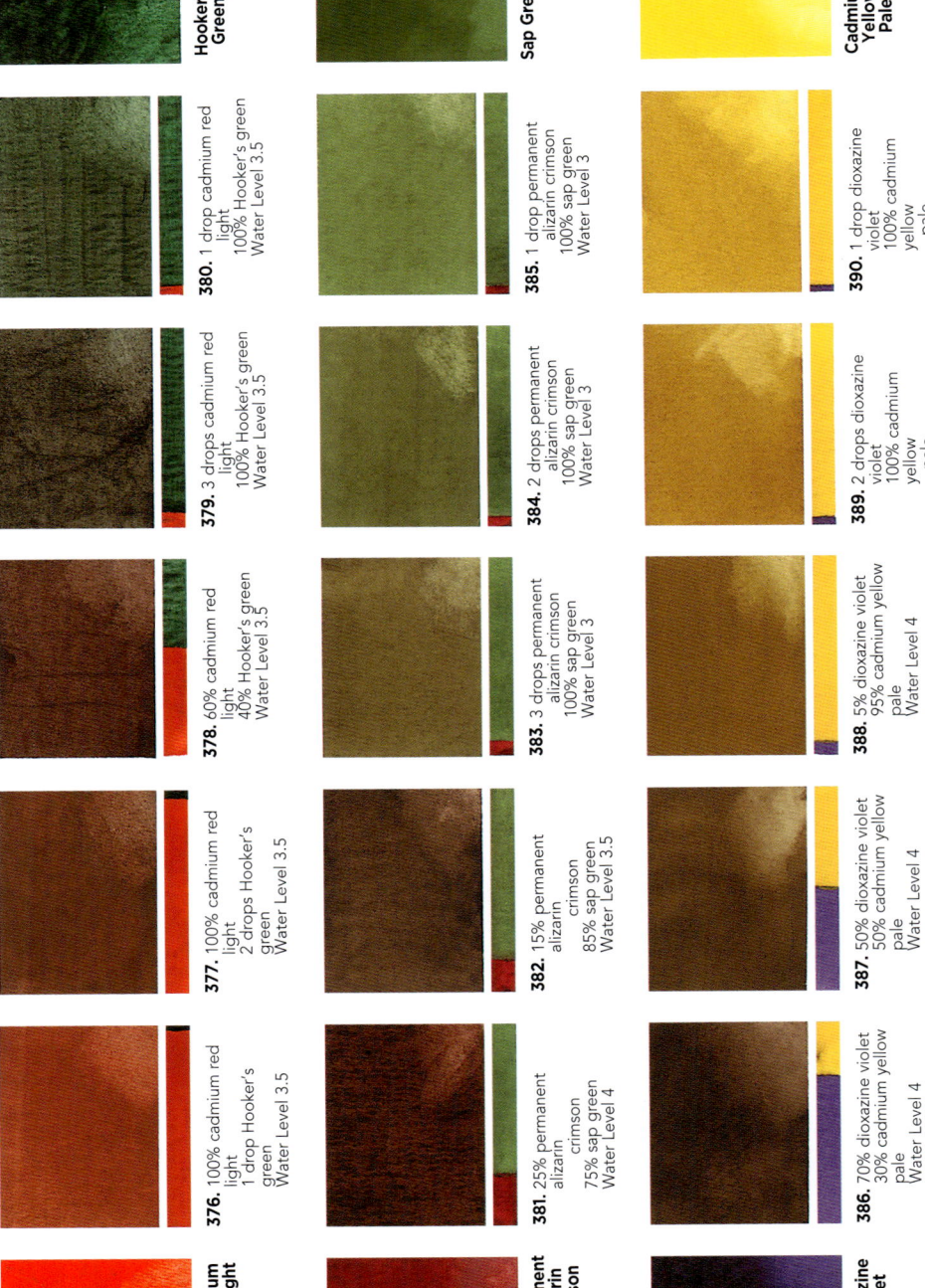

Hooker's Green

Sap Green

Cadmium Yellow Pale

380. 1 drop cadmium red light
100% Hooker's green
Water Level 3.5

385. 1 drop permanent alizarin crimson
100% sap green
Water Level 3

390. 1 drop dioxazine violet
100% cadmium yellow pale
Water Level 4

379. 3 drops cadmium red light
100% Hooker's green
Water Level 3.5

384. 2 drops permanent alizarin crimson
100% sap green
Water Level 3

389. 2 drops dioxazine violet
100% cadmium yellow pale
Water Level 4

378. 60% cadmium red light
40% Hooker's green
Water Level 3.5

383. 3 drops permanent alizarin crimson
100% sap green
Water Level 3

388. 5% dioxazine violet
95% cadmium yellow pale
Water Level 4

377. 100% cadmium red light
2 drops Hooker's green
Water Level 3.5

382. 15% permanent alizarin crimson
85% sap green
Water Level 3.5

387. 50% dioxazine violet
50% cadmium yellow pale
Water Level 4

376. 100% cadmium red light
1 drop Hooker's green
Water Level 3.5

381. 25% permanent alizarin crimson
75% sap green
Water Level 4

386. 70% dioxazine violet
30% cadmium yellow pale
Water Level 4

Cadmium Red Light

Permanent Alizarin Crimson

Dioxazine Violet

Color Mixing for
Portraits

PAINT COLORS NEEDED

Below you'll find all the paint colors needed to create the skin, eye, lip, and hair color tones in this section. Keep in mind that some color names will vary depending on the manufacturer, and some of these oil colors aren't available in acrylic and therefore must be mixed. (See the Oil/Acrylic Conversion Chart on page 174 for color equivalents.) As you follow the recipes, you may also find that hues and strengths vary slightly from brand to brand, so you may need to adjust the recipes accordingly.

OIL/ACRYLIC

Alizarin crimson

Burnt sienna

Burnt umber

Cadmium orange

Cadmium red light

Cadmium vermilion

Cadmium yellow light

Cadmium yellow medium

Cerulean blue hue

Chrome oxide green
   (chromium oxide green in acrylic)

Cobalt blue

Ivory black
   (abbreviated "black" throughout)

Naples yellow hue

Phthalo red rose
   (abbreviated "phthalo red" throughout)
   (can be substituted with
   quinacridone red)

Raw sienna

Raw umber

Titanium white
   (abbreviated 'white" throughout)

Ultramarine blue

Venetian red

Viridian green

Yellow ochre

Zinc yellow

WATERCOLOR

Burnt sienna

Burnt umber

Cadmium orange

Cadmium red light

Cerulean blue hue

Cobalt blue

Hooker's green deep

Ivory black
   (abbreviated "black" throughout)

Lemon yellow

New gamboge
   (avoid substituting with gamboge;
   substitute with Indian yellow if
   necessary)

Permanent alizarin crimson
   (abbreviated "alizarin crimson"
   throughout)

Permanent rose

Raw sienna

Sap green

Sepia

Ultramarine blue

Viridian green

Yellow ochre

NOTE: We have abbreviated some of the color names, such as using "black" in place of "ivory black," as mentioned above. However, it is important that you use the exact color names listed to mix the recipes. For example, ivory black is a warm black, so substituting this color for a cooler lamp black would change the dynamic of the color mixture. This applies to titanium white as well; avoid substituting this color for a cooler variety, such as zinc white.

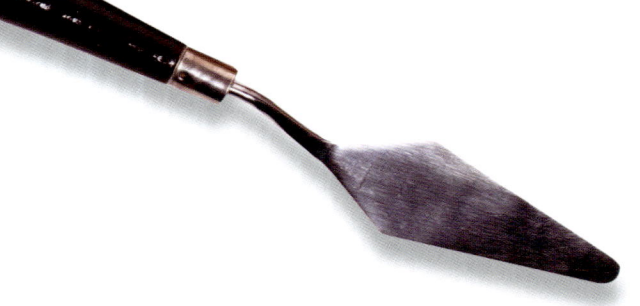

Contents

Yellow ochre is the most common color used in basic skin tone palettes. The samples below show yellow ochre mixed with different reds. First create a master recipe to the desired yellow or red tone. The recipe can be lightened, darkened, grayed, or intermixed.

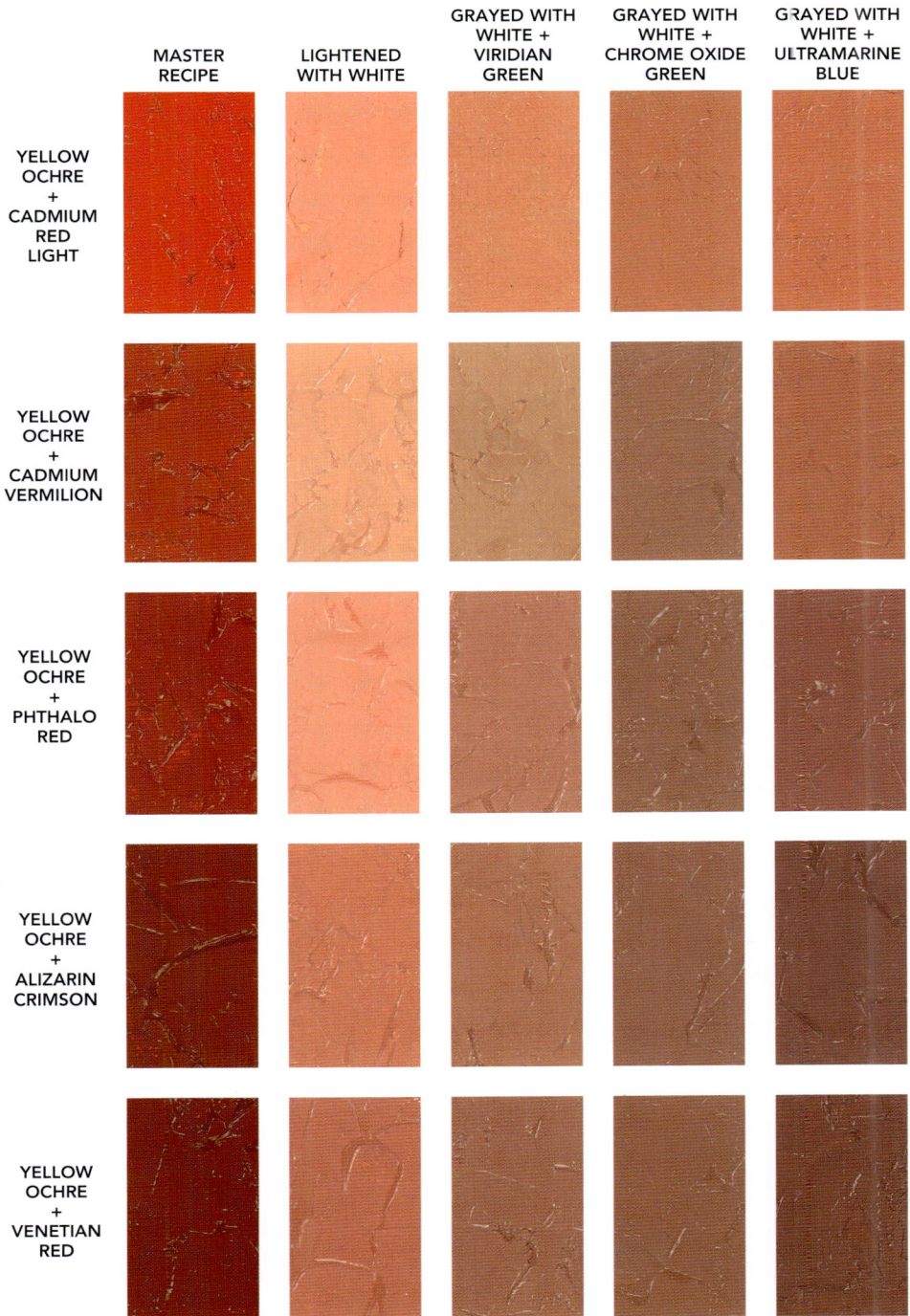

	MASTER RECIPE	LIGHTENED WITH WHITE	GRAYED WITH WHITE + VIRIDIAN GREEN	GRAYED WITH WHITE + CHROME OXIDE GREEN	GRAYED WITH WHITE + ULTRAMARINE BLUE
YELLOW OCHRE + CADMIUM RED LIGHT					
YELLOW OCHRE + CADMIUM VERMILION					
YELLOW OCHRE + PHTHALO RED					
YELLOW OCHRE + ALIZARIN CRIMSON					
YELLOW OCHRE + VENETIAN RED					

Naples yellow hue is a light, warm yellow that also mixes well with reds for skin tone palettes. The samples below show Naples yellow hue mixed with different reds. First create a master recipe to the desired yellow or red tone. The recipe can be lightened, darkened, grayed, or intermixed.

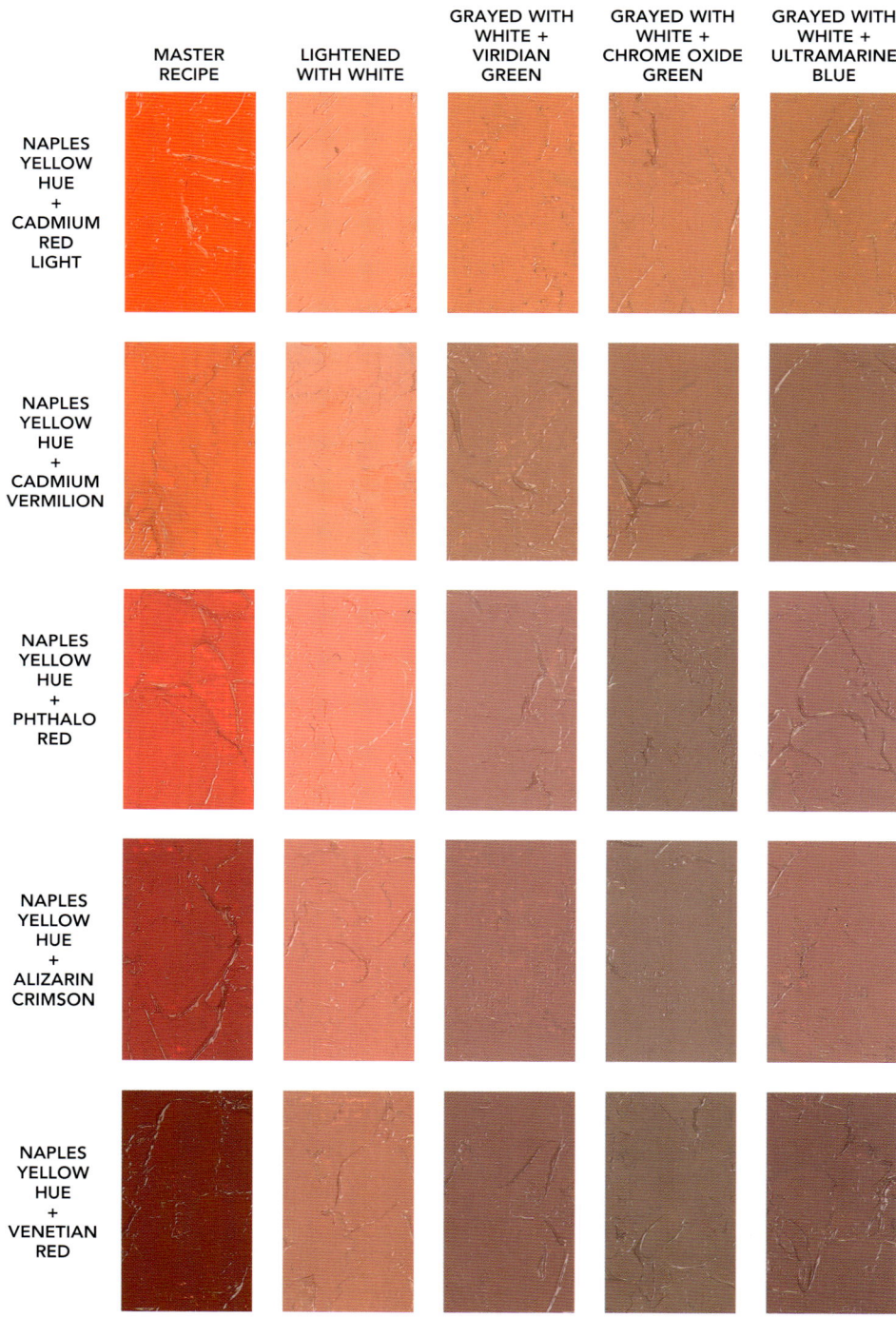

	MASTER RECIPE	LIGHTENED WITH WHITE	GRAYED WITH WHITE + VIRIDIAN GREEN	GRAYED WITH WHITE + CHROME OXIDE GREEN	GRAYED WITH WHITE + ULTRAMARINE BLUE
NAPLES YELLOW HUE + CADMIUM RED LIGHT					
NAPLES YELLOW HUE + CADMIUM VERMILION					
NAPLES YELLOW HUE + PHTHALO RED					
NAPLES YELLOW HUE + ALIZARIN CRIMSON					
NAPLES YELLOW HUE + VENETIAN RED					

As shown on page 9, a color cannot be "grayed" using black or white—it can be only tinted, toned, or shaded. Colors directly across the color wheel from each another, such as red and green, are known as "direct complements." Direct complements have the ability to neutralize or "gray" each other. When you mix two direct complementary colors, the result is a natural, neutral color. The mixture at right shows yellow ochre and cadmium vermilion mixed for a skin tone that can be grayed with viridian green (vermilion's complement) or tinted with white.

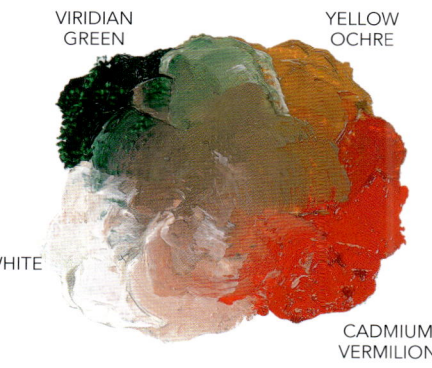

VIRIDIAN GREEN

YELLOW OCHRE

WHITE

CADMIUM VERMILION

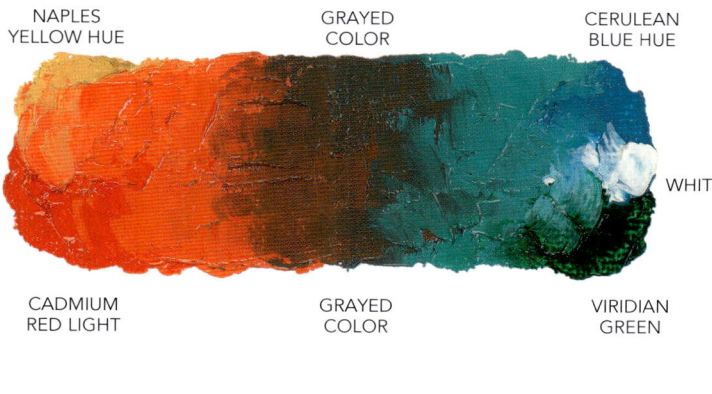

NAPLES YELLOW HUE

GRAYED COLOR

CERULEAN BLUE HUE

WHITE

CADMIUM RED LIGHT

GRAYED COLOR

VIRIDIAN GREEN

As you mix skin tones, it's a good idea to make test "smearings" to find the best mixtures. The sample at left shows cerulean blue hue mixed with viridian green and white, producing a soft blue-green. Combining these with the skin tone recipe of Naples yellow hue and cadmium red light yields a beautiful, natural gray of each.

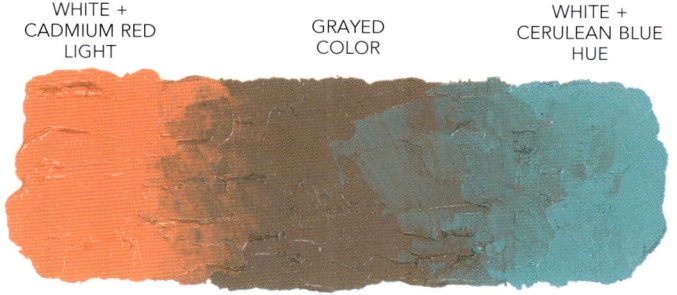

WHITE + CADMIUM RED LIGHT

GRAYED COLOR

WHITE + CERULEAN BLUE HUE

This example shows two colors (cadmium red light and cerulean blue hue) that have been tinted with white. Even though these colors are tinted, they still remain complementary to each other. Notice the grayed color in the center created by mixing the two colors.

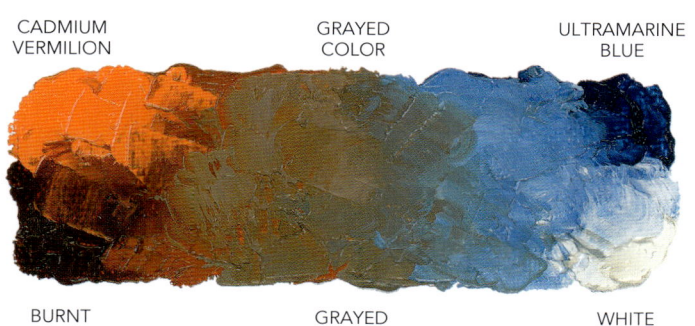

CADMIUM VERMILION

GRAYED COLOR

ULTRAMARINE BLUE

BURNT SIENNA

GRAYED COLOR

WHITE

Here you see a light, cool blue (ultramarine) mixed with a warm reddish-orange mix of burnt sienna and cadmium vermilion. Orange and blue are direct complements, so they gray each other well. Notice the graduations of grayed colors in the center of this sample.

BASIC PALETTES

If your model's skin color doesn't match any palettes in this section, you can use the color mixes on these pages as a base for mixing the exact tone you need. Start with any mix and lighten, darken, or gray as indicated below until you achieve the desired color.

To Lighten Add other, lighter skin tones, or try adding white to colors like zinc yellow, cadmium yellow light, Naples yellow hue, or cadmium orange.

To Darken Add other, darker skin tones, or try adding burnt umber, burnt sienna, alizarin crimson, ultramarine blue, or mixtures of the above colors. To shade a tone, add a touch of black.

To Gray Add one or more of the following colors: white plus ultramarine blue, chrome oxide green, cadmium yellow light, cerulean blue hue, or cadmium orange. Also add a complementary color: If the tone is red, add green; if yellow, add purple.

1. Medium Mix

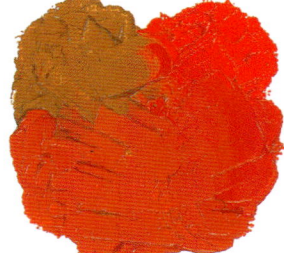

YELLOW OCHRE +
CADMIUM RED LIGHT

2. Light Mix

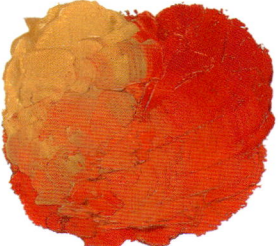

NAPLES YELLOW HUE +
CADMIUM RED LIGHT

3. Ruddy Mix

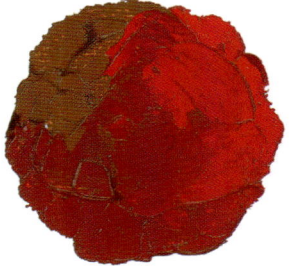

BURNT SIENNA +
CADMIUM RED LIGHT

4. Medium-Dark Mix

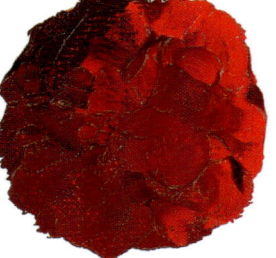

RAW SIENNA +
CADMIUM VERMILION

5. Dark Mix

BURNT UMBER +
CADMIUM VERMILION

MODIFYING COLORS

The two mixtures at right, modifying colors, can be used to tone down light flesh colors, to deepen and bronze reddish colors, and to warm or cool shadow colors.

1. Cool Purple Mix

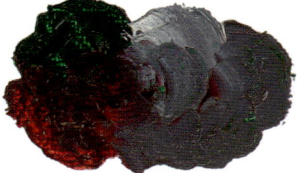

ALIZARIN CRIMSON +
VIRIDIAN GREEN + WHITE

2. Warm Purple Mix

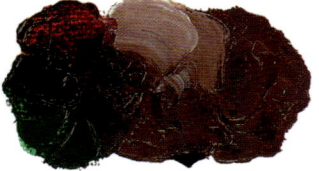

ALIZARIN CRIMSON + WHITE +
BURNT UMBER + VIRIDIAN
GREEN

FAIR SKIN TONES

The combination of colors below can be used as a base for fair skin tones. You can create many skin tones using this palette. Phthalo red is the key color here—mix it with white to produce pink, or add white and the other colors shown to change the value. Gray or warm the mixes as a base for fair skin tones.

Try to keep the colors delicate and not too harsh or pure. Play with these colors first, and then develop some original palettes. (Note: When painting a flesh color, never use any red in its pure state.)

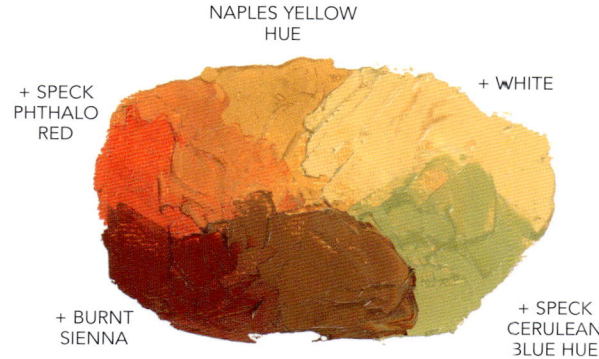

NAPLES YELLOW HUE

+ SPECK PHTHALO RED

+ WHITE

+ BURNT SIENNA

+ SPECK CERULEAN BLUE HUE

BURNT UMBER TO BRONZE TONES

The palette at right is a base for skin tones that range in hue from burnt umber to bronze. Manipulate the colors to create a wide variety of skin tones. Note that some skin tones have a rich, warm undertone; others are delicately cool. Also take note of subtle colors that can appear under various lighting; look for delicate colors in the shadows and lively tints in the light areas. Depending on the model, shadows can be warm, cool, or even purple or green.

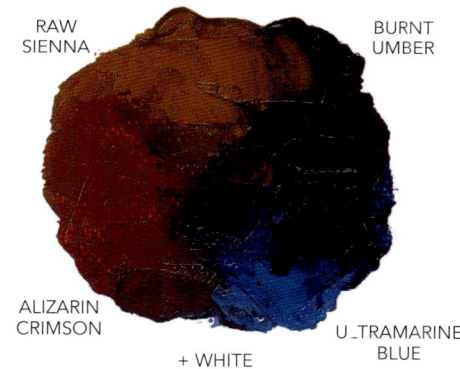

RAW SIENNA

BURNT UMBER

ALIZARIN CRIMSON

+ WHITE

ULTRAMARINE BLUE

LIGHT BRONZE TO YELLOW OCHRE TONES

You can use this palette as a base for skin tones that range in hue from light bronze to yellow ochre. The more burnt sienna and red in the mix, the more bronze the color will be. Adding more yellow ochre moves the mix toward lighter tones. You can lighten these mixes with a bit of white, but be careful when adding white to darker tones, as it can make them appear milky. Adding a speck of Venetian red will warm the colors. Experiment and remember that these introductory colors can lead to an endless number of skin tone palettes.

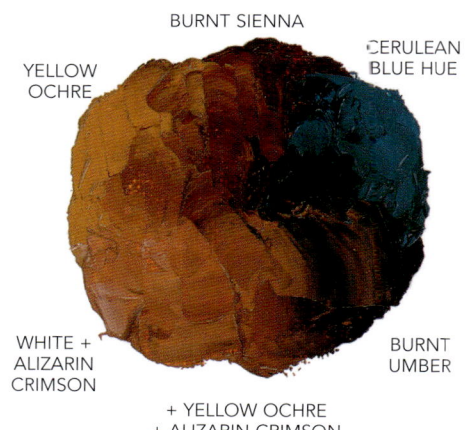

BURNT SIENNA

YELLOW OCHRE

CERULEAN BLUE HUE

WHITE + ALIZARIN CRIMSON

BURNT UMBER

+ YELLOW OCHRE + ALIZARIN CRIMSON

79

Variations in value create form and the illusion of depth, so it's important to learn to control these values. Comparing tonal values of black and white to color tones is a helpful exercise. Start with pure white and pure black at the two ends of your value scale; then mix the sample values at right in the following order to obtain a smooth graduation: 9, 8, 6, 7, 5, 4, 2, and 3.

TONAL VALUES

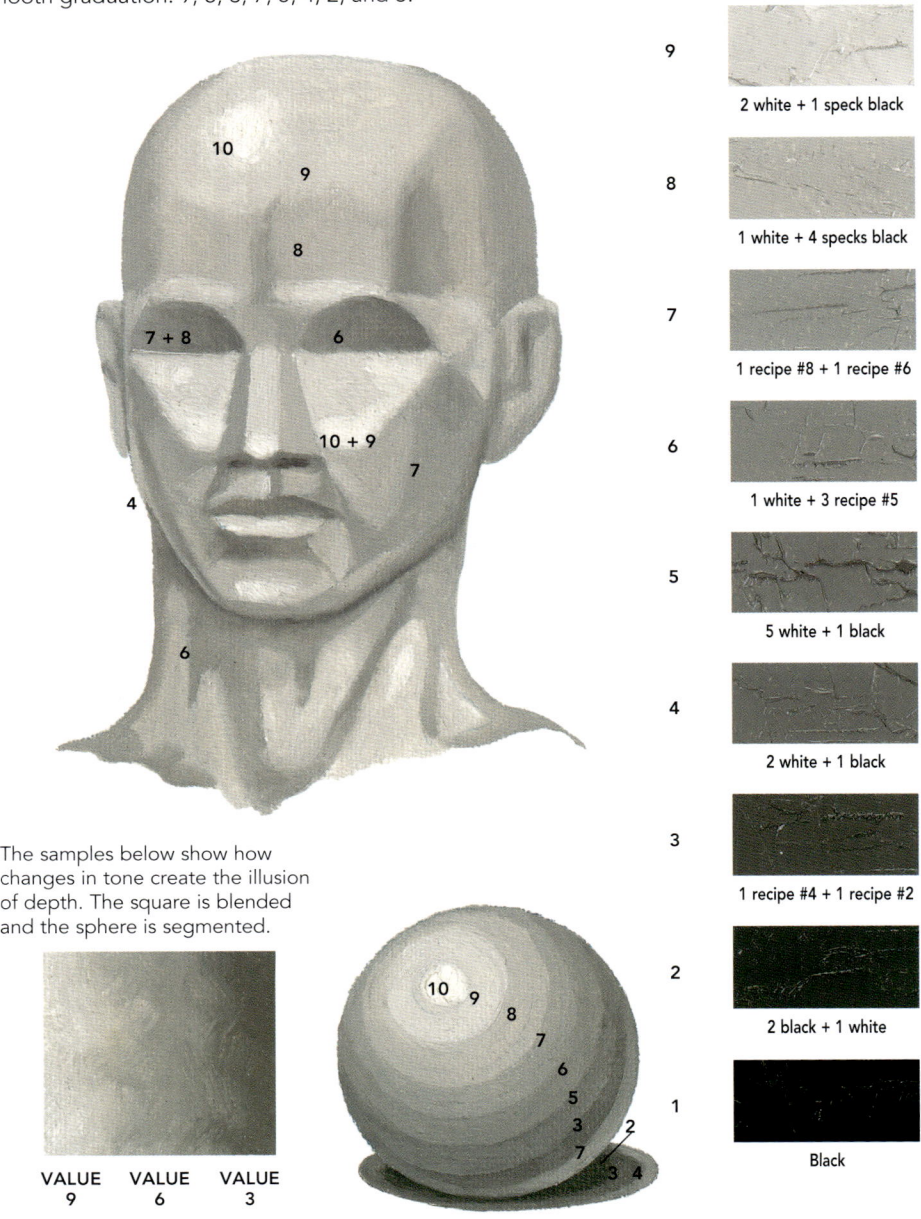

White

2 white + 1 speck black

1 white + 4 specks black

1 recipe #8 + 1 recipe #6

1 white + 3 recipe #5

5 white + 1 black

2 white + 1 black

1 recipe #4 + 1 recipe #2

2 black + 1 white

Black

The samples below show how changes in tone create the illusion of depth. The square is blended and the sphere is segmented.

VALUE 9   VALUE 6   VALUE 3

This value scale is based on the Munsell Value System, with 10 representing white (or "light," a combination of all colors created by light), graduating to 1, or black (the absence of light and color). Some artists reverse these numbers. The head study above, painted from an artist's wooden mannequin, has a few references on it as a visual guide to the scale.

COLOR VALUES

Page 84, recipe #11 — 10

Page 84, recipe #2 — 9

Page 84, recipe #3 — 8

Page 84, recipe #4 — 7

Page 84, recipe #5 — 6

Page 84, recipe #6 — 5

Page 84, recipe #7 — 4

Page 84, recipe #8 — 3

Page 84, recipe #9 — 2

Page 84, recipe #10 — 1

Seeing the value of colors is crucial to creating realistic forms. Tonal value scales, like the one on page 80, also are wonderful guides for comparing color values. For your reference, the colors in this scale are numbered to match their corresponding gray values on the other scale. The colors featured on this page are from the palette on page 84.

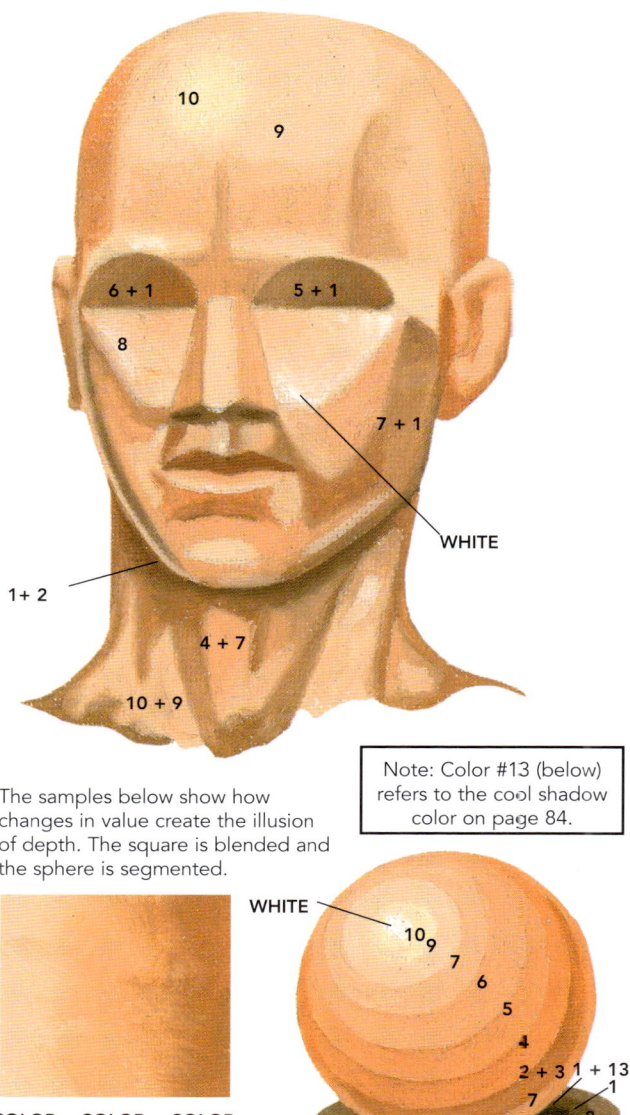

The samples below show how changes in value create the illusion of depth. The square is blended and the sphere is segmented.

COLOR 8   COLOR 5   COLOR 2

Note: Color #13 (below) refers to the cool shadow color on page 84.

Notice that the color value number placements on this head study vary slightly from the gray-scale study on page 80. This is because different skin tone palettes vary in value and tone from warm and cool to creamy and bronze. Due to these differences, use the value scale as a reference, not an absolute. Some palettes may relate only to limited portions of the scale; nonetheless, the scale is a great guide for color tone control. Study each palette and relate each color to a value on the scale.

WARM AND COOL AREAS IN AND AROUND THE MOUTH

The skin is thinner on the mouth and blood is closer to the surface, which can make this area redder than other areas of skin. At times, areas in and around the mouth can appear to be warmer than the rest of the face, as weather and emotions can flush the lips.

The upper lip is usually more shadowed than the lower lip, and it casts a shadow on the top of the lower lip. The mixtures shown on this page work as ideal basic lip color mixes that can be darkened, lightened, or grayed, depending on the model.

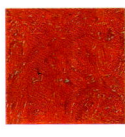

1. Warming Color
3 yellow ochre +
2 cadmium red light +
1 speck alizarin crimson

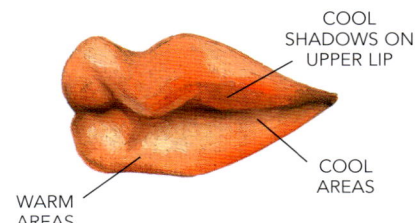

COOL SHADOWS ON UPPER LIP

HIGHLIGHT ON LOWER LIP

LOWER LIP WARM

COOL SHADOWS ON UPPER LIP

WARM AREAS

COOL AREAS

Add Venetian red and white to soften the lip colors where needed. Keep highlights soft to prevent the lips from appearing shiny. The highlight on the lower lip should be the lightest light.

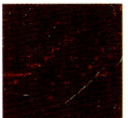

2. Warm Shadow
1 burnt umber +
1 alizarin crimson +
1 cadmium red light

Alter these mixes using a master skin tone recipe plus white, burnt sienna, Naples yellow hue, and cobalt blue; add Venetian red and burnt umber to deepen.

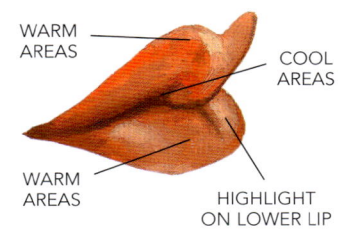

WARM AREAS

COOL AREAS

WARM AREAS

HIGHLIGHT ON LOWER LIP

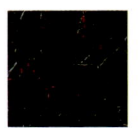

3. Cool Shadow
2 alizarin crimson +
1 ultramarine blue

4. Lightening Color
2 white +
1 speck Naples yellow hue

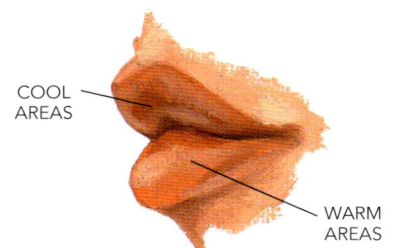

COOL AREAS

WARM AREAS

Varying edge lines add life to the mouth. Some lines are soft and "lost," whereas others are hard and definite. Use alizarin crimson and burnt umber for the deep shadows at the corners. Add specks of ultramarine blue and alizarin crimson for cooler purple shadows. For lower lip highlights, use a pale pink with the lightening color and different reds. White plus Venetian red makes a nice natural pink. The lightening color plus any pink can make an effective lip highlight. White plus alizarin crimson makes a cool pink, whereas white plus a speck of cadmium red light creates a warm pink. Remember to keep all value changes subtle for a realistic look.

WARM AND COOL AREAS IN AND AROUND THE EARS AND NOSE

Many delicate color changes can take place in the creases and curves of the ears and nose. The tops of the ears can become red with the flow of blood, whereas the nose can become red at the tip. The following basic mixes can be deepened or lightened, depending on the model.

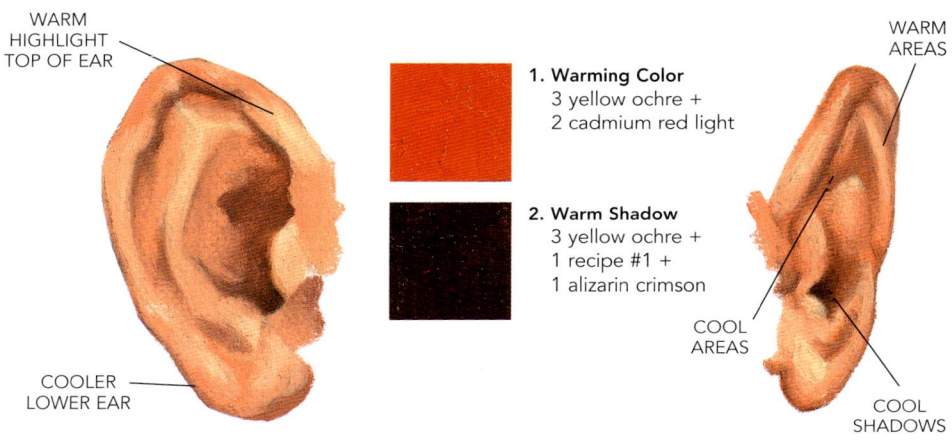

WARM HIGHLIGHT TOP OF EAR

WARM AREAS

1. Warming Color
3 yellow ochre +
2 cadmium red light

2. Warm Shadow
3 yellow ochre +
1 recipe #1 +
1 alizarin crimson

COOL AREAS

COOL SHADOWS

COOLER LOWER EAR

Colors selected for these warmer areas should be muted in intensity. Cadmium red light is very bright if used too strongly. Cadmium vermilion and Venetian red are more muted and will tone down the color. If shadow colors become too strong, gray them with a speck of burnt umber, ultramarine blue, viridian green, or chrome oxide green. As with the mouth, use a variety of reds for different tones. Keep purple mixes for the shadows delicate and not too strong—or they may give a bruised appearance. Colors used in the mouth, ears, and nose must be harmonious with the flesh tone of the subject. Simply use these basic mixes to manipulate the overall skin tones.

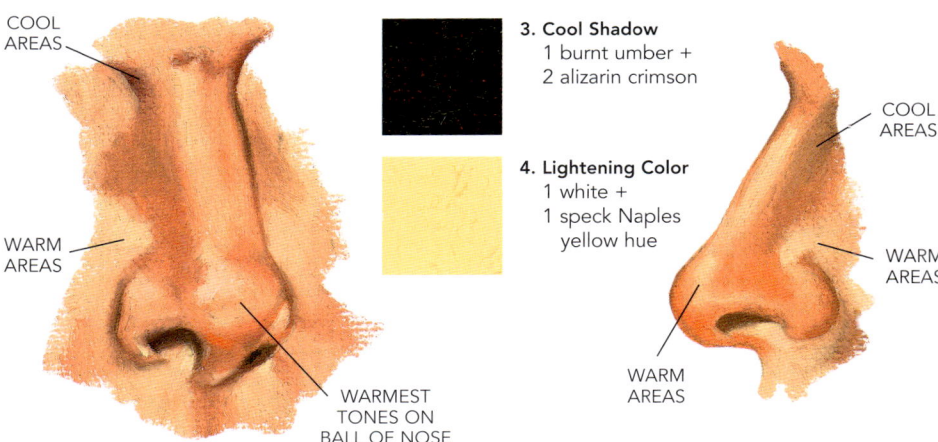

COOL AREAS

3. Cool Shadow
1 burnt umber +
2 alizarin crimson

COOL AREAS

4. Lightening Color
1 white +
1 speck Naples
yellow hue

WARM AREAS

WARM AREAS

WARMEST TONES ON BALL OF NOSE

WARM AREAS

The placement of the mouth, eyes, nose, and ears in relationship to one another on the cranial mass is of the utmost importance. Even the slightest variation of a feature's position can change the expression of the portrait. Any slight misplacement will also change the features of the subject enough to lose the likeness. Study the subject closely and take note of even the subtlest tone changes in the flesh of the ears, nose, and mouth.

COLORS USED

- Burnt Sienna
- Cadmium Red Light
- Ivory Black
- Naples Yellow Hue
- Raw Umber
- Titanium White
- Viridian Green
- Yellow Ochre

Mix until the color matches the **Master Skin Tone Recipe** shown at right.

1. 3 cadmium red light
2 yellow ochre

Cadmium red light

Yellow ochre

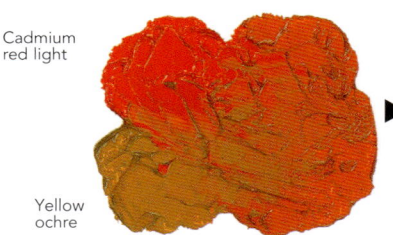

MASTER SKIN TONE RECIPE

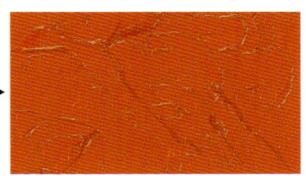

LIGHT VALUES

2. 2 white
1 speck master recipe
1 speck Naples yellow hue

3. 1 white
3 specks master recipe
1 speck Naples yellow hue

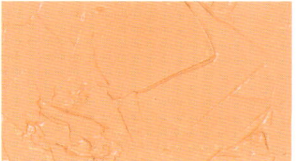

4. 10 white
1 master recipe

MIDDLE VALUES

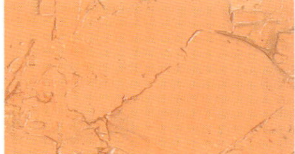

5. 8 white
1 master recipe

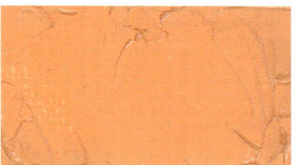

6. 6 white
1 master recipe

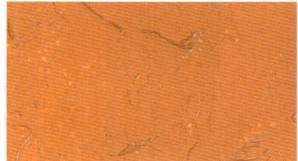

7. 5 white
2 master recipe
2 specks recipe #12

DARK/GRAYED VALUES

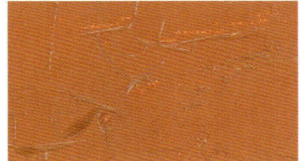

8. 3 white
1 master recipe
1 recipe #12

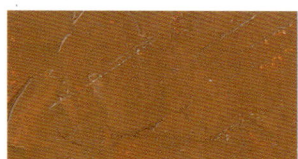

9. 2 white
1 master recipe
1 recipe #12
1 speck recipe #14

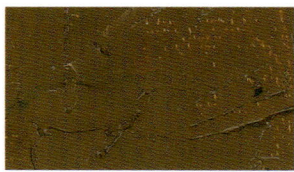

10. 1 white
1 master recipe
1 recipe #13
1 speck recipe #14

HIGHLIGHT VALUE

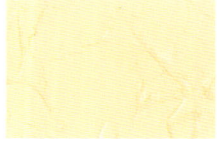

11. 1 white
2 specks Naples yellow hue

WARM SHADOW

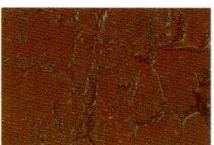

12. 4 burnt sienna
1 white
1 master recipe

COOL SHADOW

13. 4 raw umber
1 white
1 master recipe

GRAYING COLOR

14. 2 viridian green
1 white
1 speck black

COLORS USED

- Burnt Umber
- Cadmium Red Light
- Cerulean Blue Hue
- Naples Yellow Hue
- Titanium White
- Venetian Red
- Yellow Ochre

Mix until the color matches the **Master Skin Tone Recipe** shown at right.

1. 5 cadmium red light
2 yellow ochre
3 white

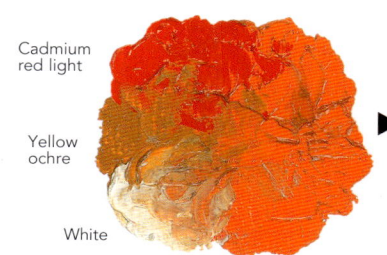

Cadmium red light

Yellow ochre

White

MASTER SKIN TONE RECIPE

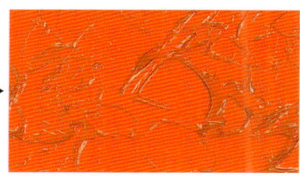

LIGHT VALUES

2. 9 white
1 Naples yellow hue

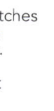

3. 2 recipe #2
1 speck Venetian red

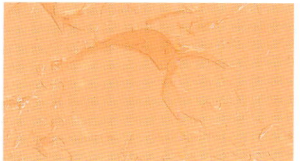

4. 13 recipe #2
1 master recipe

MIDDLE VALUES

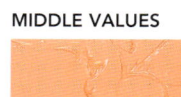

5. 5 white
3 recipe #2
2 specks cadmium red light
1 speck master recipe

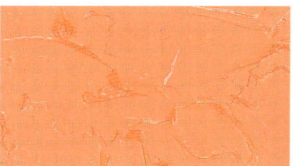

6. 6 white
1 recipe #2
1 master recipe
4 specks cadmium red light

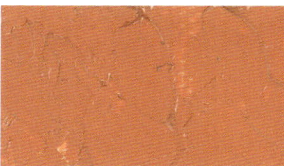

7. 4 recipe #5
3 specks Venetian red
1 speck master recipe

DARK/GRAYED VALUES

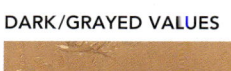

8. 7 white
2 master recipe
1 recipe #14
1 speck recipe #13

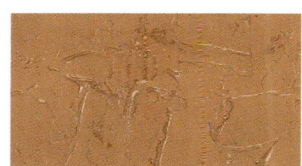

9. 5 recipe #8
1 master recipe
2 specks recipe #13

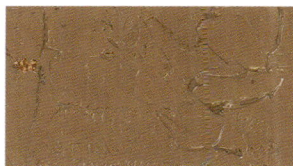

10. 5 recipe #9
1 recipe #12
1 recipe #14

HIGHLIGHT VALUE

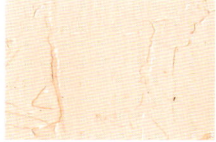

11. 2 white
1 speck cadmium red light

WARM SHADOW

12. 4 recipe #2
2 master recipe
1 Venetian red
1 burnt umber

COOL SHADOW

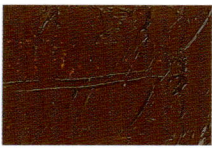

13. 2 master recipe
1 burnt umber

GRAYING COLOR

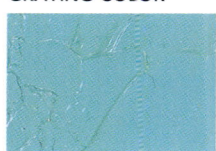

14. 4 white
1 cerulean blue hue

OIL & ACRYLIC SKIN TONES

COLORS USED

- Alizarin Crimson
- Cadmium Red Light
- Raw Sienna
- Titanium White
- Viridian Green

Mix until the color matches the **Master Skin Tone Recipe** shown at right.

1. 1 raw sienna
3 white

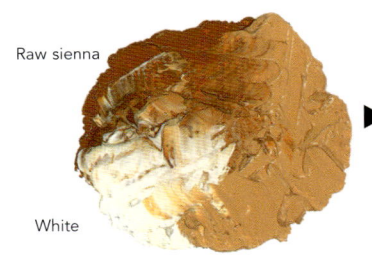

Raw sienna

White

MASTER SKIN TONE RECIPE

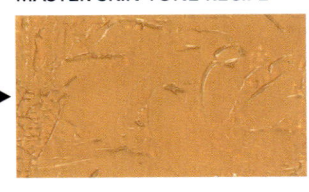

LIGHT VALUES

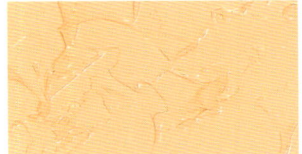

2. 5 white
1 master recipe

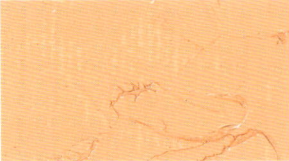

3. 5 recipe #2
3 specks cadmium red light

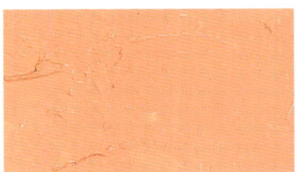

4. 1 recipe #3
1 speck alizarin crimson

MIDDLE VALUES

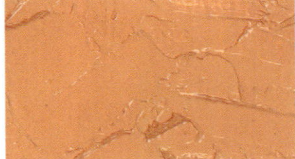

5. 1 white
1 master recipe
2 specks recipe #12

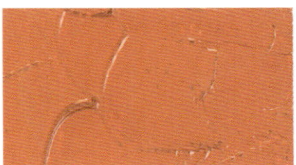

6. 3 white
5 master recipe
1 recipe #12

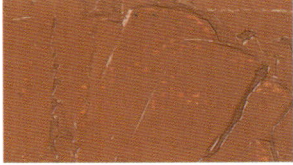

7. 6 recipe #6
1 recipe #13

DARK/GRAYED VALUES

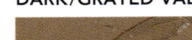
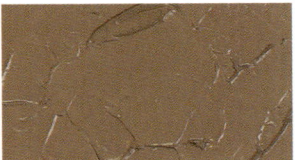

8. 3 recipe #7
1 recipe #14

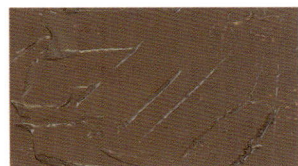

9. 2 recipe #7
1 recipe #12
3 recipe #14
2 specks recipe #13

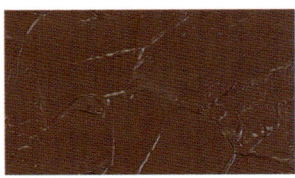

10. 5 recipe #9
3 recipe #13
1 speck raw sienna

HIGHLIGHT VALUE

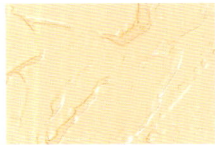

11. 1 white
3 specks master recipe

WARM SHADOW

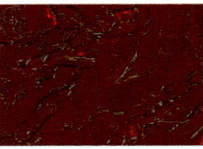

12. 1 raw sienna
1 alizarin crimson

COOL SHADOW

13. 1 raw sienna
1 alizarin crimson
1 viridian green

GRAYING COLOR

14. 3 white
1 viridian green

COLORS USED

- Burnt Umber
- Cobalt Blue
- Ivory Black
- Naples Yellow Hue
- Phthalo Red
- Titanium White
- Viridian Green

Mix until the color matches the **Master Skin Tone Recipe** shown at right.

1. 3 Naples yellow hue
1 phthalo red

Naples yellow hue

Phthalo red

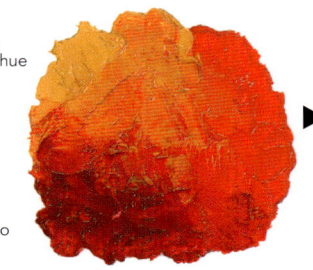

MASTER SKIN TONE RECIPE

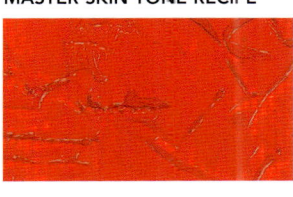

LIGHT VALUES

2. 2 white
1 speck master recipe
1 speck Naples yellow hue

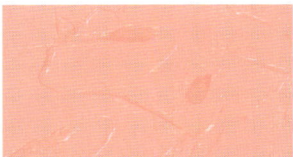

3. 6 white
1 master recipe

4. 6 white
1 master recipe
1 Naples yellow hue

MIDDLE VALUES

5. 5 recipe #3
1 recipe #14

6. 7 white
1 master recipe
2 Naples yellow hue
1 recipe #12

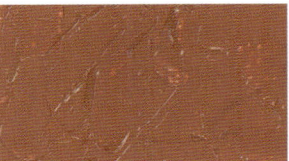

7. 5 white
2 master recipe
1 Naples yellow hue
3 specks burnt umber

DARK/GRAYED VALUES

8. 1 master recipe
1 viridian green
1 recipe #11

9. 1 master recipe
1 recipe #13
1 recipe #14

10. 3 master recipe
1 white
2 recipe #13

HIGHLIGHT VALUE

11. 3 white
1 speck Naples yellow hue
1 tiny speck phthalo red

WARM SHADOW

12. 1 burnt umber
1 Naples yellow hue
1 phthalo red
2 white

COOL SHADOW

13. 3 master recipe
1 viridian green

GRAYING COLOR

14. 4 white
1 cobalt blue
1 speck black

OIL & ACRYLIC SKIN TONES

- Alizarin Crimson
- Burnt Sienna
- Burnt Umber
- Cerulean Blue Hue
- Naples Yellow Hue
- Raw Sienna
- Titanium White
- Viridian Green

Mix until the color matches the **Master Skin Tone Recipe** shown at right.

1. 1 raw sienna
1 alizarin crimson
1 white

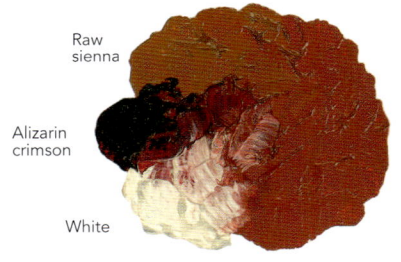

Raw sienna

Alizarin crimson

White

MASTER SKIN TONE RECIPE

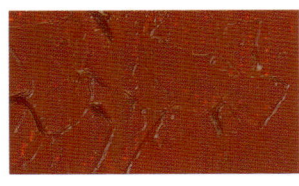

LIGHT VALUES

2. 2 white
1 speck raw sienna

3. 3 white
1 speck Naples yellow hue
1 speck master recipe

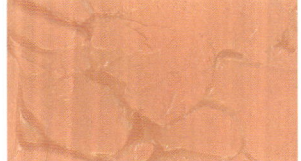

4. 9 white
1 master recipe
2 specks raw sienna

MIDDLE VALUES

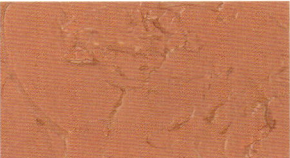

5. 3 white
1 master recipe
2 specks raw sienna

6. 3 recipe #5
1 recipe #12

7. 3 recipe #5
1 burnt sienna
1 alizarin crimson
2 specks burnt umber

DARK/GRAYED VALUES

8. 6 master recipe
3 white
2 recipe #13

9. 3 recipe #8
1 recipe #14

10. 2 master recipe
3 burnt umber
1 burnt sienna
1 alizarin crimson

HIGHLIGHT VALUE

11. 1 white
1 speck Naples yellow hue

WARM SHADOW

12. 3 master recipe
1 burnt umber

COOL SHADOW

13. 3 master recipe
2 viridian green

GRAYING COLOR

14. 1 cerulean blue hue
1 viridian green
1 white

COLORS USED

- Burnt Sienna
- Cadmium Orange
- Cadmium Red Light
- Cadmium Vermilion
- Cadmium Yellow Medium
- Cerulean Blue Hue
- Raw Sienna
- Titanium White
- Viridian Green

Mix until the color matches the **Master Skin Tone Recipe** shown at right.

1. 5 raw sienna
2 cadmium red light

Raw sienna

Cadmium red light

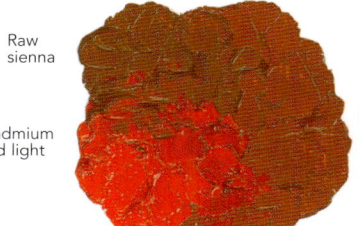

MASTER SKIN TONE RECIPE

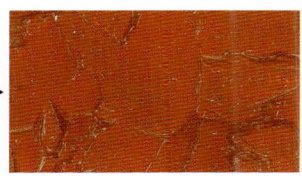

LIGHT VALUES

2. 2 white
1 speck master recipe
2 specks recipe #11

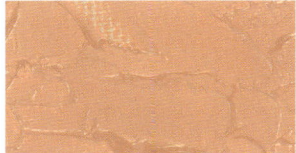

3. 10 white
1 master recipe

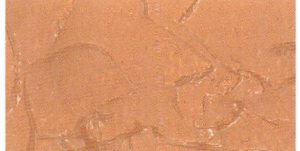

4. 6 white
1 master recipe

MIDDLE VALUES

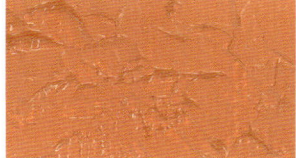

5. 3 white
1 master recipe
1 speck cadmium orange

6. 2 white
1 master recipe
2 specks cadmium vermilion

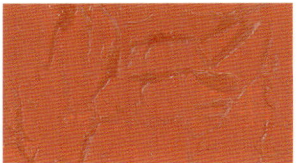

7. 2 white
1 master recipe
1 cadmium vermilion

DARK/GRAYED VALUES

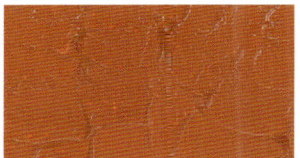

8. 1 white
1 master recipe
1 recipe #12

9. 1 master recipe
1 recipe #13

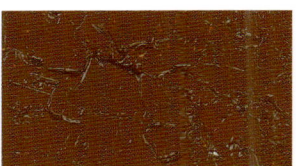

10. 1 master recipe
2 recipe #14
1 speck cadmium vermilion

HIGHLIGHT VALUE

11. 1 white
1 speck cadmium yellow medium

WARM SHADOW

12. 1 master recipe
1 burnt sienna

COOL SHADOW

13. 1 white
1 cerulean blue hue
1 cadmium vermilion

GRAYING COLOR

14. 2 master recipe
1 viridian green

OIL & ACRYLIC SKIN TONES

- Alizarin Crimson
- Burnt Sienna
- Burnt Umber
- Cadmium Orange
- Cadmium Yellow Medium
- Naples Yellow Hue
- Phthalo Red
- Raw Sienna
- Titanium White
- Ultramarine Blue

Mix until the color matches the **Master Skin Tone Recipe** shown at right.

1. 6 Naples yellow hue
1 cadmium yellow medium
1 raw sienna
1 speck phthalo red

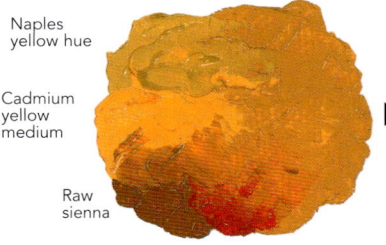

Naples yellow hue

Cadmium yellow medium

Raw sienna

Phthalo red

MASTER SKIN TONE RECIPE

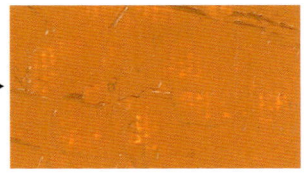

LIGHT VALUES

2. 2 white
1 speck master recipe

3. 1 recipe #2
1 recipe #4

4. 3 white
1 master recipe

MIDDLE VALUES

5. 8 white
2 master recipe
1 cadmium orange

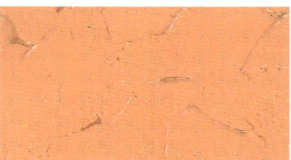

6. 1 recipe #5
1 speck phthalo red

7. 2 recipe #6
2 specks recipe #14

DARK/GRAYED VALUES

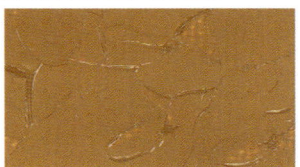

8. 2 master recipe
1 recipe #14
1 speck phthalo red

9. 3 master recipe
1 recipe #14
1 recipe #12

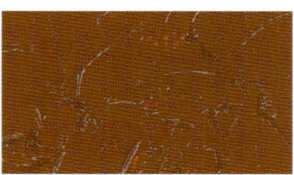

10. 4 master recipe
1 recipe #13
1 recipe #11

HIGHLIGHT VALUE

11. 2 white
1 speck cadmium yellow medium

WARM SHADOW

12. 1 white
2 burnt sienna

COOL SHADOW

13. 1 white
1 burnt umber
1 alizarin crimson

GRAYING COLOR

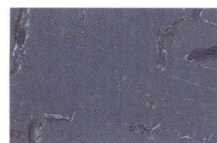

14. 3 white
1 ultramarine blue
3 specks alizarin crimson

OIL & ACRYLIC SKIN TONES

COLORS USED

- Alizarin Crimson
- Burnt Sienna
- Burnt Umber
- Cadmium Orange
- Cadmium Vermilion
- Cadmium Yellow Medium
- Ivory Black
- Naples Yellow Hue
- Raw Sienna
- Titanium White
- Ultramarine Blue

Mix until the color matches the **Master Skin Tone Recipe** shown at right.

1. 8 Naples yellow hue
1 cadmium yellow medium
3 raw sienna
2 specks cadmium vermilion

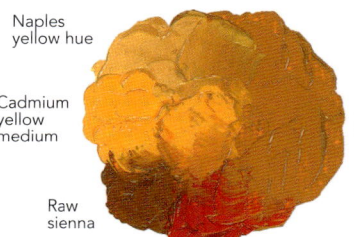

Naples yellow hue

Cadmium yellow medium

Raw sienna

Cadmium vermilion

MASTER SKIN TONE RECIPE

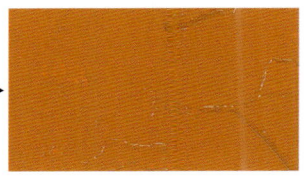

LIGHT VALUES

2. 2 white
1 speck master recipe

3. 1 recipe #2
1 recipe #4

4. 2 white
1 master recipe

MIDDLE VALUES

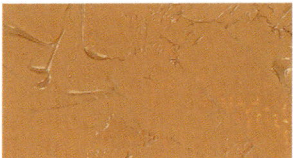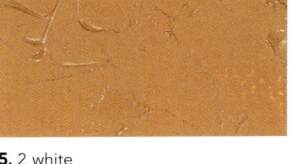

5. 2 white
1 master recipe
1 burnt sienna
1 recipe #11

6. 5 recipe #5
1 cadmium orange
1 recipe #12

7. 2 recipe #5
1 recipe #13

DARK/GRAYED VALUES

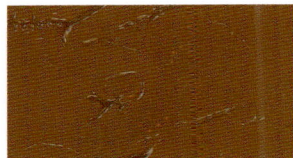

8. 3 master recipe
2 specks cadmium vermilion
1 speck alizarin crimson

9. 2 master recipe
1 recipe #13

10. 6 master recipe
1 alizarin crimson
3 specks ultramarine blue

HIGHLIGHT VALUE

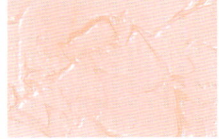

11. 1 white
1 speck cadmium vermilion

WARM SHADOW

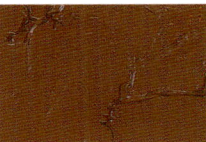

12. 2 white
2 burnt sienna
1 black

COOL SHADOW

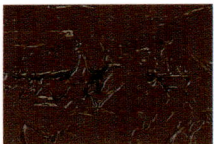

13. 2 white
2 burnt umber
1 alizarin crimson

GRAYING COLOR

14. 2 white
1 ultramarine blue

91

COLORS USED

- Alizarin Crimson
- Burnt Sienna
- Burnt Umber
- Cadmium Orange
- Cadmium Vermilion
- Naples Yellow Hue
- Raw Sienna
- Titanium White
- Ultramarine Blue

Mix until the color matches the **Master Skin Tone Recipe** shown at right.

1. 1 raw sienna
1 cadmium orange
1 white

Raw sienna

Cadmium orange + white

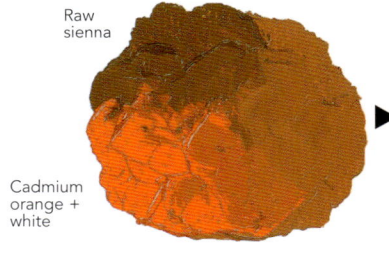

MASTER SKIN TONE RECIPE

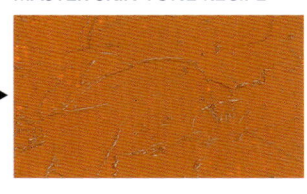

LIGHT VALUES

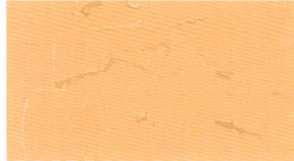

2. 2 recipe #11
1 speck master recipe

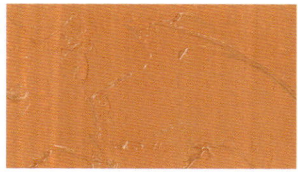

3. 2 white
1 master recipe

4. 1 recipe #3
1 speck burnt sienna
1 speck cadmium vermilion

MIDDLE VALUES

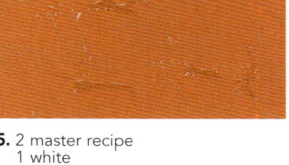

5. 2 master recipe
1 white
2 specks cadmium vermilion

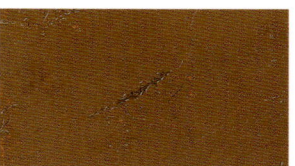

6. 2 recipe #5
1 recipe #12

7. 2 recipe #5
1 recipe #13

DARK/GRAYED VALUES

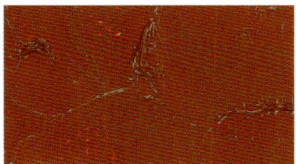

8. 2 master recipe
1 burnt umber
1 cadmium orange

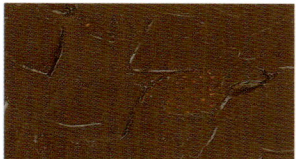

9. 1 master recipe
1 recipe #12

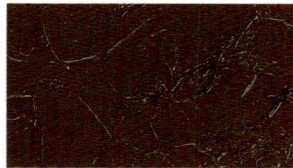

10. 1 master recipe
1 recipe #12
1 recipe #13
1 speck #14

HIGHLIGHT VALUE

11. 3 white
1 speck cadmium orange

WARM SHADOW

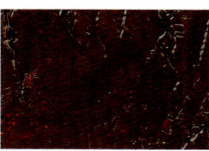

12. 2 burnt sienna
1 alizarin crimson
1 Naples yellow hue

COOL SHADOW

13. 2 burnt umber
1 alizarin crimson
1 Naples yellow hue

GRAYING COLOR

14. 1 white
1 ultramarine blue
1 alizarin crimson

OIL & ACRYLIC SKIN TONES

- Alizarin Crimson
- Burnt Sienna
- Burnt Umber
- Cadmium Red Light
- Cadmium Vermilion
- Chrome Oxide Green
- Cobalt Blue
- Titanium White
- Yellow Ochre

Mix until the color matches the **Master Skin Tone Recipe** shown at right.

1. 4 yellow ochre
   2 burnt sienna
   1 chrome oxide green
   3 cadmium red light

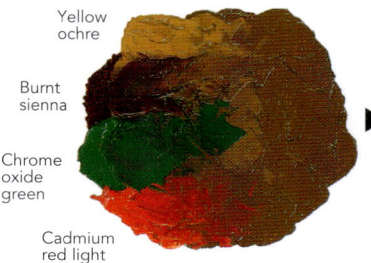

Yellow ochre
Burnt sienna
Chrome oxide green
Cadmium red light

MASTER SKIN TONE RECIPE

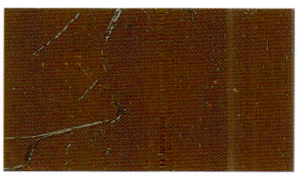

LIGHT VALUES

2. 1 recipe #11
   1 speck master recipe

3. 3 white
   1 master recipe

4. 3 white
   1 master recipe
   2 specks cadmium vermilion

MIDDLE VALUES

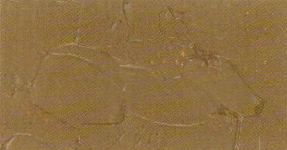

5. 4 white
   1 master recipe

6. 1 recipe #5
   1 recipe #7

7. 3 recipe #5
   1 master recipe

DARK/GRAYED VALUES

8. 2 recipe #4
   1 recipe #12

9. 2 recipe #11
   1 master recipe
   1 recipe #14

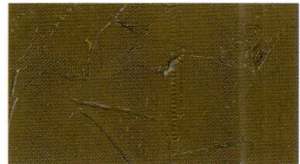

10. 2 recipe #9
   1 recipe #13

HIGHLIGHT VALUE

11. 1 white
   1 speck cadmium vermilion

WARM SHADOW

12. 2 master recipe
   1 burnt sienna
   1 speck alizarin crimson

COOL SHADOW

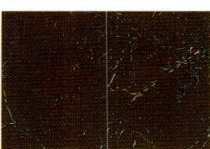

13. 2 master recipe
   1 burnt umber

GRAYING COLOR

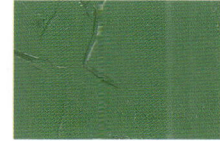

14. 2 white
   1 chrome oxide green
   2 specks cobalt blue

OIL & ACRYLIC SKIN TONES

COLORS USED

- Alizarin Crimson
- Burnt Sienna
- Burnt Umber
- Cadmium Orange
- Cadmium Vermilion
- Cadmium Yellow Medium
- Ivory Black
- Titanium White
- Ultramarine Blue
- Yellow Ochre

Mix until the color matches the **Master Skin Tone Recipe** shown at right.

1. 2 white
1 yellow ochre
2 burnt sienna
1 black

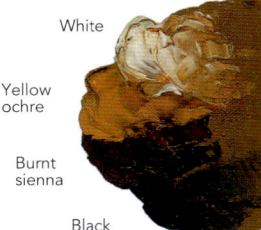

White
Yellow ochre
Burnt sienna
Black

MASTER SKIN TONE RECIPE

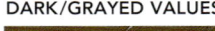

LIGHT VALUES

2. 2 white
1 recipe #11
1 speck master recipe

3. 1 master recipe
1 white
1 recipe #11

4. 2 recipe #3
1 master recipe

MIDDLE VALUES

5. 1 white
1 master recipe
2 specks recipe #12

6. 2 white
3 master recipe
3 specks cadmium vermilion

7. 2 master recipe
1 burnt sienna

DARK/GRAYED VALUES

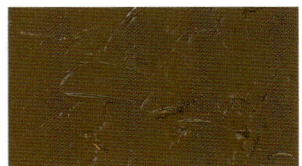

8. 6 recipe #14
2 master recipe
1 cadmium vermilion

9. 4 master recipe
2 recipe #14
1 alizarin crimson

10. 2 master recipe
1 recipe #13

HIGHLIGHT VALUE

11. 3 white
1 speck cadmium orange
1 speck cadmium yellow medium

WARM SHADOW

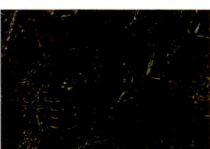

12. 2 burnt umber
1 cadmium vermilion

COOL SHADOW

13. 2 white
1 black
1 burnt umber
1 speck alizarin crimson

GRAYING COLOR

14. 2 white
1 ultramarine blue

COLORS USED

- Alizarin Crimson
- Burnt Sienna
- Burnt Umber
- Cadmium Orange
- Cadmium Red Light
- Cadmium Yellow Medium
- Naples Yellow Hue
- Raw Sienna
- Titanium White
- Ultramarine Blue

Mix until the color matches the **Master Skin Tone Recipe** shown at right.

1. 4 Naples yellow hue
1 burnt sienna
3 specks cadmium orange

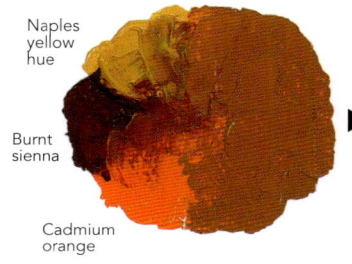

Naples yellow hue

Burnt sienna

Cadmium orange

MASTER SKIN TONE RECIPE

LIGHT VALUES

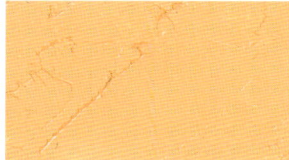

2. 1 white
1 recipe #11
1 speck master recipe

3. 2 white
2 recipe #11
1 master recipe

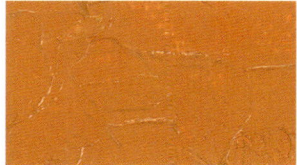

4. 3 recipe #11
1 master recipe

MIDDLE VALUES

5. 3 recipe #14
1 master recipe
1 speck cadmium orange

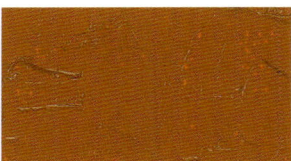

6. 1 recipe #14
1 master recipe
1 speck recipe #12

7. 3 master recipe
1 recipe #12

DARK/GRAYED VALUES

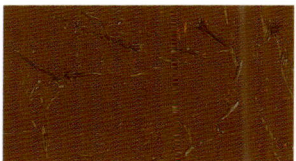

8. 2 master recipe
1 recipe #14

9. 2 master recipe
1 recipe #12
1 speck cadmium red light

10. 1 master recipe
1 recipe #13

HIGHLIGHT VALUE

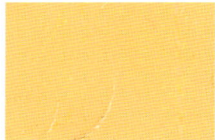

11. 3 white
1 Naples yellow hue
1 speck cadmium yellow medium

WARM SHADOW

12. 2 burnt umber
1 alizarin crimson
1 raw sienna

COOL SHADOW

13. 1 burnt umber
1 speck cadmium orange

GRAYING COLOR

14. 1 white
1 ultramarine blue
1 alizarin crimson

95

OIL & ACRYLIC SKIN TONES

- Burnt Sienna
- Burnt Umber
- Cadmium Red Light
- Cobalt Blue
- Ivory Black
- Naples Yellow Hue
- Titanium White
- Venetian Red
- Viridian Green

Mix until the color matches the **Master Skin Tone Recipe** shown at right.

1. 3 Venetian red
   1 burnt sienna

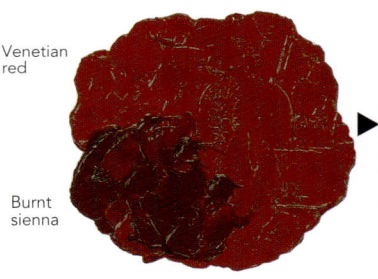

Venetian red

Burnt sienna

MASTER SKIN TONE RECIPE

LIGHT VALUES

2. 1 Naples yellow hue
   1 speck master recipe
   1 speck cadmium red light

3. 1 recipe #11
   1 speck master recipe

4. 1 recipe #11
   2 specks master recipe

MIDDLE VALUES

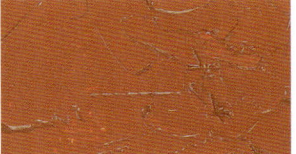

5. 1 recipe #11
   4 specks master recipe

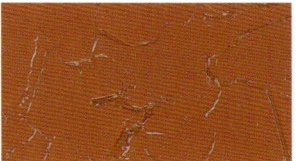

6. 4 recipe #11
   1 master recipe
   3 Naples yellow hue

7. 2 recipe #11
   1 master recipe

DARK/GRAYED VALUES

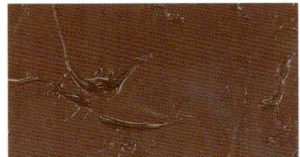

8. 5 recipe #14
   1 master recipe

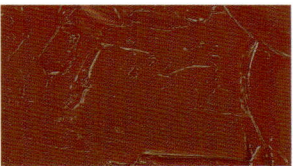

9. 1 white
   1 master recipe
   1 recipe #12

10. 3 recipe #13
   1 master recipe
   2 recipe #14

HIGHLIGHT VALUE

11. 6 white
   5 Naples yellow hue
   1 cadmium red light

WARM SHADOW

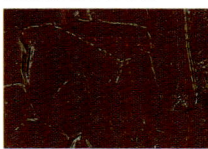

12. 1 master recipe
   2 burnt umber

COOL SHADOW

13. 2 black
   3 viridian green
   1 master recipe

GRAYING COLOR

14. 2 white
   1 cobalt blue

COLORS USED

- Alizarin Crimson
- Burnt Sienna
- Burnt Umber
- Cadmium Orange
- Cadmium Red Light
- Cadmium Yellow Medium
- Chrome Oxide Green
- Raw Sienna
- Titanium White
- Viridian Green

Mix until the color matches the **Master Skin Tone Recipe** shown at right.

1. 3 burnt sienna
2 raw sienna
1 speck cadmium red light

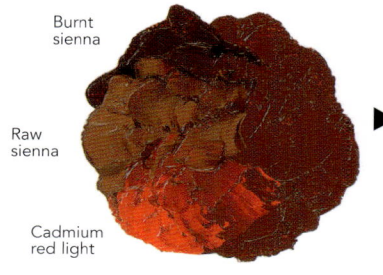

Burnt sienna

Raw sienna

Cadmium red light

MASTER SKIN TONE RECIPE

LIGHT VALUES

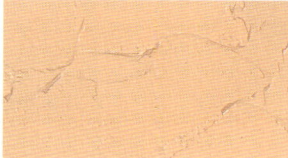

2. 2 white
1 recipe #11
1 speck master recipe

3. 1 recipe #11
2 specks master recipe

4. 2 recipe #11
1 master recipe

MIDDLE VALUES

5. 1 white
1 master recipe

6. 3 recipe #5
1 recipe #12

7. 1 recipe #6
1 recipe #12
1 speck cadmium orange

DARK/GRAYED VALUES

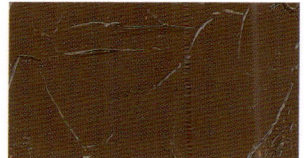

8. 4 master recipe
1 recipe #14

9. 1 master recipe
1 recipe #12

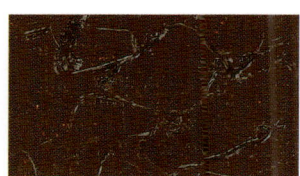

10. 1 master recipe
1 recipe #13

HIGHLIGHT VALUE

11. 5 white
1 cadmium yellow medium
1 speck cadmium red light

WARM SHADOW

12. 2 burnt umber
1 alizarin crimson

COOL SHADOW

13. 2 burnt sienna
3 viridian green

GRAYING COLOR

14. 1 white
1 chrome oxide green

OIL & ACRYLIC SKIN TONES

- Alizarin Crimson
- Burnt Sienna
- Burnt Umber
- Cadmium Orange
- Cadmium Vermilion
- Ivory Black
- Titanium White
- Ultramarine Blue
- Yellow Ochre

Mix until the color matches the **Master Skin Tone Recipe** shown at right.

1. 2 burnt sienna
2 cadmium orange
1 yellow ochre
1 burnt umber

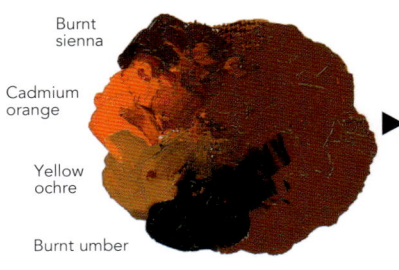

Burnt sienna

Cadmium orange

Yellow ochre

Burnt umber

MASTER SKIN TONE RECIPE

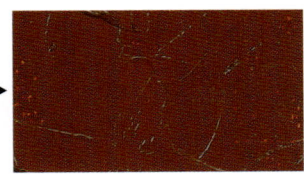

LIGHT VALUES

2. 1 recipe #11
1 speck master recipe

3. 1 recipe #11
1 master recipe

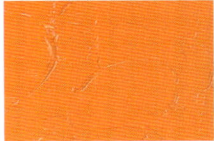

4. 1 recipe #11
1 master recipe
2 specks alizarin crimson

MIDDLE VALUES

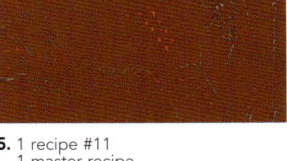

5. 1 recipe #11
1 master recipe
3 specks alizarin crimson
2 specks recipe #12

6. 1 recipe #5
1 recipe #7

7. 1 master recipe
1 burnt sienna

DARK/GRAYED VALUES

8. 1 master recipe
1 recipe #14

9. 1 master recipe
1 recipe #12
1 speck recipe #14

10. 2 master recipe
1 recipe #13

HIGHLIGHT VALUE

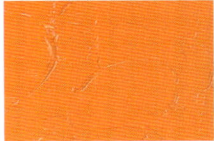

11. 1 white
1 yellow ochre
1 cadmium orange

WARM SHADOW

12. 2 burnt sienna
1 burnt umber

COOL SHADOW

13. 2 black
1 cadmium vermilion

GRAYING COLOR

14. 2 white
1 ultramarine blue
1 alizarin crimson

COLORS USED

- Alizarin Crimson
- Burnt Sienna
- Burnt Umber
- Cadmium Orange
- Cadmium Red Light
- Cadmium Vermilion
- Ivory Black
- Naples Yellow Hue
- Titanium White
- Ultramarine Blue
- Yellow Ochre

Mix until the color matches the **Master Skin Tone Recipe** shown at right.

1. 4 Naples yellow hue
2 burnt sienna
1 cadmium orange
1 white

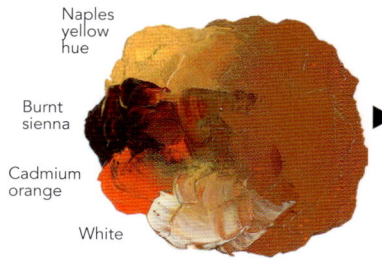

Naples yellow hue

Burnt sienna

Cadmium orange

White

MASTER SKIN TONE RECIPE

LIGHT VALUES

2. 1 recipe #11
1 speck master recipe

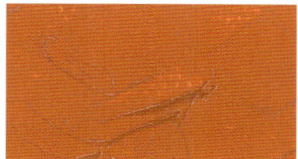

3. 1 recipe #11
1 master recipe

4. 2 master recipe
3 recipe #11
2 specks alizarin crimson
2 specks burnt umber

MIDDLE VALUES

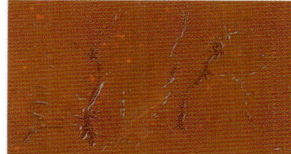

5. 3 master recipe
1 burnt umber

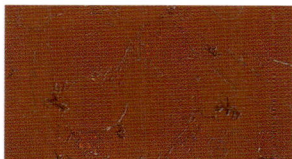

6. 3 master recipe
1 cadmium vermilion
1 recipe #14

7. 5 recipe #14
1 master recipe
1 recipe #12

DARK/GRAYED VALUES

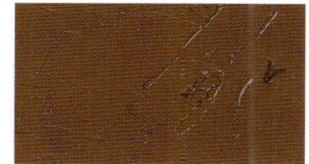

8. 1 master recipe
1 recipe #14

9. 2 master recipe
1 recipe #12
1 recipe #14

10. 2 master recipe
1 recipe #13

HIGHLIGHT VALUE

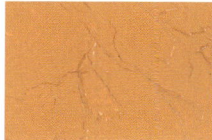

11. 2 white
1 Naples yellow hue
1 yellow ochre
1 speck cadmium
red light

WARM SHADOW

12. 3 burnt sienna
1 black
2 specks cadmium
vermilion

COOL SHADOW

13. 3 burnt umber
2 alizarin crimson

GRAYING COLOR

14. 4 white
1 alizarin crimson
1 ultramarine blue

COLORS USED

- Alizarin Crimson
- Burnt Sienna
- Burnt Umber
- Cadmium Orange

- Cobalt Blue
- Ivory Black
- Raw Umber

- Titanium White
- Venetian Red
- Viridian Green

Mix until the color matches the **Master Skin Tone Recipe** shown at right.

1. 2 raw umber
1 burnt sienna
3 white

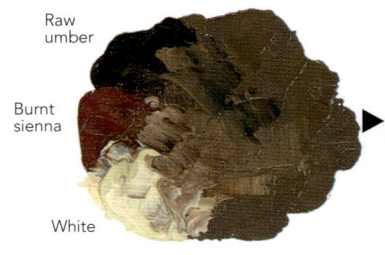

Raw umber

Burnt sienna

White

MASTER SKIN TONE RECIPE

LIGHT VALUES

2. 3 white
1 recipe #11
1 master recipe

3. 2 recipe #11
2 white
1 master recipe

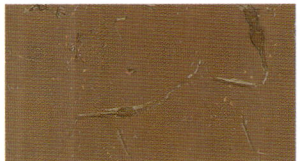

4. 3 recipe #11
1 master recipe

MIDDLE VALUES

5. 1 master recipe
2 white
1 speck alizarin crimson

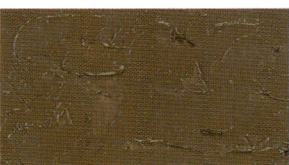

6. 1 recipe #5
2 specks black

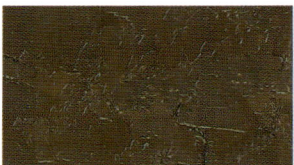

7. 1 recipe #6
2 specks black
2 specks burnt umber

DARK/GRAYED VALUES

8. 2 master recipe
1 recipe #12

9. 2 master recipe
1 recipe #13

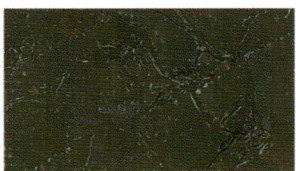

10. 2 master recipe
1 viridian green

Highlight Value

11. 3 white
1 alizarin crimson
1 cadmium orange

Warm Shadow

12. 2 black
1 Venetian red

Cool Shadow

13. 1 black
1 cobalt blue

Graying Color

14. Viridian green (pure)

COLORS USED

- Alizarin Crimson
- Burnt Sienna
- Burnt Umber
- Cadmium Orange
- Cadmium Red Light
- Cobalt Blue
- Raw Umber
- Titanium White

Mix until the color matches the **Master Skin Tone Recipe** shown at right.

1. 2 raw umber
1 burnt sienna
6 white

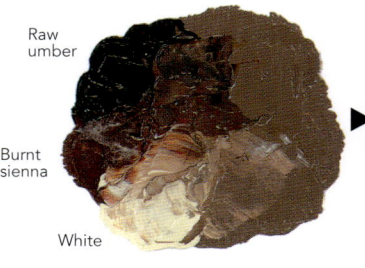

Raw umber

Burnt sienna

White

MASTER SKIN TONE RECIPE

LIGHT VALUES

2. 5 white
1 master recipe
1 recipe #11

3. 2 master recipe
2 recipe #11
3 white

4. 1 recipe #3
2 specks alizarin crimson

MIDDLE VALUES

5. 4 white
1 master recipe
1 burnt sienna
1 recipe #11

6. 2 recipe #5
1 white
1 burnt sienna

7. 1 white
1 recipe #6
2 specks alizarin crimson

DARK/GRAYED VALUES

8. 1 master recipe
1 recipe #14

9. 2 white
2 master recipe
1 recipe #12

10. 3 white
2 master recipe
1 recipe #13

Highlight Value

11. 3 white
1 cadmium orange
1 speck cadmium
red light

Warm Shadow

12. 1 burnt sienna
1 speck cobalt blue

Cool Shadow

13. Burnt umber (pure)

Graying Color

14. 12 white
4 cobalt blue
1 cadmium red light

BASIC COLOR RECIPES FOR THE EYES

These basic color recipes offer good starting mixes that can be lightened, darkened, or grayed according to your model.

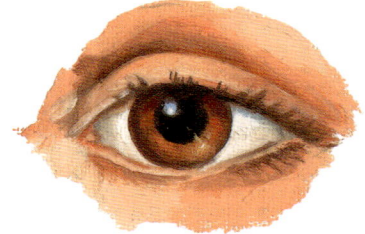

THE UPPER LID CASTS A SHADOW ON THE EYEBALL

The white of the eye is not pure white. Mix a bit of skin tone and a tiny bit of ultramarine blue into white. Keep the mix warm and light. Then highlight a small area on each side of the iris with a spot of pure white. The surface reflection on the eye should be soft. Paint a light blue circle first (white + 1 speck of ultramarine blue), and then place the white highlight spot in it. Titanium white and flake white are both warm whites and work well for skin tones and eyes in portrait painting.

LIGHT BROWN

There is a wide range of light brown eyes. Warm these colors with a tiny speck of cadmium red light, or cool them with a speck of ultramarine blue.

1. Pupil
1 burnt sienna + 1 speck burnt umber

2. Iris Main
2 raw sienna + 1 speck cadmium red light

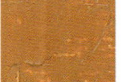

3. Iris Medium
4 Naples yellow hue + 1 raw sienna

4. Iris Light
1 Naples yellow hue + 1 speck cadmium orange

5. Iris Highlight
2 white + 1 recipe #4

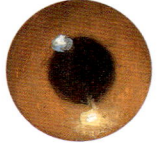

MAIN COLOR BLENDS

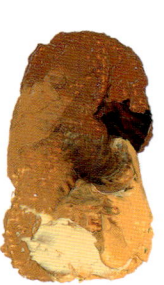

BROWN

Eyes in this book are lit from the upper left. Light is caught in the lower right of the iris, creating a liquid appearance and a reflection on the surface in the upper left pupil.

1. Pupil
1 burnt umber + 1 speck ultramarine blue

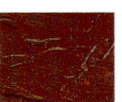

2. Iris Main
2 burnt sienna + 1 raw sienna

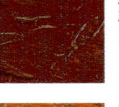

3. Iris Medium
3 recipe #2 + 5 yellow ochre + 2 cadmium orange

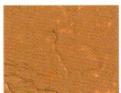

4. Iris Light
yellow ochre + 2 white + 1 recipe #3

5. Iris Highlight
2 white + 1 speck yellow ochre + 1 speck recipe #4

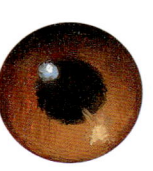

MAIN COLOR BLENDS

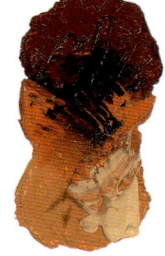

DARK BROWN

Keep all dark brown mixes warm in color tone. As with all the eyes, the iris is darker at the top because of the shadow cast by the upper eyelid and lashes.

1. Pupil
2 burnt umber + 1 black

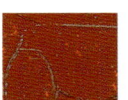

2. Iris Main
1 burnt umber + 1 burnt sienna

3. Iris Medium
1 burnt umber + 1 cadmium orange

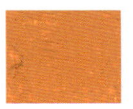

4. Iris Light
1 recipe #3 + 1 white

5. Iris Highlight
1 yellow ochre + 1 cadmium orange + 1 white

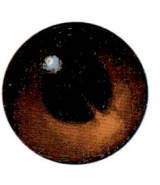

MAIN COLOR BLENDS

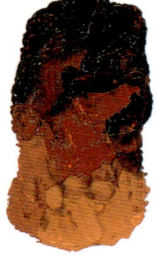

BLUE

Blue eyes can range from a light crystal color to a deep sapphire. The basic recipes here can be lightened with white; darkened with deeper blues, such as cobalt or ultramarine blue; or grayed with burnt umber, raw sienna, or a speck of cadmium orange.

1. Pupil
1 black +
1 ultramarine blue
+ 1 recipe #2

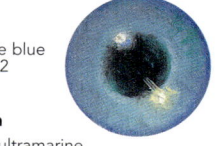

2. Iris Main
2 white + 1 ultramarine blue + 1 speck cadmium red light

MAIN COLOR BLENDS

3. Iris Medium
3 white +
1 cerulean blue hue
+ 1 recipe #2

4. Iris Light
2 white +
1 recipe #3

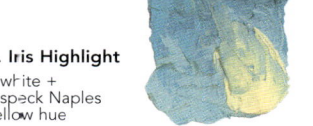

5. Iris Highlight
2 white +
1 speck Naples
yellow hue

GREEN

There are many variations of green eyes—some even appear to have small flecks of brown or yellow. Use raw sienna and yellow ochre warmed with a speck of cadmium orange to create this effect.

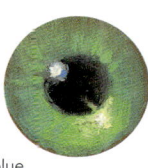

1. Pupil
1 burnt umber +
1 recipe #2

2. Iris Main
3 white + 1 cerulean blue hue + 1 raw sienna + 1 speck Naples yellow hue

MAIN COLOR BLENDS

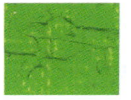

3. Iris Medium
3 white + 1 cerulean blue hue + 1 speck Naples yellow hue

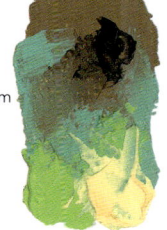

4. Iris Light
2 white + 1 recipe #3 + 1 speck cadmium yellow light

5. Iris Highlight
2 white +
1 speck Naples
yellow hue

HAZEL

Hazel eyes can be warm, cool, or slightly gray in color. Manipulate these basic mixes with cadmium orange to warm; viridian green to cool; and a warm purple mix to gray.

1. Pupil
1 burnt umber +
1 raw sienna

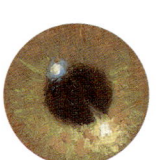

2. Iris Main
1 white +
1 raw sienna

MAIN COLOR BLENDS

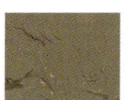

3. Iris Medium
3 white + 1 raw sienna + 1 speck ultramarine blue

4. Iris Light
1 white + 2 Naples yellow hue + 1 speck viridian green

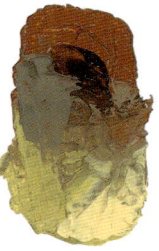

5. Iris Highlight
2 white +
1 speck Naples
yellow hue

GRAY

Some gray eyes appear to have a cold look, whereas others appear warmer. For a cool, steely look, add a speck of cerulean blue hue and raw umber to the mix. Use ultramarine blue or cobalt blue for a warmer color.

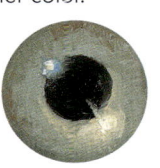

1. Pupil
9 viridian green +
1 cadmium red
light

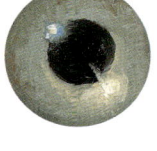

2. Iris Main
1 recipe #1 +
2 white

MAIN COLOR BLENDS

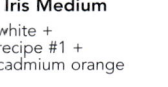

3. Iris Medium
6 white +
2 recipe #1 +
1 cadmium orange

4. Iris Light
4 white +
1 recipe #1

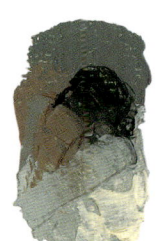

5. Iris Highlight
2 white + 1 speck
Naples yellow hue +
1 speck cadmium orange

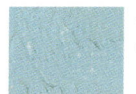

DARK BROWN

Dark brown hair is usually warm in color. If your model has hair that is a bit cooler, add a small speck of viridian green or ultramarine blue to the mix.

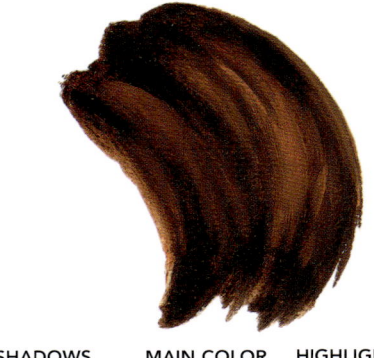

SHADOWS	MAIN COLOR	HIGHLIGHTS
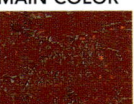 (wait)		

SHADOWS	MAIN COLOR	HIGHLIGHTS

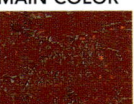 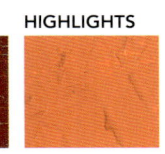

1. 3 burnt umber
2 burnt sienna

2. 1 burnt sienna
1 raw sienna

3. 1 white
1 raw sienna
1 cadmium orange

BROWN

This is just slightly lighter in value than dark brown, but it is also warm in color. Keep value changes subtle. Do not use pure white as a highlight—instead add white to the light recipe.

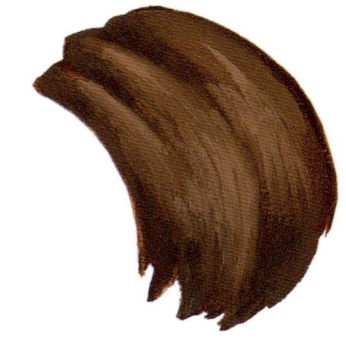

SHADOWS	MAIN COLOR	HIGHLIGHTS

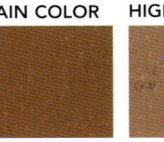 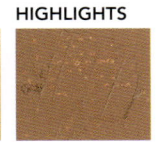

1. 2 burnt sienna
2 burnt umber
1 white

2. 1 recipe #1
1 yellow ochre
1 white

3. 1 recipe #2
2 white

GOLDEN BROWN

Golden brown is a bit richer in yellow than the two previous browns. Raw sienna is the dominant color in these recipes. Again, don't use only white to lighten; remember to add color as well (see page 9).

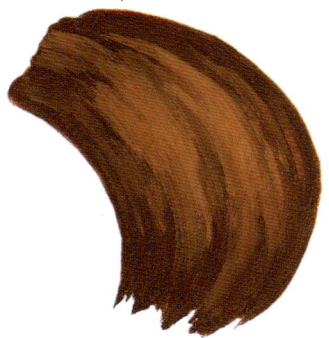

SHADOWS	MAIN COLOR	HIGHLIGHTS

  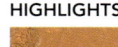 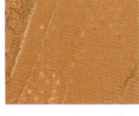

1. 3 raw sienna
2 burnt sienna
1 burnt umber

2. 2 raw sienna
1 white

3. 6 Naples yellow hue
1 white
1 raw sienna

LIGHT BROWN

The colors in light brown hair can be a bit cooler than those in brown or dark brown. Use a little viridian green or a touch of cerulean blue hue to cool colors, if necessary.

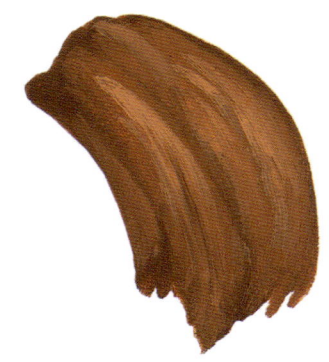

SHADOWS	MAIN COLOR	HIGHLIGHTS

 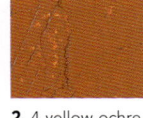 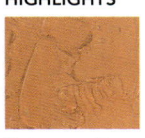

1. 4 raw sienna
1 burnt umber
2 white
2 specks burnt sienna

2. 4 yellow ochre
4 Naples yellow hue
1 burnt sienna

3. 1 recipe #2
2 white

AUBURN

Auburn hair is very rich in dark reds mingled with deep browns. Notice that this set of recipes includes both a warm red (cadmium red light) and a cool red (alizarin crimson).

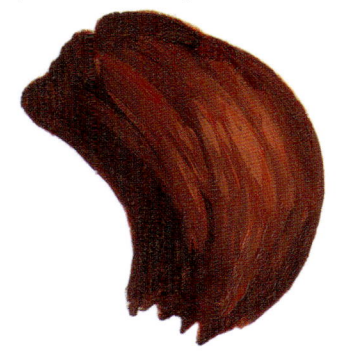

SHADOWS	MAIN COLOR	HIGHLIGHTS
	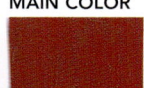	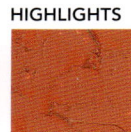
1. 2 alizarin crimson 2 burnt sienna 1 burnt umber	**2.** 1 burnt sienna 1 cadmium red light	**3.** 2 yellow ochre 1 cadmium red light

RED

Reds can range from rich, deep reds to carrotlike orange tones. In these recipes, cool phthalo red tones down the warmth of cadmium orange without losing color intensity.

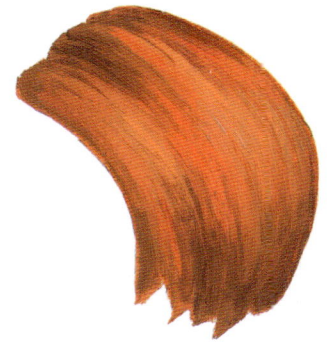

SHADOWS	MAIN COLOR	HIGHLIGHTS
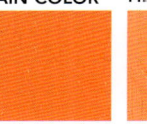		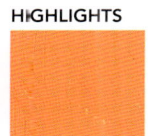
1. 2 raw sienna 1 cadmium orange 1 speck cadmium red light 1 speck burnt umber	**2.** 1 cadmium orange 1 speck phthalo red	**3.** 1 Naples yellow hue 2 specks cadmium orange 1 speck cad. yellow light

STRAWBERRY BLOND

This color can be tricky. Some hair leans toward the reds without being "red," whereas other hair leans toward the orange-tan range of color. Add a speck of cadmium vermilion to these mixes if you need a redder tint.

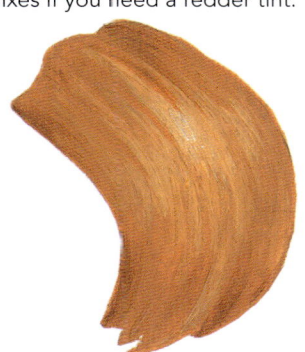

SHADOWS	MAIN COLOR	HIGHLIGHTS
		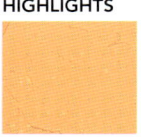
1. 1 raw sienna 1 Naples yellow hue 1 speck cad. red light	**2.** 1 Naples yellow hue 1 speck cad. red light	**3.** 1 recipe #2 2 white

GOLDEN BLOND

The colors in some golden blond hair can be fairly strong. The value is usually lighter than strawberry blond and is a little less red in hue. Use cadmium yellow medium to make these colors appear more golden.

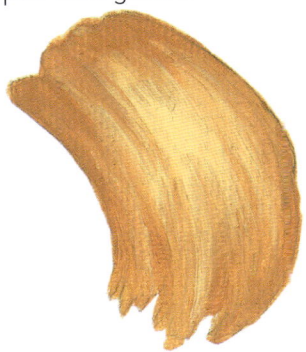

SHADOWS	MAIN COLOR	HIGHLIGHTS
	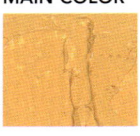	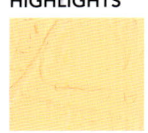
1. 2 Naples yellow hue 1 raw sienna	**2.** 2 Naples yellow hue 1 speck cad. yellow med.	**3.** 6 white 1 cac. yellow med. 1 speck Naples yellow hue

PALE BLOND

Keep the colors fresh by limiting the use of white. Naples yellow hue, cadmium yellow medium, and raw sienna mixed with white make good combinations for this hair color.

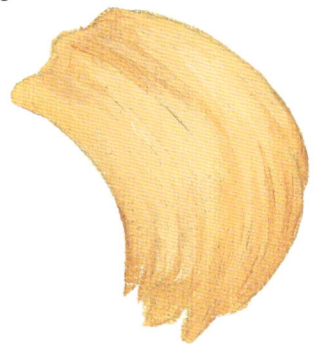

SHADOWS	MAIN COLOR	HIGHLIGHTS

1. 1 white
1 Naples yellow hue
1 raw sienna

2. 1 white
1 Naples yellow hue

3. 6 white
1 Naples yellow hue
1 speck cad. yellow med.

ASH BLOND

This hair color contains more green than the others do. However, it must be very subtle and used only to affect the other colors in creating the ash appearance.

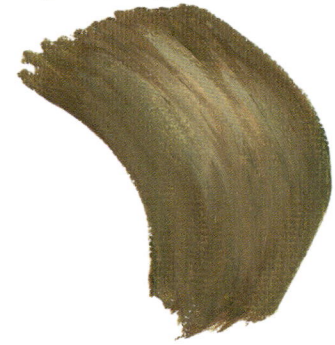

SHADOWS	MAIN COLOR	HIGHLIGHTS

  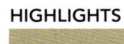

1. 4 white
3 raw sienna
1 chrome oxide green

2. 4 white
1 yellow ochre
1 chrome oxide green

3. 1 white
1 speck raw sienna
1 speck chrome oxide green

WARM WHITE

When painting white hair, try to keep the colors from appearing chalky. Also limit the use of yellows in white hair, as they can cause the hair to appear heavy and unclean.

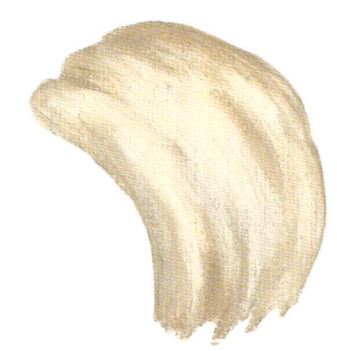

SHADOWS	MAIN COLOR	HIGHLIGHTS

 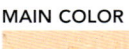  

1. 1 white
1 speck burnt umber

2. 1 white
1 speck burnt sienna

3. 1 white
1 speck cadmium orange

COOL WHITE

Colors in cool white must also be kept to a minimum. Ultramarine blue is a warm blue. It contains a bit of red, making it a purplish-blue that is perfect for cool white hair.

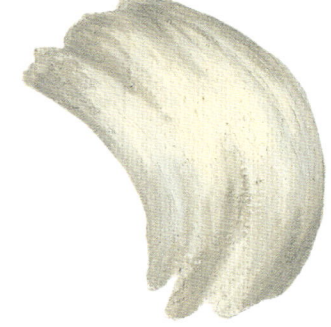

SHADOWS	MAIN COLOR	HIGHLIGHTS

 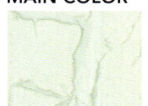 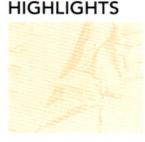

1. 1 white
1 speck burnt umber
1 speck ultramarine blue

2. 1 white
1 speck ultramarine blue

3. White (pure)

WARM GRAY

Gray hair also contains color. As in white hair, keep the colors soft. If your model has warm gray with more brown-red tones, use burnt umber and a speck of cadmium red light.

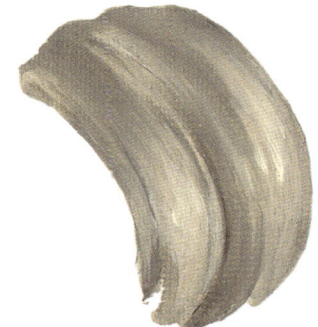

SHADOWS	MAIN COLOR	HIGHLIGHTS
	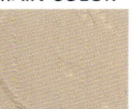	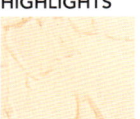
1. 6 white 1 burnt umber 1 ultramarine blue	**2.** 1 white 1 speck burnt umber 1 speck alizarin crimson	**3.** 2 white 1 speck burnt sienna

COOL GRAY

Use ivory black for this hair color. It is a warm black, and it's weaker than other blacks. When mixed with the other recipes here (all of which contain ultramarine blue), it works perfectly.

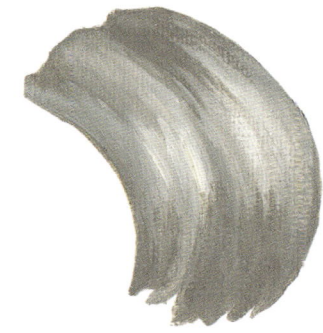

SHADOWS	MAIN COLOR	HIGHLIGHTS
	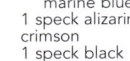	
1. 8 white 1 black	**2.** 2 white 1 speck ultra- marine blue 1 speck alizarin crimson 1 speck black	**3.** 2 white 1 speck ultra- marine blue

WARM BLACK

This hair color contains recipes that reflect warm highlights. Make your own black for the dark recipe with burnt umber and ultramarine blue. This way you can make it cooler with more blue or warmer with more umber.

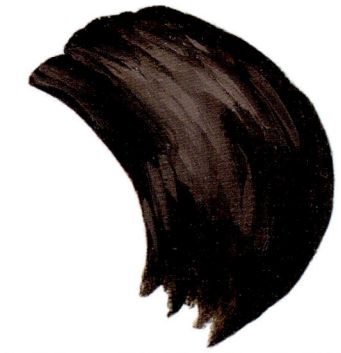

SHADOWS	MAIN COLOR	HIGHLIGHTS
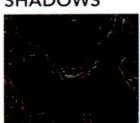	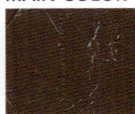	
1. 1 burnt umber 1 ultramarine blue	**2.** 1 recipe #1 2 white 3 specks burnt sienna	**3.** 1 recipe #2 2 white 2 specks alizarin crimson

COOL BLACK

For cool black, use a mix of black and ultramarine blue. The addition of ultramarine blue along with alizarin crimson in the light recipe gives the color a slight purplish tone.

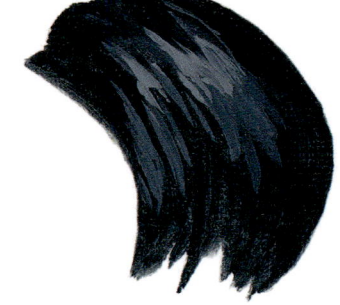

SHADOWS	MAIN COLOR	HIGHLIGHTS

1. 1 black 1 ultramarine blue	**2.** 1 recipe #1 1 white	**3.** 1 recipe #2 1 white 1 speck alizarin crimson

WATERCOLORSKIN TONES

- Burnt Umber
- Burnt Sienna
- Cadmium Red Light
- Hooker's Green Deep
- Permanent Rose
- Ultramarine Blue
- Yellow Ochre

Mix until the color matches the **Master Skin Tone Recipe** shown at right.

1. 50% yellow ochre
50% cadmium red light
Water: level 5

1. MASTER SKIN TONE RECIPE

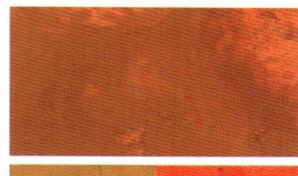

COLOR/WATER LEVELS

Level 1 Pale Color

Level 2 Weak Color

Level 3 Medium Color

Level 4 Strong Color

Level 5 Very Strong Color

LIGHT VALUES

2. 100% master recipe
Water: level 1

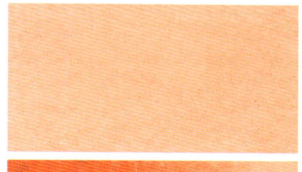

MIDDLE VALUES

5. 80% master recipe
20% recipe #12
Water: level 3

DARK/GRAYED VALUES

8. 80% master recipe
20% recipe #14
Water: level 3

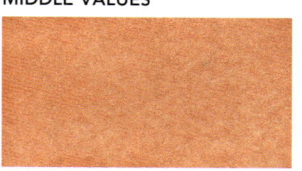

3. 100% master recipe
Water: level 2

6. 70% master recipe
30% recipe #12
Water: level 3

9. 60% master recipe
25% recipe #14
15% recipe #12
Water: level 4

4. 95% master recipe
5% recipe #11
Water: level 2

7. 60% master recipe
40% recipe #13
Water: level 4

10. 60% master recipe
30% recipe #13
10% ultramarine blue
Water: level 4

HIGHLIGHT VALUE

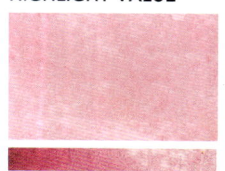

11. 1 speck permanent rose
Water: level 1

WARM SHADOW

12. 75% burnt sienna
25% burnt umber
Water: level 4

COOL SHADOW

13. 60% burnt sienna
20% burnt umber
20% ultramarine blue
Water: level 4

GRAYING COLOR

14. 100% Hooker's green deep
Water: level 4

<table>
<tr><td>

WATERCOLOR COLORS USED
</td><td>

• Cadmium Red Light
• Cerulean Blue Hue
• Cobalt Blue
</td><td>

• Burnt Sienna
• Burnt Umber
• Permanent Rose
</td><td>

• Raw Sienna
• Sepia
• Viridian Green
</td></tr>
</table>

Mix until the color matches the **Master Skin Tone Recipe** shown at right.

1. 85% raw sienna
15% cerulean blue hue
Water: level 5

1. MASTER SKIN TONE RECIPE

COLOR/WATER LEVELS

Level 1 Pale Color

Level 2 Weak Color

Level 3 Medium Color

Level 4 Strong Color

Level 5 Very Strong Color

LIGHT VALUES

2. 95% master recipe
5% cadmium red light
Water: level 2

3. 90% master recipe
10% cadmium red light
Water: level 3

4. 80% master recipe
20% burnt sienna
Water: level 3

MIDDLE VALUES

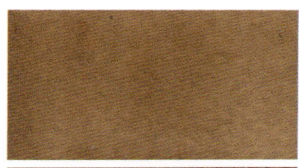

5. 60% master recipe
40% burnt umber
Water: level 3

6. 85% master recipe
15% viridian green
Water: level 3

7. 60% master recipe
40% recipe #14
Water: level 3

DARK/GRAYED VALUES

8. 45% master recipe
45% recipe #12
10% permanent rose
Water: level 3

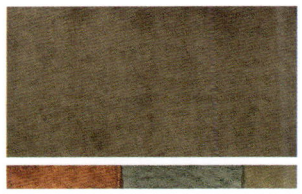

9. 40% burnt sienna
40% recipe #14
20% master recipe
Water: level 4

10. 50% master recipe
50% recipe #12
Water: level 4

HIGHLIGHT VALUE

11. 1 speck any color above
Water: level 1

WARM SHADOW

12. 100% sepia
Water: level 3

COOL SHADOW

13. 50% sepia
50% viridian green
Water: level 3

GRAYING COLOR

14. 80% cobalt blue
20% master recipe
Water: level 3

WATERCOLOR SKIN TONES

WATERCOLOR COLORS USED		
• Burnt Sienna	• Cerulean Blue Hue	• Viridian Green
• Burnt Umber	• Cobalt Blue	• Yellow Ochre
• Cadmium Orange	• Permanent Rose	

Mix until the color matches the **Master Skin Tone Recipe** shown at right.

1. 60% yellow ochre
30% cadmium orange
10% permanent rose
Water: level 5

1. MASTER SKIN TONE RECIPE

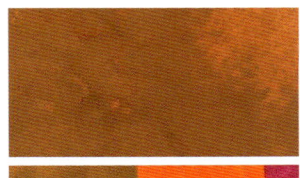

COLOR/WATER LEVELS

Level 1 Pale Color

Level 2 Weak Color

Level 3 Medium Color

Level 4 Strong Color

Level 5 Very Strong Color

LIGHT VALUES

2. 100% master recipe
Water: level 1

3. 100% master recipe
Water: level 2

4. 100% master recipe
Water: level 2.5

MIDDLE VALUES

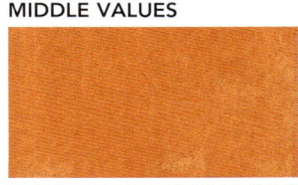

5. 100% master recipe
Water: level 3

6. 70% master recipe
30% burnt sienna
Water: level 3

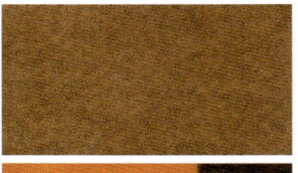

7. 70% master recipe
30% burnt umber
Water: level 3

DARK/GRAYED VALUES

8. 80% master recipe
20% recipe #14
Water: level 4

9. 70% master recipe
30% recipe #12
Water: level 4

10. 75% recipe #13
25% master recipe
Water: level 4

HIGHLIGHT VALUE

11. 1 speck any color above
Water: level 1

WARM SHADOW

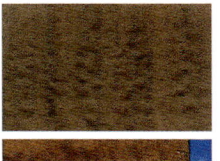

12. 90% burnt sienna
10% cobalt blue
Water: level 4

COOL SHADOW

13. 90% burnt umber
10% cobalt blue
Water: level 4

GRAYING COLOR

14. 95% viridian green
5% cerulean blue hue
Water: level 4

WATERCOLOR COLORS USED

- Alizarin Crimson
- Burnt Sienna
- Burnt Umber
- Cadmium Orange
- Cobalt Blue
- Permanent Rose
- Raw Sienna

Mix until the color matches the **Master Skin Tone Recipe** shown at right.

1. 40% raw sienna
40% cadmium orange
20% burnt umber
Water: level 5

1. MASTER SKIN TONE RECIPE

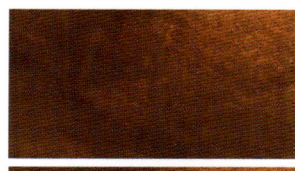

COLOR/WATER LEVELS

Level 1 Pale Color

Level 2 Weak Color

Level 3 Medium Color

Level 4 Strong Color

Level 5 Very Strong Color

LIGHT VALUES

2. 100% master recipe
Water: level 1

3. 97% master recipe
3% permanent rose
Water: level 2

4. 95% master recipe
5% permanent rose
Water: level 3

MIDDLE VALUES

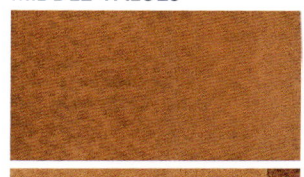

5. 90% master recipe
10% burnt sienna
Water: level 3

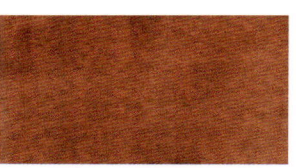

6. 85% master recipe
10% burnt sienna
5% alizarin crimson
Water: level 4

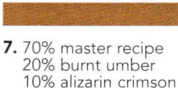

7. 70% master recipe
20% burnt umber
10% alizarin crimson
Water: level 4

DARK/GRAYED VALUES

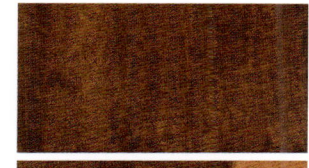

8. 75% recipe #12
25% master recipe
Water: level 4

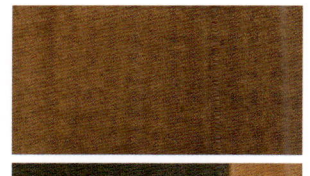

9. 75% recipe #13
25% master recipe
Water: level 4

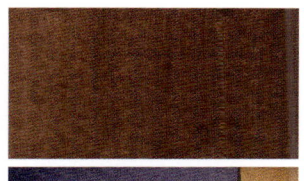

10. 80% recipe #14
20% master recipe
Water: level 4

HIGHLIGHT VALUE

11. 1 speck cadmium
orange
Water: level 1

WARM SHADOW

12. 75% burnt umber
25% alizarin crimson
Water: level 4

COOL SHADOW

13. 60% burnt umber
40% cobalt blue
Water: level 4

GRAYING COLOR

14. 70% cobalt blue
30% alizarin crimson
Water: level 3

<table>
<tr><td>

WATERCOLOR COLORS USED

</td><td>

- Burnt Sienna
- Burnt Umber
- Cerulean Blue Hue

</td><td>

- Ivory Black
- Lemon Yellow

</td><td>

- Permanent Rose
- Sap Green

</td></tr>
</table>

Mix until the color matches the **Master Skin Tone Recipe** shown at right.

1. 60% permanent rose
40% lemon yellow
Water: level 5

1. MASTER SKIN TONE RECIPE

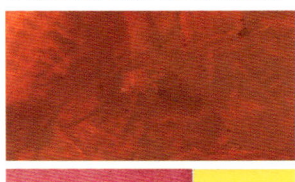

COLOR/WATER LEVELS

Level 1 Pale Color

Level 2 Weak Color

Level 3 Medium Color

Level 4 Strong Color

Level 5 Very Strong Color

LIGHT VALUES

2. 90% master recipe
10% lemon yellow
Water: level 1

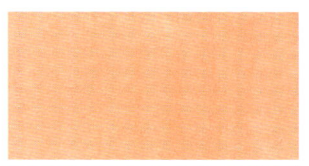

3. 100% master recipe
Water: level 1.5

4. 100% master recipe
Water: level 2

MIDDLE VALUES

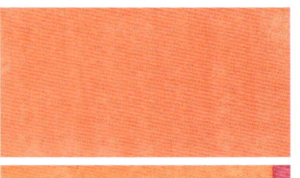

5. 95% master recipe
5% permanent rose
Water: level 3

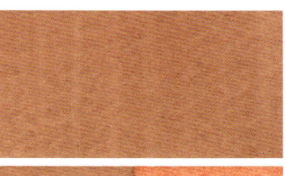

6. 50% recipe #12
50% master recipe
Water: level 3

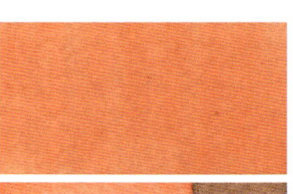

7. 70% master recipe
30% recipe #13
Water: level 3

DARK/GRAYED VALUES

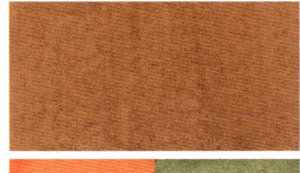

8. 50% master recipe
50% recipe #14
Water: level 3.5

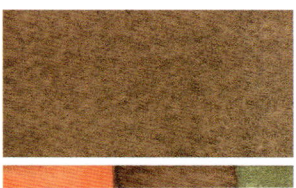

9. 40% master recipe
40% burnt umber
20% recipe #14
Water: level 4

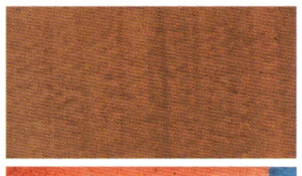

10. 90% master recipe
10% cerulean blue hue
Water: level 4

HIGHLIGHT VALUE

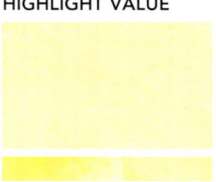

11. 1 speck lemon yellow
Water: level 1

WARM SHADOW

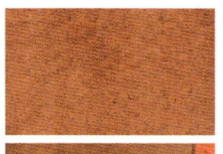

12. 90% burnt sienna
10% master recipe
Water: level 3

COOL SHADOW

13. 70% master recipe
30% black
Water: level 4

GRAYING COLOR

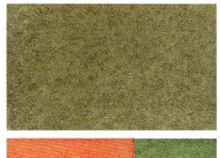

14. 60% master recipe
40% sap green
Water: level 3

- Burnt Sienna
- Burnt Umber
- Cadmium Red Light
- Lemon Yellow
- New Gamboge
- Viridian Green

Mix until the color matches the
Master Skin Tone Recipe
shown at right.

1. 60% cadmium red light
40% new gamboge
Water: level 5

1. MASTER SKIN TONE RECIPE

COLOR/WATER LEVELS

Level 1   Pale Color

Level 2   Weak Color

Level 3   Medium Color

Level 4   Strong Color

Level 5   Very Strong Color

LIGHT VALUES

2. 100% master recipe
Water: level 1

3. 100% master recipe
Water: level 2

4. 90% master recipe
10% lemon yellow
Water: level 2

MIDDLE VALUES

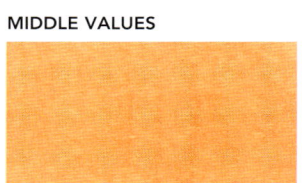

5. 90% master recipe
10% new gamboge
Water: level 3

6. 95% master recipe
5% new gamboge
Water: level 3

7. 100% master recipe
Water: level 3.5

DARK/GRAYED VALUES

8. 50% master recipe
50% recipe #12
Water: level 3

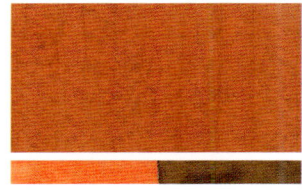

9. 50% master recipe
50% recipe #13
Water: level 3

10. 65% master recipe
35% recipe #14
Water: level 3

HIGHLIGHT VALUE

11. 1 speck any color above
Water: level 1

WARM SHADOW

12. 50% burnt sienna
50% burnt umber
Water: level 3

COOL SHADOW

13. 100% burnt umber
Water: level 4

GRAYING COLOR

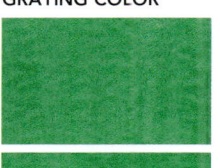

14. 100% viridian green
Water: level 3

CREATING COLORS NEW MASTER RECIPES

You can create your own master recipes for a completely new variation of skin tones. Use the examples here and create your own combinations. You can even create your own original master recipes. By adding additional colors to the selected master recipe, the combinations are endless.

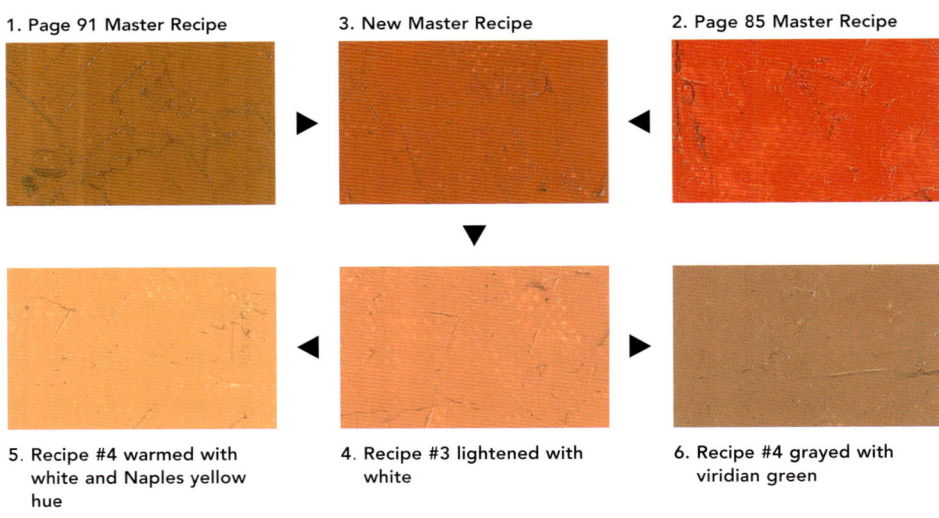

1. Page 91 Master Recipe

3. New Master Recipe

2. Page 85 Master Recipe

5. Recipe #4 warmed with white and Naples yellow hue

4. Recipe #3 lightened with white

6. Recipe #4 grayed with viridian green

By selecting master recipes that are very different in tone, you can achieve almost any color. You can even lighten, darken, warm, cool, or gray the recipes. Mixing Page 85's Master Recipe with Page 98's Master Recipe creates some beautiful skin tones. Vary the mix amounts for even a wider range of skin tone colors.

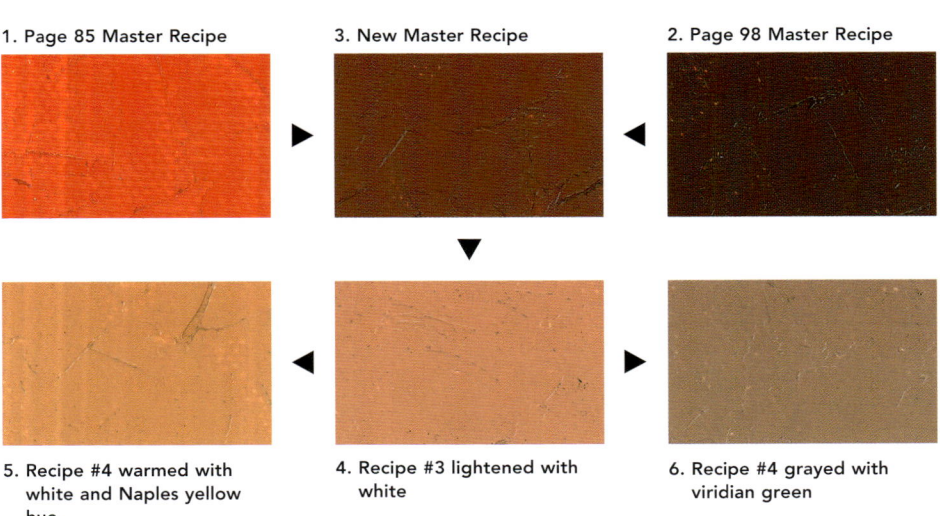

1. Page 85 Master Recipe

3. New Master Recipe

2. Page 98 Master Recipe

5. Recipe #4 warmed with white and Naples yellow hue

4. Recipe #3 lightened with white

6. Recipe #4 grayed with viridian green

Like the master recipes, subsequent value recipes also can be altered. They can be intermixed (creating a new color), lightened, darkened, grayed, and so on. This first example is golden tones mixed with ruddy tones. This creates a new and beautiful color mix. Add more of the ruddy tones for a redder color.

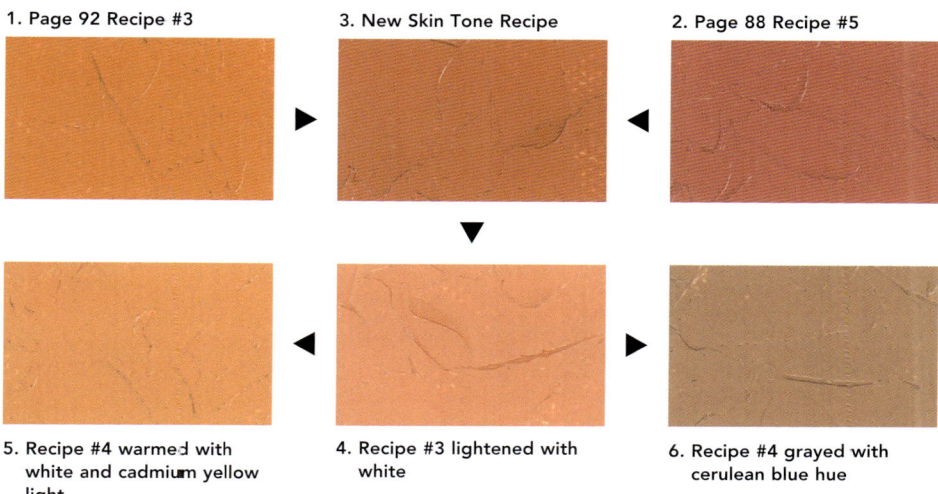

1. Page 92 Recipe #3

3. New Skin Tone Recipe

2. Page 88 Recipe #5

5. Recipe #4 warmed with white and cadmium yellow light

4. Recipe #3 lightened with white

6. Recipe #4 grayed with cerulean blue hue

You will notice similarities in the recipes. However, there are slight tonal differences that are extremely important in matching a model's skin tone. You can also add raw colors to these recipes. For instance, if your model has a reddish skin tone, find and add the correct red, warm, cool, dark, light, and so on.

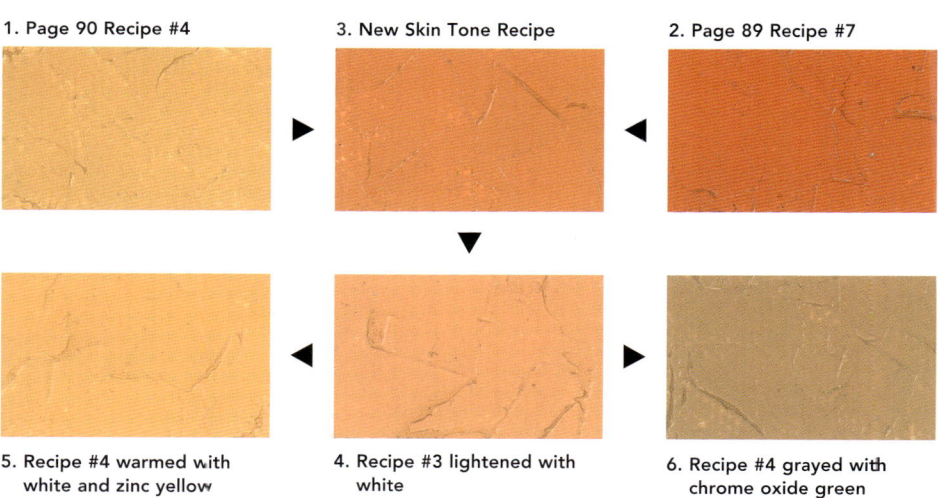

1. Page 90 Recipe #4

3. New Skin Tone Recipe

2. Page 89 Recipe #7

5. Recipe #4 warmed with white and zinc yellow

4. Recipe #3 lightened with white

6. Recipe #4 grayed with chrome oxide green

Color Mixing for
Landscapes

PAINT COLORS NEEDED

You will need all of the following colors to create the color mixing recipes in this section. Note: Some acrylic color names will vary depending on the manufacturer; also, some of these colors are not available in acrylic so they must be mixed. Please refer to the conversion chart below.

OIL COLOR NAME	ACRYLIC COLOR NAME	EQUIVALENT MIXTURE
Alizarin crimson	Alizarin crimson	
Burnt sienna	Burnt sienna	
Burnt umber	Burnt umber	
Cadmium orange	Cadmium orange	
Cadmium red light	Cadmium red light	
Cadmium vermilion	not available (use mixture)	2 parts indo-red= 1 part Naphthol crimson
Cadmium yellow light	Cadmium yellow light	
Cadmium yellow medium	Cadmium yellow medium	
Cerulean blue	Cerulean blue	
Cobalt blue	Cobalt blue	
Cobalt violet	Cobalt violet	
Ivory black	Ivory black	
Magenta	Medium magenta	
Naples yellow	Naples yellow (or use mixture)	4 parts yellow ochre/oxide+ 1 part titanium white 2 specks cadmium orange
Permanent blue	Ultramarine blue	
Permanent green light	Permanent green light	
Raw sienna	Raw sienna	
Raw umber	Raw umber	
Thalo® blue	Phthalo blue	
Thalo® green (blue shade) *can be substituted with phthalo green or Winsor green	Phthalo green	
Thalo® red rose *can be substituted with quinacridone red	Naphthol crimson, phthalo crimson, or quinacridone red	
Titanium white	Titanium white	
Venetian red	Venetian red or red oxide	
Viridian green	Viridian green or viridian hue permanent	
Yellow ochre	Yellow ochre or yellow oxide	
Zinc yellow	Yellow light hansa	

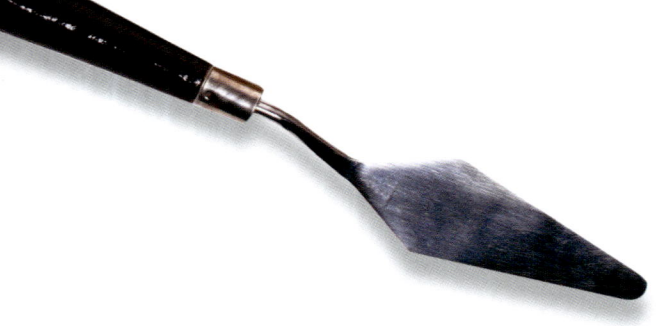

Contents

SKIES AND CLOUDS

The sky is the most important element in a painting because it influences the entire landscape composition, controlling the light, time of day, season, weather, color palette, and mood of a scene. Colors and lighting also vary in terms of color temperature, with the palette leaning either warm or cool. Early morning light is cooler than mid-afternoon or a warm evening sunset. Because of this, we use different color combinations and palettes for each skyscape. Different cloud formations also dictate weather and sky moods.

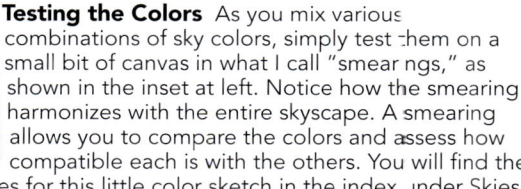

Testing the Colors As you mix various combinations of sky colors, simply test them on a small bit of canvas in what I call "smearings," as shown in the inset at left. Notice how the smearing harmonizes with the entire skyscape. A smearing allows you to compare the colors and assess how compatible each is with the others. You will find the recipes for this little color sketch in the index under Skies & Clouds, "Daybreak Pinkish Sky." The color recipes used in this little painting are as follows: zenith #67, secondary color #68, and horizon colors #65 and #69. The clouds are as follows: main color #72, highlight colors #65 and #74, and shadow color #70.

Comparing Sky Moods The three small color sketches on this page are similar in composition and cloud formations. However, the time of day and color mood is completely different in each. Compare them and notice the difference.

Finding Recipes Complete recipes for the color sketches below are in the index under Skies & Clouds, "Daybreak Blue Sky" (A) and "Dusk Blue Sky" (B). Index recipes range from daybreak to sunsets along with moonlight, stormy skies, and many other mood combinations. You can create complete, detailed paintings of any size using these color recipes.

Another method of using the color recipe swatches and index is to simply scan through the pages of recipe mixtures. Compare the swatches to the colors you see in your photo or subject. Select the dominant colors first, and then use the book to search for secondary and subtle color tones seen throughout your composition. Make notes and smearings of recipes you are considering to make certain they work well together. Create small non-detailed color sketches, such as these examples. Once you have selected your colors, you can create a larger painting with great success.

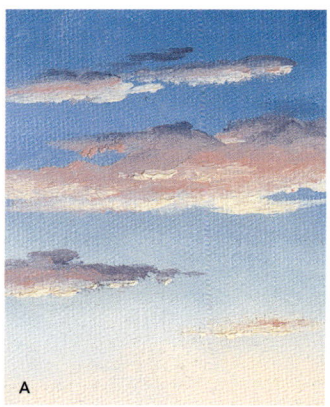

A

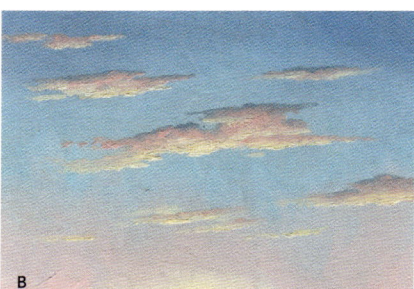

B

USINGTHERECIPES

Below are several sky mood sketches. The index name of each sketch is listed beneath. Select the one in the index that you would like to paint and follow the corresponding recipe numbers. The four thumbnail color sketches below are shown at the exact size they were painted.

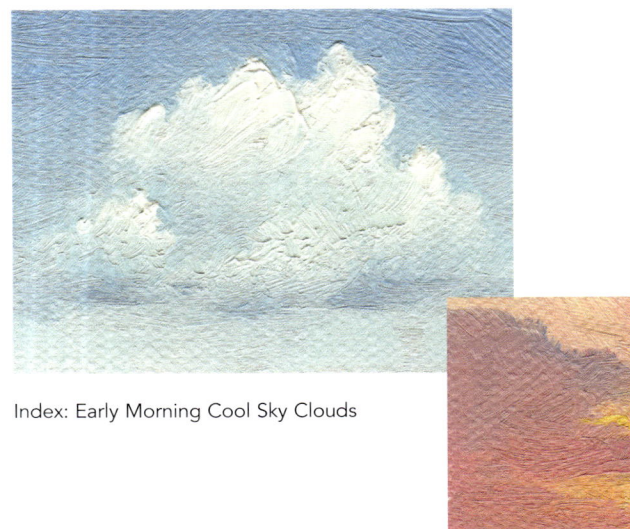

Index: Early Morning Cool Sky Clouds

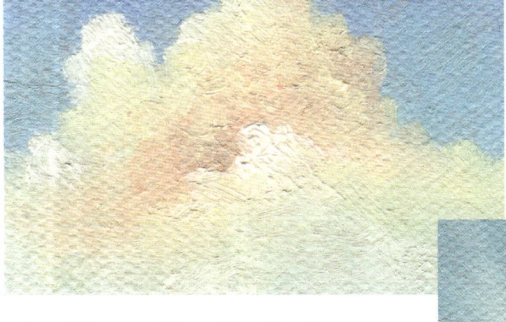

Index: Afternoon Warm Sky Clouds

Index: Sunset, Reddish Clouds

Index: Evening Sky, Clouds & Light Rays

120

The rough color sketch of the desert rock below shows the versatility of using color recipes from different parts of the book to create a composition. The mood involves a warm, low-light source on the desert red rock.

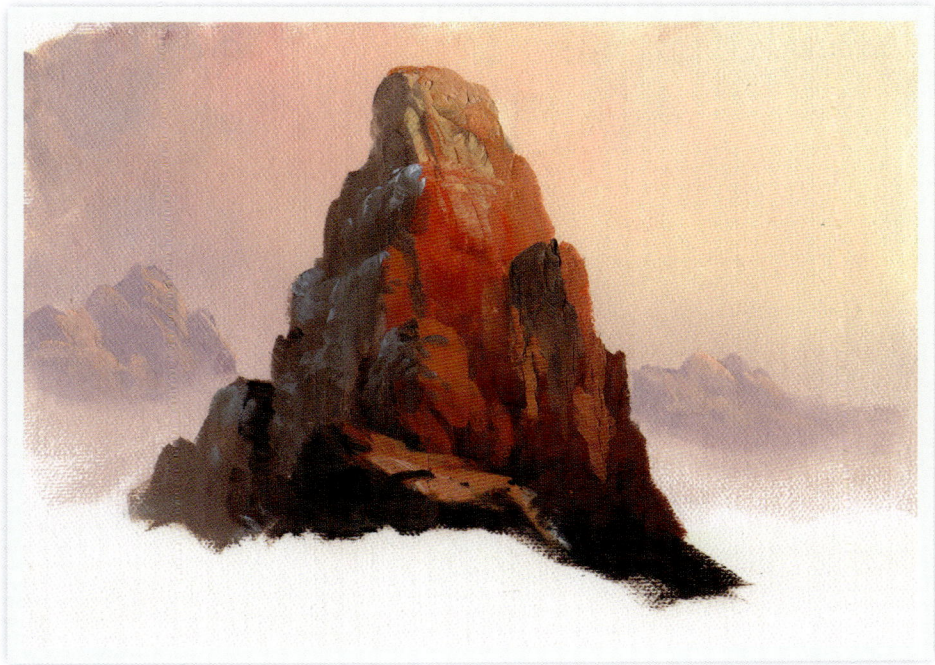

Color recipes used in this sketch include the following:

Sky: Begin at right and blend color mixtures toward the left. Start with #65 blended into #117 blended into #120.

Distant Rocks: Base color is #120 with highlights of #105. Main Rock: Paint the dark base shape using #43. Then add progressively lighter areas using recipes #22, #57, #30, #55, #18, and #40. Use a bit of #49 and #106 on the shadowed side. These mixes can be used to create any number of desert or seascape scenes with dramatic mood lighting. Remember to build colors from dark to light in this sketch.

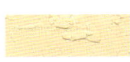

Sky Recipe #65

Sky Recipe #117

Sky Recipe #120

Light Recipe #30

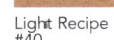

Light Recipe #40

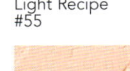

Light Recipe #55

Light Recipe #57

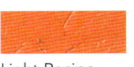

Light Recipe #18

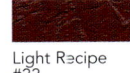

Light Recipe #22

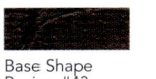

Base Color Recipe #120

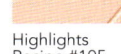

Base Shape Recipe #43

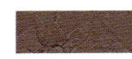

Highlights Recipe #105

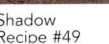

Shadow Recipe #49

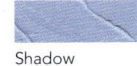

Shadow Recipe #106

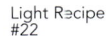

TREES AND MOUNTAINS

When we think of colors in nature, we usually say that skies are blue, trees are green, and so on. However, when we look closely and analyze the colors in an object, we find that not only does it contain a variety of color tones, but each object also contains a number of color *values* (the lightness or darkness of a color) within it.

Painting Trees When we look at a tree, our first impression is that it is made up of one overall color: green. Upon closer observation, we find it is made up of numerous tones of greens; several are a basic mass color, a secondary lighter color, a dark shadow color, and a highlight color. In some instances, there are additional subtle values within the tree mass. This variation in color tones is what allows the artist to create the illusion of form and dimension within an object on a flat painting surface. All objects in nature are made up of a number of color tones, whether a tree trunk, rock, or mountain. Even a small leaf contains numerous tones. The simple example at right shows how the recipes for a coniferous tree have been selected and applied to develop a very realistic tree. Compare the recipe colors used to paint the pine tree at right, and you will see how easily you can use the color guidance landscape index to find the colors of the subject and then paint it using those colors. You can also just scan through the mixtures and select colors you see in your subject. Below is a broadleaf bough that has been created using some of the same color mixtures used on the coniferous tree, plus a few added mixtures for warmth.

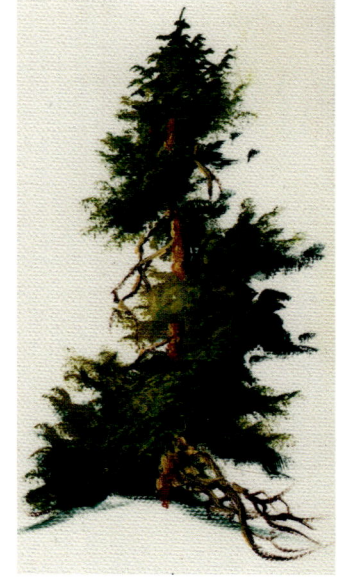
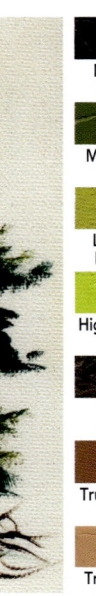
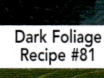

Dark Foliage
Recipe #81

Middle Foliage
Recipe #98

Light Foliage
Recipe #100

Highlight Foliage
Recipe #85

Trunk Dark
Recipe #26

Trunk Secondary
Recipe #31

Trunk Highlight
Recipe #40

Branches Gray
Recipe #39

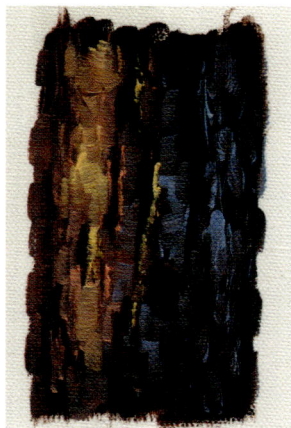

Pine Tree Trunk Dark brown #43, secondary warm #48, middle light #59, highlight #40, and #141 for the cool accent color used within the shadow on the right side.

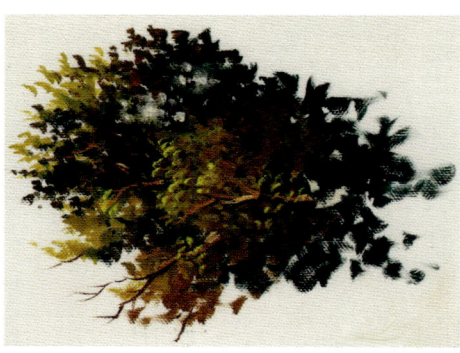

Broadleaf Bough Foliage: Dark green #81, secondary green #83, light green #95, highlight green #85, bright light green #87. Branches: Dark #43, secondary #55, and highlight #40.

Tip: In all exercises, allow your brushstrokes and colors to blend into one another to create realistic form.

USING RECIPES TO PAINT MOUNTAINS

There are many types and colors of mountains, but one of the most common is gray. This entire exercise uses only recipe mixes from this book. Below you can see how easily you can create an entire scene using the recipes. Go to the index and find Mountain Scene Colors, "Gray Mountain Scene with Snow." You will discover the full set of mixtures for this painting. Follow the steps below to re-create it yourself.

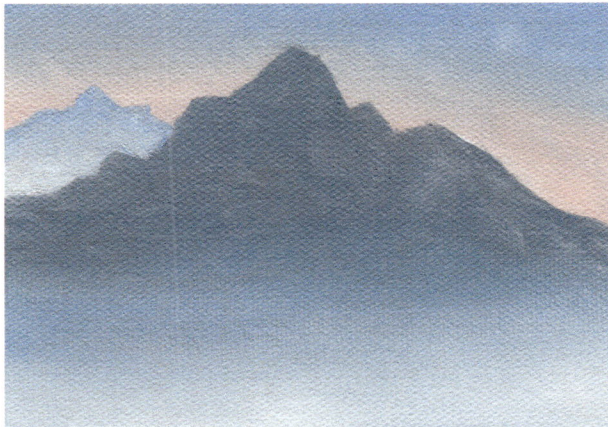

Step 1. Begin by painting the sky blue using recipe #106. Then paint the pink horizon using recipe #64, and blend it into the previous mixture. Next, paint the distant mountain with recipe #106, and blend #108 at the base for haze. Next, paint the main mountain shape using #101. To create a haze at the bottom of the main mountain, blend #107 into the base.

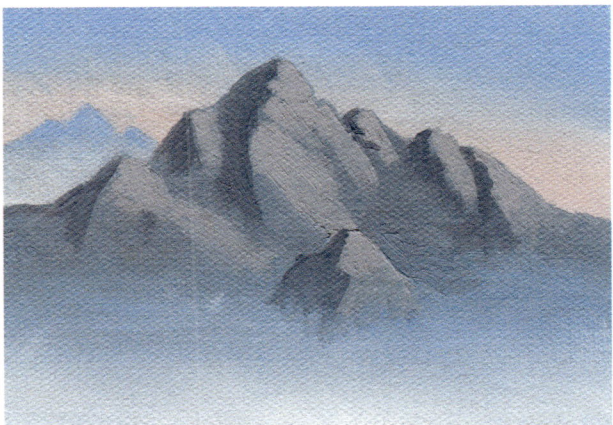

Step 2. Paint in the mountain forms using recipes #102 for the lighter side and #103 for the shadow side. This step is very important since you create the basic forms and depth of the entire mountain. Notice how a smaller peak has been developed in front of the mountain using these mixes.

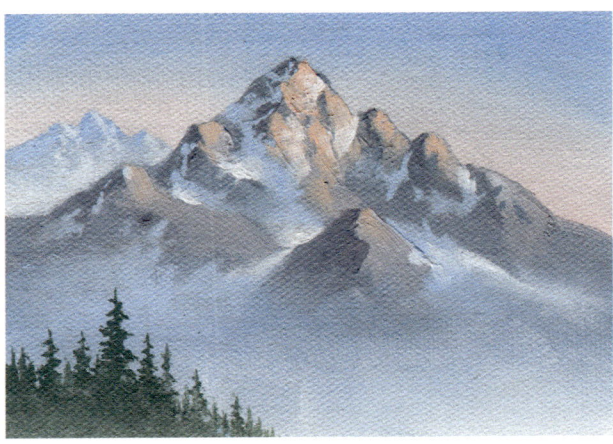

Step 3. Next, begin painting the warm, peach sunlit snow on the right sides of the mountain using recipe #105. Then use #106 for the blue shadowed snow. Add the highlights using recipe #108. Use a mix of #107 and #108 to enhance the base haze. Finally, paint the distant pine trees using #104.

COLORS USED

- Alizarin Crimson
- Burnt Umber
- Cadmium Orange
- Cadmium Red Light
- Cadmium Vermilion
- Cadmium Yellow Light
- Cerulean Blue
- Ivory Black
- Permanent Blue
- Raw Sienna
- Thalo® Blue
- Titanium White
- Venetian Red
- Yellow Ochre
- Zinc Yellow

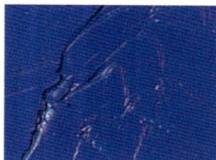

1. 1 white
4 permanent blue

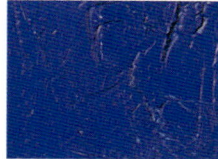

2. 2 permanent blue
1 white
1 • alizarin crimson

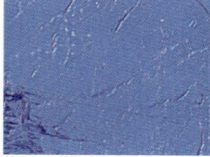

3. 2 white
1 permanent blue
1 • cerulean blue

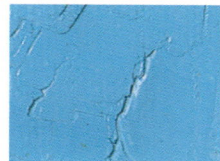

4. 1 white
1 • Thalo® blue

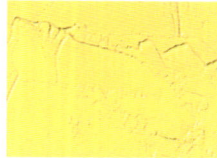

5. 2 white
1 zinc yellow
1 • cadmium orange

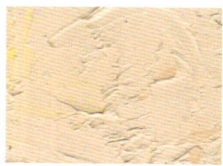

6. 1 white
1 • yellow ochre

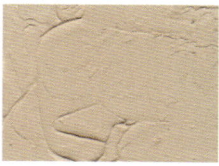

7. 8 white
1 yellow ochre
1 • permanent blue

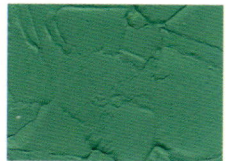

8. 6 white
1 Thalo® blue
4 zinc yellow

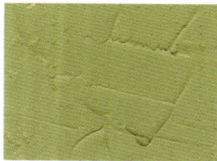

9. 7 white
1 ivory black
3 cadmium yellow light

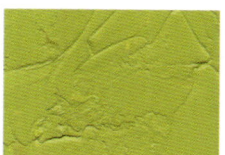

10. 4 zinc yellow
1 • cerulean blue
1 • raw sienna

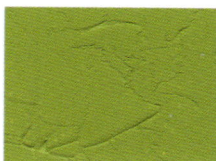

11. 8 cadmium yellow light
1 cerulean blue

12. 5 zinc yellow hue
1 Thalo® blue

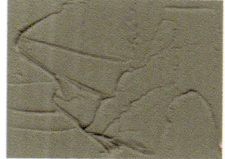

13. 5 white
3 yellow ochre
1 permanent blue

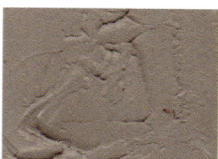

14. 5 white
1 • burnt umber

15. 2 cadmium vermilion
1 ivory black

16. 8 cadmium vermilion
1 ivory black

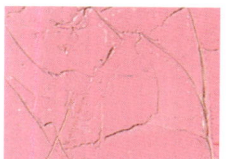

17. 5 white
1 • alizarin crimson

18. 4 white
1 cadmium red light
7 zinc yellow

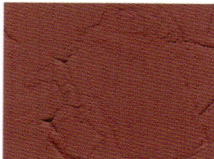

19. 3 white
1 Venetian red

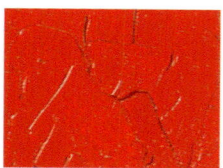

20. cadmium vermilion

COLORS USED

- Burnt Sienna
- Cadmium Orange
- Cadmium Vermilion
- Cadmium Yellow Light
- Cobalt Violet
- Ivory Black
- Permanent Blue
- Permanent Green Light
- Raw Sienna
- Titanium White
- Yellow Ochre
- Zinc Yellow

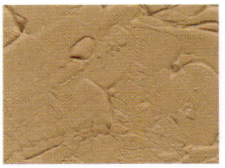

21. 3 white
1 raw sienna
1 • zinc yellow

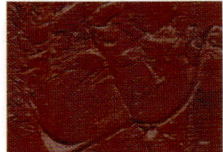

22. 2 cadmium vermilion
1 ivory black

23. 1 cobalt violet
1 cadmium orange
1 zinc yellow

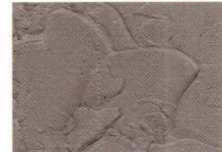

24. 7 white
1 ivory black
1 • cadmium vermilion

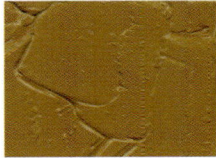

25. 1 cadmium yellow light
1 cobalt violet

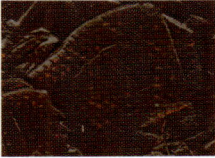

26. 1 burnt sienna
2 permanent green light

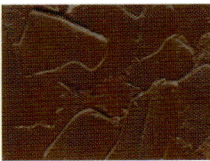

27. 3 permanent green light
1 cadmium vermilion

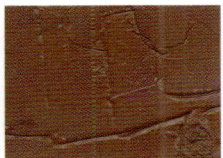

28. 1 cadmium vermilion
1 ivory black
4 raw sienna
1 white

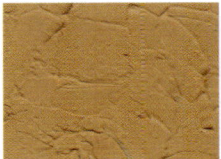

29. 1 white
2 yellow ochre

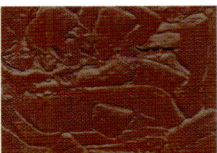

30. 1 burnt sienna
1 raw sienna

31. 3 raw sienna
1 white

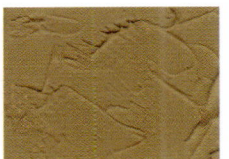

32. 2 white
2 cadmium orange
1 permanent green light

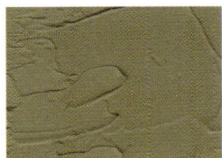

33. 5 white
3 yellow ochre
1 permanent blue

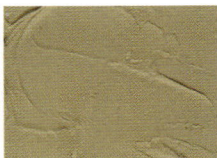

34. 5 white
2 yellow ochre
3 • permanent blue

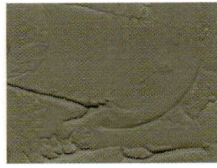

35. 3 white
2 raw sienna
1 permanent blue
1 • burnt sienna

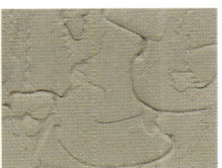

36. 3 white
1 #35
1 • raw sienna

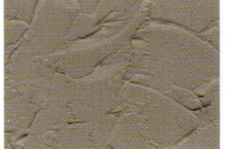

37. 5 white
1 burnt sienna
1 permanent blue

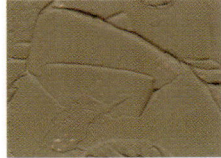

38. 8 white
2 burnt sienna
1 permanent blue

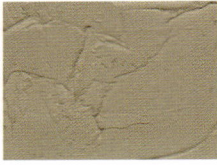

39. 2 white
1 #38

40. 3 white
1 yellow ochre

COLORS USED

- Burnt Sienna
- Burnt Umber
- Cadmium Orange
- Cadmium Red Light
- Cadmium Vermilion
- Cadmium Yellow Light
- Cadmium Yellow Medium
- Cerulean Blue
- Cobalt Violet
- Ivory Black
- Naples Yellow
- Permanent Blue
- Permanent Green Light
- Raw Sienna
- Titanium White
- Yellow Ochre

41. 2 raw sienna
1 cobalt violet
1 • cadmium vermilion

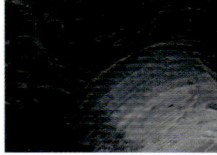

42. 1 ivory black
1 • permanent blue

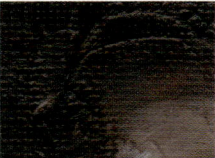

43. 1 burnt umber
1 • cadmium vermilion

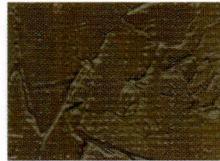

44. 2 raw sienna
1 permanent green light

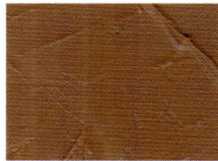

45. 3 Naples yellow
2 burnt sienna
1 • cadmium vermilion

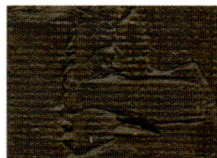

46. 1 cadmium yellow
medium
1 burnt umber
1 • cadmium orange

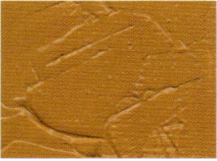

47. 1 cadmium yellow
medium
1 cobalt violet
1 • burnt sienna

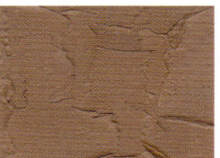

48. 4 white
1 burnt sienna
2 • burnt umber

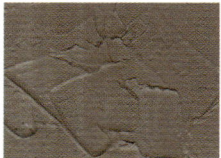

49. 3 white
1 burnt umber
2 • burnt sienna

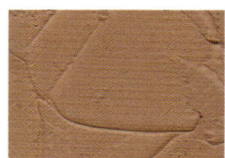

50. 6 white
1 burnt sienna
2 raw sienna

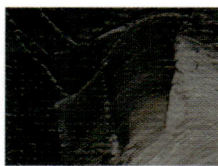

51. 1 burnt umber
1 permanent blue
1 • Naples yellow

52. 1 white
1 burnt umber
1 • burnt sienna

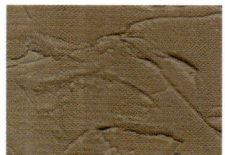

53. 2 white
1 burnt sienna
1 raw sienna
2 • permanent blue

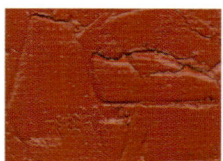

54. 1 cadmium vermilion
2 • ivory black

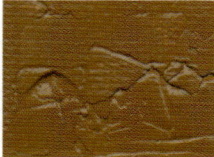

55. 4 cadmium orange
1 cerulean blue

56. 8 white
1 yellow ochre
1 • permanent blue

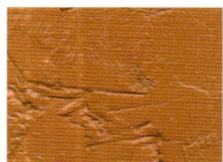

57. 2 cadmium yellow
medium
1 cadmium vermilion
1 • burnt umber

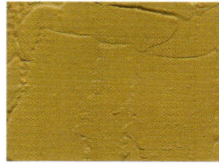

58. 2 cadmium yellow light
1 cobalt violet

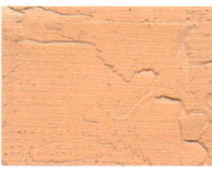

59. 6 white
7 Naples yellow
1 cadmium red light

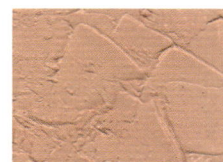

60. 3 white
1 burnt sienna

COLORS USED

- Alizarin Crimson
- Cadmium Orange
- Cadmium Red Light
- Cerulean Blue
- Cobalt Blue
- Cobalt Violet
- Ivory Black
- Naples Yellow
- Permanent Blue
- Titanium White
- Venetian Red
- Zinc Yellow

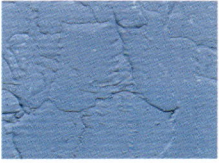

61. 6 white
1 cerulean blue
1 cobalt blue
1 cobalt violet

62. 8 white
1 cerulean blue

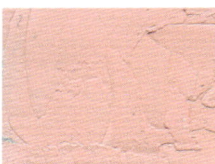

63. 3 white
2 • alizarin crimson
1 • zinc yellow

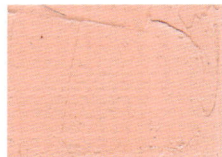

64. 3 white
1 • cadmium red light

65. 2 white
3 • Naples yellow

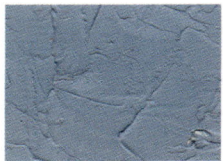

66. 2 white
1 cobalt blue
1 • cadmium red light

67. 2 white
2 • cobalt blue
1 • cadmium red light

68. 5 white
3 • cerulean blue
1 • cadmium red light
1 • cadmium orange

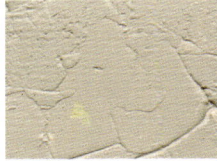

69. 2 white
1 • cadmium orange
1 • cerulean blue

70. 7 white
1 permanent blue
2 • Venetian red

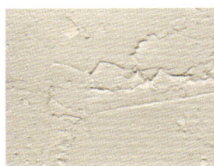

71. 2 white
1 • cadmium orange
1 • cobalt blue

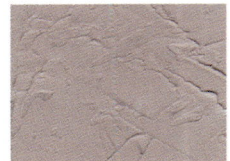

72. 2 white
2 • ivory black
1 • cadmium red light

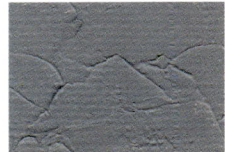

73. 1 #72
1 • cobalt blue
1 • ivory black

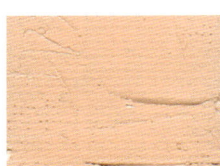

74. 2 white
1 • cadmium orange

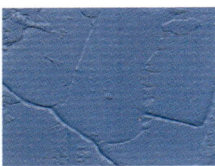

75. 3 white
4 • ivory black
3 • cobalt violet

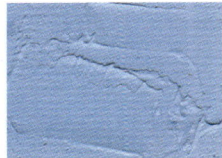

76. 4 white
1 cobalt blue
3 • cobalt violet

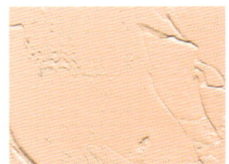

77. 6 white
1 • cadmium orange
1 • alizarin crimson

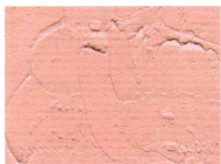

78. 2 white
1 • alizarin crimson
1 • cadmium orange

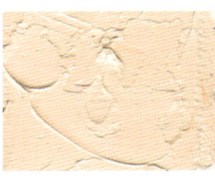

79. 4 white
1 • cadmium orange

80. 1 #75
1 • ivory black
1 • alizarin crimson

COLORS USED

- Burnt Umber
- Cadmium Orange
- Cadmium Red Light
- Cadmium Yellow Light
- Cadmium Yellow Medium
- Cerulean Blue
- Ivory Black
- Naples Yellow
- Permanent Blue
- Permanent Green Light
- Raw Sienna
- Thalo® Blue
- Titanium White
- Yellow Ochre
- Zinc Yellow

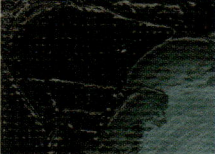

81. 2 burnt umber
1 Thalo® blue

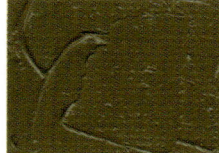

82. 3 yellow ochre
1 permanent blue

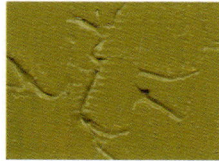

83. 1 cadmium yellow medium
3 • permanent blue

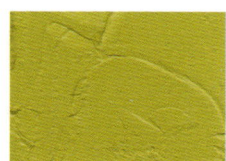

84. 1 cadmium yellow light
2 • permanent blue

85. 2 zinc yellow
1 • cerulean blue

86. 1 zinc yellow
2 • #85
2 • white

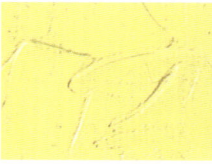

87. 1 #86
1 white

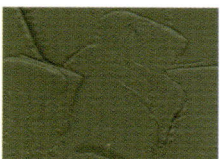

88. 2 cerulean blue
2 Naples yellow
1 cadmium orange

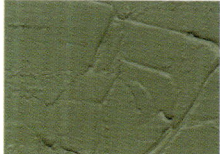

89. 1 #88
1 #90
1 • cerulean blue

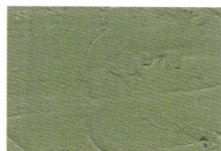

90. 1 #88
1 white
1 • cadmium yellow light

91. 1 white
3 • cadmium yellow light
1 • ivory black
1 • cerulean blue

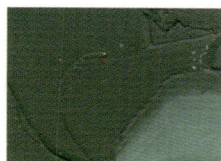

92. 3 cerulean blue
1 raw sienna
1 • Naples yellow

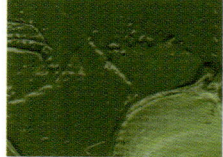

93. 1 permanent green light
2 • cadmium red light

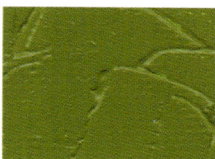

94. 3 cadmium yellow medium
1 • Thalo® blue

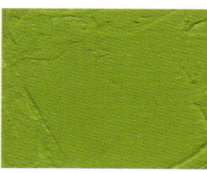

95. 3 cadmium yellow light
1 permanent green light
3 • white

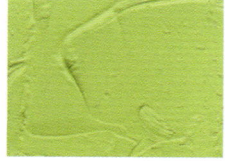

96. 1 #95
1 white

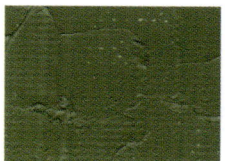

97. 3 cerulean blue
1 Naples yellow
1 cadmium orange

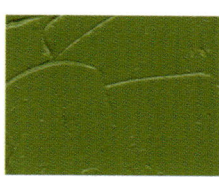

98. 1 cadmium yellow medium
1 • Thalo® blue
1 • cadmium red light

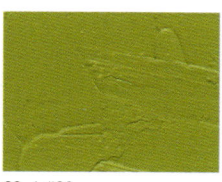

99. 1 #98
2 cadmium yellow light
1 • cadmium orange

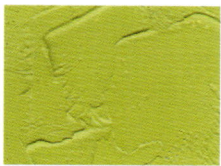

100. 2 zinc yellow
2 • permanent green light
2 • cadmium orange
1 white

COLORS USED

- Alizarin Crimson
- Burnt Umber
- Cadmium Orange
- Cadmium Red Light

- Cadmium Vermilion
- Cadmium Yellow Light
- Cerulean Blue
- Cobalt Blue

- Ivory Black
- Naples Yellow
- Permanent Blue

- Titanium White
- Yellow Ochre
- Zinc Yellow

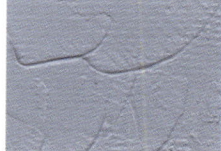

101. 5 white
1 • permanent blue
1 • cadmium red light

102. 3 white
1 • cadmium red light
4 • permanent blue

103. 1 #101
1 • permanent blue
2 • cadmium red light

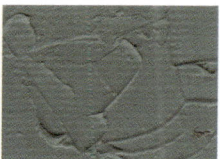

104. 2 white
2 • permanent blue
1 • yellow ochre

105. 2.5 white
1 • cadmium orange

106. 10 white
1 • permanent blue

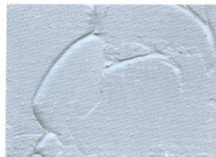

107. 2 white
3 • permanent blue

108. 6 white
1 • Naples yellow

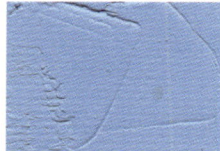

109. 4 white
1 • cobalt blue

110. 2 white
4 • cerulean blue

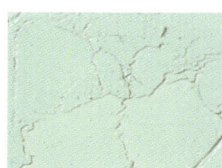

111. 2 white
1 • cerulean blue
1 • Naples yellow

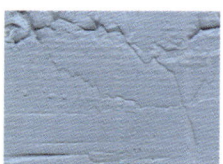

112. 2 #109
1 • ivory black

113. 3 white
2 • zinc yellow

114. 7 white
1 cerulean blue

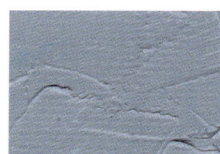

115. 3 white
2 cobalt blue
3 • ivory black

116. 1 #115
3 • cobalt blue
2 • ivory black

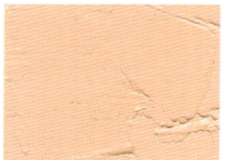

117. 2 white
1 • cadmium orange

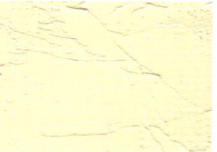

118. 1 white
1 • cadmium yellow light

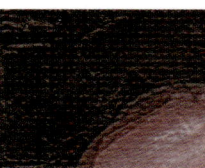

119. 1 burnt umber
1 alizarin crimson

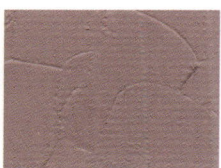

120. 1 white
2 • #119
2 • permanent blue

129

COLORS USED

- Alizarin Crimson
- Burnt Umber
- Cadmium Orange
- Cadmium Red Light
- Cadmium Yellow Light
- Cadmium Yellow Medium
- Cerulean Blue
- Cobalt Blue
- Ivory Black
- Naples Yellow
- Permanent Blue
- Raw Sienna
- Raw Umber
- Titanium White
- Venetian Red
- Zinc Yellow

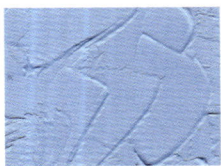

121. 2 white
1 • permanent blue

122. 1 white
1 #121

123. 4 white
1 permanent blue
2 • cerulean blue

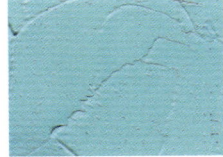

124. 2 white
1 cerulean blue

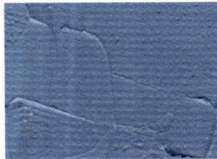

125. 3 white
3 cobalt blue
3 • ivory black

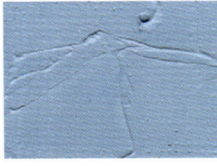

126. 1 #125
1 white
1 • cerulean blue

127. 3 white
3 • cerulean blue
2 • cobalt blue

128. 3 white
2 • cobalt blue
2 • ivory black
1 • raw umber

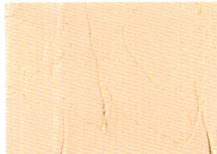

129. 4 white
2 • Naples yellow
1 • cadmium orange

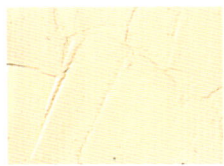

130. 3 white
2 • Naples yellow

131. 1.5 white
1 • cadmium yellow
light
1 • zinc yellow

132. 2 white
2 • cadmium yellow
med.

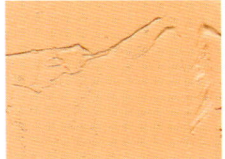

133. 2 #132
1 • cadmium red light

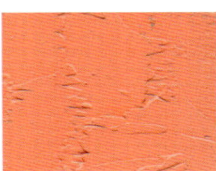

134. 2 white
3 • cadmium red light
2 • cadmium orange

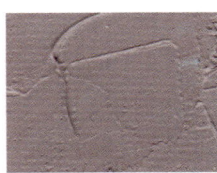

135. 2 white
4 • cobalt blue
1 • Venetian red

136. 2 white
2 • cerulean blue
1 • #133
1 • raw sienna

137. 4 white
3 • alizarin crimson

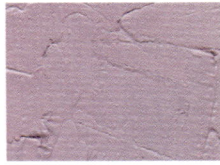

138. 1 #137
1 • permanent blue

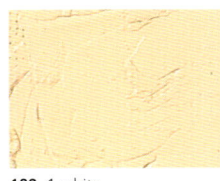

139. 1 white
1 • cadmium yellow
light
1 • #137

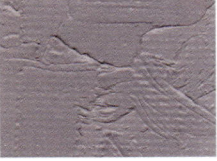

140. 1 #137
2 • permanent blue
1 • burnt umber

COLORS USED

- Alizarin Crimson
- Burnt Umber
- Cadmium Orange
- Cadmium Red Light
- Cadmium Yellow Light
- Cobalt Blue
- Ivory Black
- Naples Yellow
- Permanent Blue
- Raw Umber
- Thalo® Blue
- Titanium White
- Yellow Ochre

141. 1 white
1 • burnt umber
1 • alizarin crimson

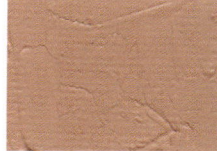

142. 2 white
1 Naples yellow
1 • alizarin crimson
1 • cadmium yellow light

143. 2 Naples yellow
2 • alizarin crimson
1 • burnt umber

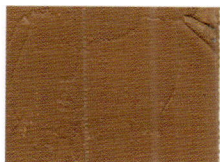

144. 1 #143
1 • alizarin crimson
1 • permanent blue

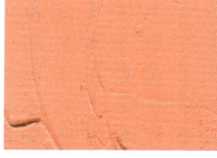

145. 3 white
4 • cadmium orange
1 • alizarin crimson
2 • cadmium red light

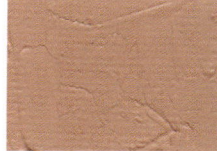

146. 2 #145
1 • permanent blue

147. 3 white
1 permanent blue
3 • alizarin crimson
1 • raw umber

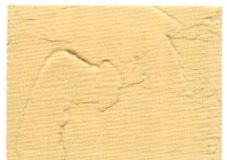

148. 2 white
1 Naples yellow

149. 2 white
2 • Thalo® blue
1 • ivory black

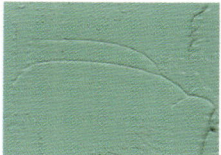

150. 1 #148
1 #149

151. 10 white
1 Thalo® blue
2 ivory black

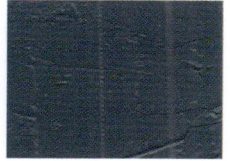

152. 1 #151
3 • ivory black

153. 3 #148
1 #149

154. 2 white
1 • raw umber
1 • cobalt blue

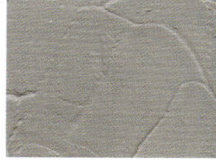

155. 2 white
2 • raw umber
1 • cobalt blue

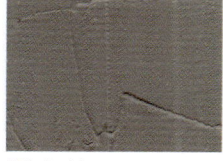

156. 2 white
4 • burnt umber
4 • permanent blue

157. 4 white
1 • cadmium orange
1 • cobalt blue

158. 2 white
1   #157

159. 10 white
1 burnt umber

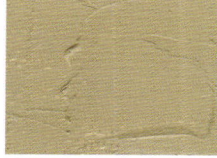

160. 8 white
1 yellow ochre
2 • permanent blue

LANDSCAPERECIPES

COLORS USED

- Alizarin Crimson
- Burnt Sienna
- Burnt Umber
- Cadmium Yellow Light
- Cadmium Yellow Medium
- Cerulean Blue
- Cobalt Blue
- Ivory Black
- Naples Yellow
- Permanent Blue
- Permanent Green Light
- Raw Sienna
- Raw Umber
- Thalo® Blue
- Titanium White
- Yellow Ochre

161. 8 cadmium yellow
medium
1 Thalo® blue
2 • alizarin crimson

162. 2 Naples yellow
1 #161

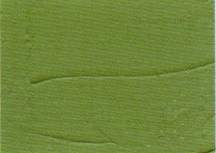

163. 1 #162
4 • cadmium yellow
light
4 • white

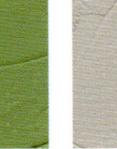

164. 2 white
2 • raw umber

165. 8 white
1 • yellow ochre
1 • cerulean blue

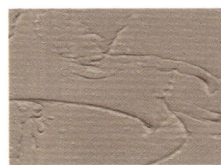

166. 2 white
3 • burnt umber

167. 1 white
1 raw umber
2 • ivory black

168. 8 white
1 • yellow ochre

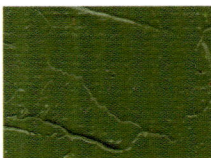

169. 2 permanent green
light
1 yellow ochre
2 • permanent blue

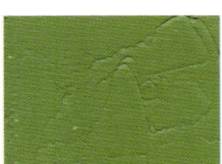

170. 1 Naples yellow
1 permanent green
light

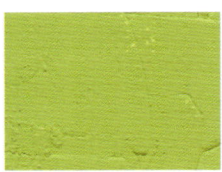

171. 1 white
1 cadmium yellow light
3 • permanent green
light

172. 2 white
4 burnt umber
3 • cobalt blue

173. 1 cobalt blue
2 Naples yellow

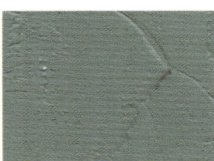

174. 2 cobalt blue
1 Naples yellow
1 white
3 • raw sienna

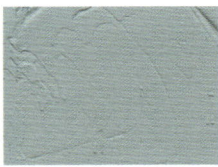

175. 1 white
2 • cobalt blue
2 • cerulean blue
1 • raw sienna

176. 1 raw sienna
1 cerulean blue
2 white

177. 2 #176
1 cerulean blue
3 • burnt sienna

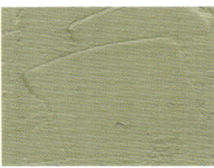

178. 1 #176
3 • cadmium yellow
light
1 white

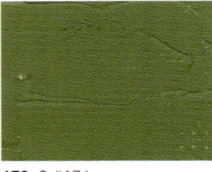

179. 2 #176
1 cadmium yellow light
3 • Naples yellow

180. 2 white
2 • raw sienna
1 • cerulean blue
2 • Naples yellow

COLORS USED

- Burnt Sienna
- Burnt Umber
- Cadmium Yellow Light
- Cadmium Yellow Medium
- Cerulean Blue
- Cobalt Blue
- Naples Yellow
- Permanent Blue
- Permanent Green Light
- Raw Sienna
- Thalo® Blue
- Titanium White
- Venetian Red
- Viridian Green
- Zinc Yellow

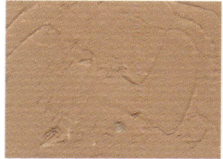

181. 2 white
1 raw sienna
1 • burnt sienna

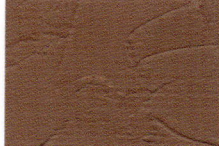

182. 2 #181
1 burnt umber
2 burnt sienna

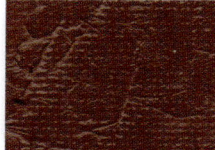

183. 6 burnt umber
1 Venetian red
4 • permanent blue

184. 3 white
3 • viridian green
1 • #188

185. 2 permanent blue
2 cadmium yellow medium
3 • cadmium yellow light

186. 2 permanent blue
1 cadmium yellow light
2 Naples yellow
1 cadmium yellow medium

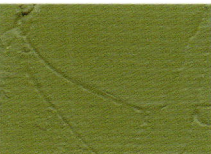

187. 1 #186
3 • cadmium yellow light
2 • white

188. 2 cerulean blue
1 cadmium yellow light
2 • white
1 • burnt sienna

189. 1 #188
2 Naples yellow

190. 1 zinc yellow
2 • #189
2 white
2 • cobalt blue

191. 2 permanent blue
2 cadmium yellow medium
3 • Thalo® blue
3 • burnt sienna

192. 2 #191
1 cadmium yellow medium

193. 2 #192
1 cadmium yellow light
1 • white

194. 1 permanent green light
2 • cadmium yellow med.

195. 1 #194
2 #196

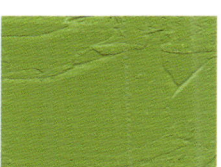

196. 1 permanent green light
2 cadmium yellow light
1 • white

197. 1.5 cadmium yellow light
2 permanent blue

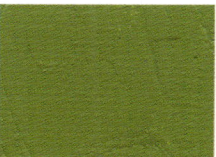

198. 1 #197
1 #199

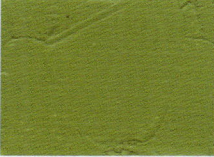

199. 1 #197
1 cadmium yellow light
1 • white

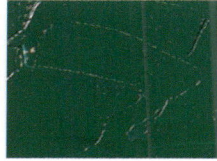

200. 1 cadmium yellow medium
1 Thalo® blue
1 white

COLORS USED

- Burnt Sienna
- Burnt Umber
- Cadmium Yellow Light
- Cadmium Yellow Medium
- Cerulean Blue
- Cobalt Blue
- Cobalt Violet
- Ivory Black
- Naples Yellow
- Permanent Blue
- Permanent Green Light
- Raw Umber
- Titanium White
- Viridian Green
- Yellow Ochre

201. 2 white
1 permanent green light

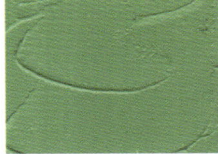

202. 3 viridian green
4 white
1 cadmium yellow medium

203. 2 permanent blue
1 cadmium yellow light
2 Naples yellow   1
cadmium yellow medium

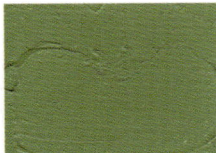

204. 1 #203
1 Naples yellow

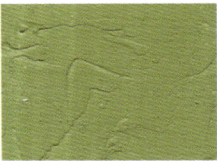

205. 1 #204
1 Naples yellow
2 • white

206. 2 white
2 • raw umber
1 • burnt umber

207. 3 white
1 raw umber

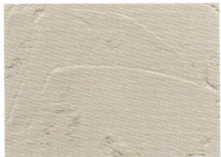

208. 2 white
1 • burnt umber

209. 3 white
1 • ivory black

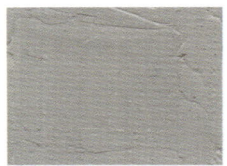

210. 3 white
3 • ivory black
1 • raw umber

211. 8 white
1 ivory black
1 • cerulean blue

212. 5 white
1 • yellow ochre

213. 1 white
4 • cobalt violet
2 • burnt umber
1 • cobalt blue

214. 1 burnt umber
1 cobalt blue
2 white
1 • burnt sienna

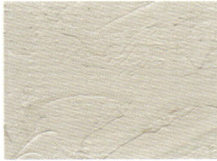

215. 2 white
2 • #214

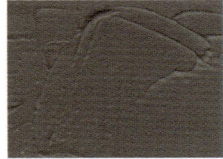

216. 2 white
1 burnt umber
1 permanent blue

217. 1 white
2 • burnt umber
1 • permanent blue

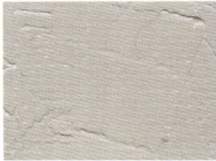

218. 4 white
1 #217
1 • cobalt violet

219. 1 white
1 burnt umber
1 burnt sienna
1 ivory black

220. 5 white
1 burnt sienna
1 burnt umber

COLORS USED

- Alizarin Crimson
- Burnt Sienna
- Burnt Umber
- Cadmium Yellow Light
- Cadmium Yellow Medium
- Cobalt Blue
- Cobalt Violet
- Ivory Black
- Naples Yellow
- Permanent Blue
- Permanent Green Light
- Raw Sienna
- Raw Umber
- Thalo® Blue
- Titanium White
- Viridian Green
- Yellow Ochre
- Zinc Yellow

221. 4 white
1 #220
2 • cobalt blue
1 • raw sienna

222. 2 ivory black
2 permanent blue
1 white

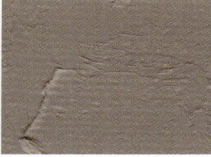

223. 1 white
4 • ivory black
1 • burnt sienna

224. 1 burnt umber
1 burnt sienna
1 white
3 • permanent blue

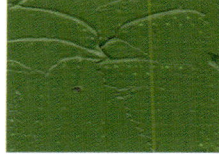

225. 2 permanent green light
2 • Thalo® blue
2 • cadmium yellow med.
2 • white

226. 2 viridian green
1 cadmium yellow light

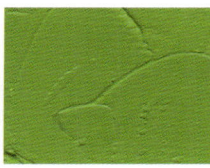

227. 1 #226
2 zinc yellow

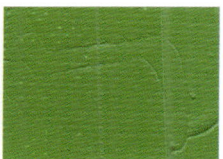

228. 2 #225
1 white
1 • zinc yellow

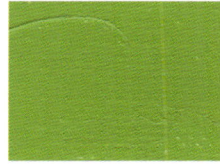

229. 1 #225
1 white
1 zinc yellow
2 cadmium yellow light

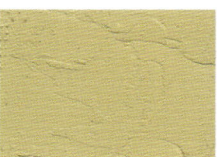

230. 1 white
1 Naples yellow
1 • permanent blue

231. 2 white
5 • raw umber
5 • Naples yellow
1 • burnt sienna

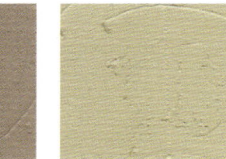

232. 2 white
2 • zinc yellow
1 • raw umber

233. 2 white
1 raw umber
1 permanent green light

234. 1 white
1 viridian green
1 raw sienna

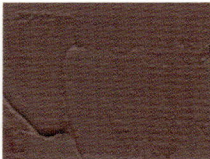

235. 1 #234
3 • alizarin crimson

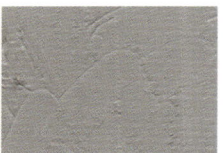

236. 1 white
3 • ivory black

237. 3 white
1 #136
1 • burnt sienna

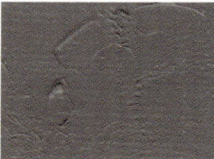

238. 2 white
1 ivory black
3 • permanent blue
2 • cobalt violet

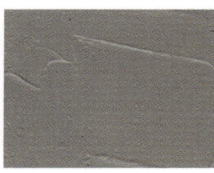

239. 3 #238
2 #237

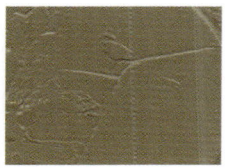

240. 6 white
4 yellow ochre
1 permanent blue

135

COLORS USED

- Alizarin Crimson
- Burnt Umber
- Cadmium Orange
- Cadmium Red Light
- Cadmium Vermilion
- Cadmium Yellow Light
- Cobalt Violet
- Ivory Black
- Naples Yellow
- Permanent Blue
- Thalo® Blue
- Thalo® Green (Blue shade)
- Thalo® Red Rose
- Titanium White
- Yellow Ochre
- Zinc Yellow

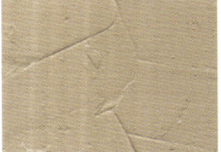

241. 2 white
3 • yellow ochre
1 • permanent blue

242. 2 burnt umber
1 Thalo® blue
4 white
2 Naples yellow

243. 2 burnt umber
2 Thalo® blue
5 Naples yellow
2 white

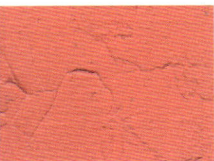

244. 4 white
1 cadmium vermilion

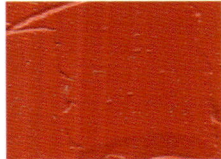

245. 1 yellow ochre
1 cadmium red light

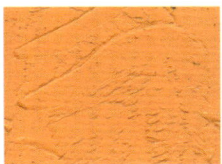

246. 2 Naples yellow
1 cadmium yellow light
2 • cadmium orange

247. 1 white
4 alizarin crimson
2 • cadmium red light

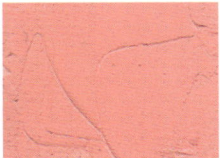

248. 1 white
2 • cadmium vermilion

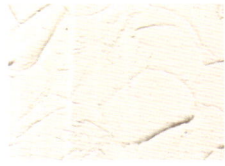

249. white

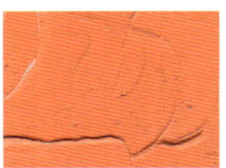

250. 6 Naples yellow
1 cadmium orange
1 white

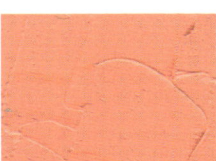

251. 2 white
4 • cadmium orange

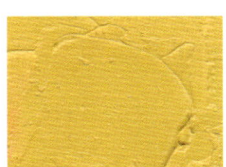

252. 3 zinc yellow
1 • cobalt violet

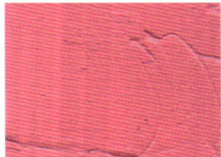

253. 3 white
1 Thalo® red rose

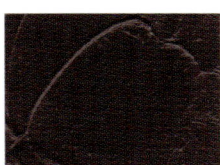

254. 3 ivory black
2 white
1 cobalt violet

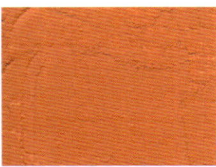

255. 1 cadmium yellow light
3 • alizarin crimson

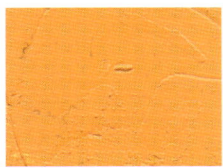

256. 2 zinc yellow
2 • cadmium orange

257. 2 permanent blue
1 burnt umber
4 white

258. ivory black

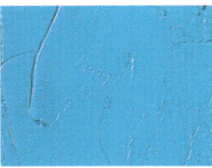

259. 1 white
2 • Thalo® blue

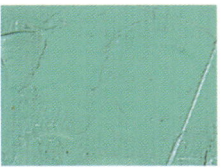

260. 2 white
2 • Thalo® green
(blue shade)

COLORS USED

- Alizarin Crimson
- Burnt Umber
- Cadmium Vermilion
- Cerulean Blue
- Cobalt Blue
- Cobalt Violet
- Ivory Black
- Magenta
- Permanent Blue
- Permanent Green Light
- Raw Umber
- Thalo® Red Rose
- Titanium White
- Viridian Green

261. 1 white
4 • permanent blue
1 • burnt umber
1 • alizarin crimson

262. 2 white
1 #261
1 • cerulean blue

263. 1 white
1 • raw umber
2 • cobalt blue

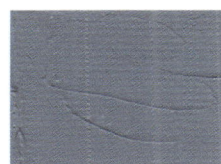

264. 1 white
2 cobalt blue
2 • cadmium vermilion

265. 1 #264
1 • ivory black

266. 1 white
2 • magenta

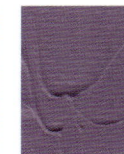

267. 6 cobalt violet
3 white
1 permanent blue

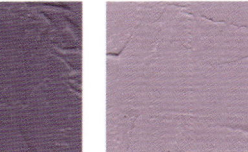

268. 2 white
1 cobalt violet
2 • permanent blue

269. 2 white
3 permanent blue
1 Thalo® red rose

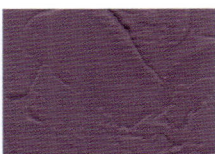

270. 5 cobalt violet
1 white
2 • permanent blue

271. 3 white
1 • cerulean blue

272. 8 white
1 cobalt violet

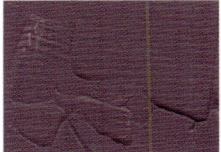

273. 3 cobalt violet
1 white
2 • burnt umber
1 • permanent blue

274. 1 #273
1 #272

275. 1 white
2 • cobalt violet

276. 10 white
1 burnt umber

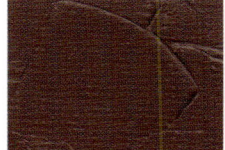

277. 2 white
1 burnt umber

278. 1 white
1 • viridian green
1 • raw umber

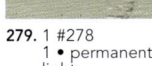

279. 1 #278
1 • permanent green light

280. 1 white
1 • cerulean blue
3 • ivory black

LANDSCAPE RECIPES

COLORS USED

- Alizarin Crimson
- Cadmium Orange
- Cadmium Red Light
- Cadmium Vermilion
- Cadmium Yellow Light
- Cadmium Yellow Medium
- Cobalt Violet
- Magenta
- Thalo® Red Rose
- Titanium White
- Zinc Yellow

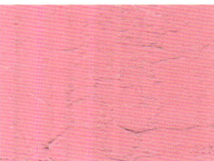

281. 1 white
4 • Thalo® red rose

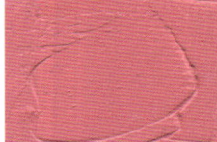

282. 1 #281
4 • alizarin crimson

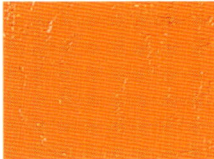

283. 2 zinc yellow
1 cadmium orange

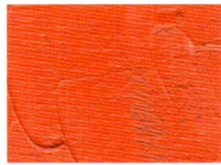

284. 2 white
1 cadmium red light

285. 2 cadmium yellow light
1 white

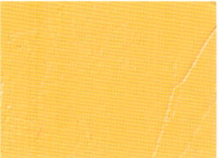

286. 2 cadmium yellow light
2 • cadmium orange
1 white

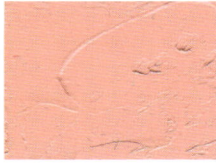

287. 1 white
1 • cadmium vermilion

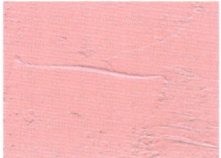

288. 1 white
2 • Thalo® red rose

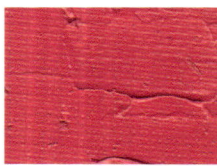

289. 4 Thalo® red rose
1 white

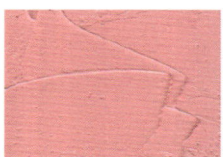

290. 1 white
3 • alizarin crimson

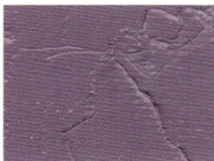

291. 2 magenta
1 white

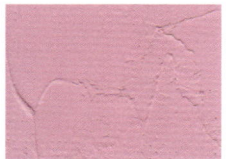

292. 1 white
2 • Thalo® red rose
2 • cobalt violet

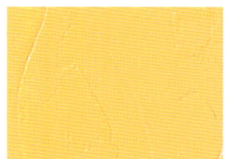

293. 5 white
1.5 cadmium yellow
med.
1 zinc yellow

294. 3 magenta
1 white

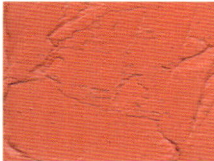

295. 1 white
1 cadmium vermilion

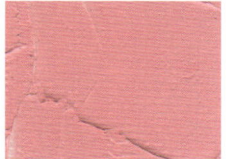

296. 20 white
1 alizarin crimson

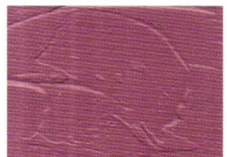

297. 8 white
8 Thalo® red rose
4 cobalt violet

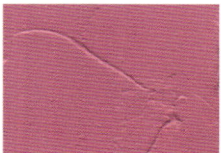

298. 8 white
8 Thalo® red rose
1 cobalt violet

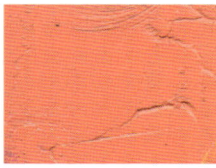

299. 7 white
1 cadmium red light

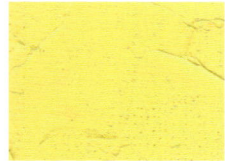

300. 1 white
1 zinc yellow

COLORS USED

- Alizarin Crimson
- Burnt Umber
- Cadmium Orange
- Cadmium Red Light
- Cadmium Vermilion

- Cadmium Yellow Light
- Cadmium Yellow Medium
- Cerulean Blue
- Ivory Black
- Naples Yellow

- Permanent Blue
- Permanent Green Light
- Raw Sienna
- Raw Umber
- Titanium White

- Viridian Green
- Yellow Ochre
- Zinc Yellow

301. 5 white
5 Naples yellow
3 cadmium yellow light

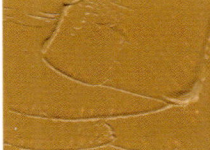

302. 1 cadmium yellow med.
1 • viridian green

303. 3 Naples yellow
1 • cadmium orange
1 • cerulean blue

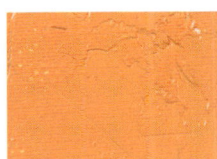

304. 6 Naples yellow
1 cadmium orange
1 white

305. 1 white
1 permanent blue
2 • alizarin crimson
2 • burnt umber

306. 1 #305
1 • alizarin crimson

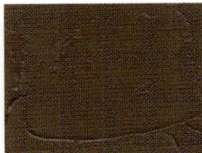

307. 1 cadmium orange
1 cerulean blue

308. 3 Naples yellow
1 cadmium orange
4 • cerulean blue

309. 5 white
3 yellow ochre
2 • permanent blue

310. 4 white
2 Naples yellow
1 cadmium yellow light

311. 1 white
2 • raw sienna
2 • zinc yellow

312. 1 white
2 • cadmium orange
3 • permanent green light

313. 1 white
3 cadmium orange
6 permanent green light

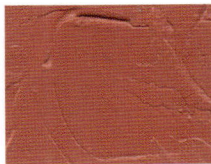

314. 1 white
3 cadmium vermilion
1 • ivory black

315. 2 cadmium vermilion
1 ivory black

316. 4 white
1 cadmium orange
3 permanent green light

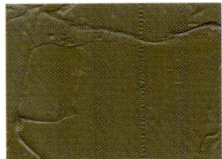

317. 1 cadmium orange
3 permanent green light
1 white

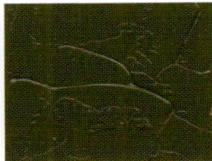

318. 3 permanent green light
2 • cadmium red light

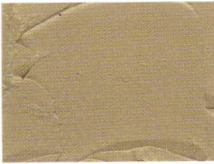

319. 2 white
1 yellow ochre
2 • cerulean blue

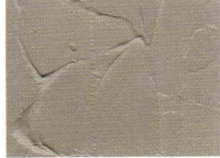

320. 8 white
1 raw umber
1 • permanent blue
1 • yellow ochre

COLORS USED

- Alizarin Crimson
- Burnt Umber
- Cerulean Blue
- Cobalt Violet
- Ivory Black
- Naples Yellow
- Permanent Blue
- Raw Sienna
- Raw Umber
- Thalo® Blue
- Thalo® Green (Blue shade)
- Thalo® Red Rose
- Titanium White

321. 1 white
1 • Thalo® green
(blue shade)

322. 2 white
1 ivory black
6 cerulean blue

323. 1 white
2 • Thalo® blue
1 raw sienna

324. 3 cerulean blue
1 white
2 • alizarin crimson

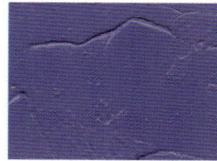

325. 2 white
3 permanent blue
2 • Thalo® red rose

326. 2 white
1 • Thalo® blue

327. 1 cerulean blue
1 permanent blue
1 white

328. 1 #327
1 • raw umber

329. 2 white
1 permanent blue
1 • burnt umber
1 • alizarin crimson

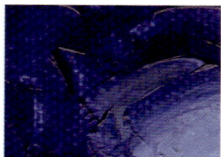

330. permanent blue (pure)

331. 1 permanent blue
1 white
2 • Thalo® red rose

332. 1 white
4 • cobalt violet
1 • permanent blue

333. 2 permanent blue
1 cerulean blue
1 white

334. 1 #333
1 • burnt umber
1 • alizarin crimson

335. 2 white
1 Naples yellow
2 • Thalo® blue
1 • burnt umber

COLORS USED

- Alizarin Crimson
- Burnt Sienna
- Burnt Umber
- Cadmium Orange
- Cadmium Yellow Medium
- Cerulean Blue
- Cobalt Violet
- Ivory Black
- Naples Yellow
- Permanent Blue
- Permanent Green Light
- Raw Sienna
- Titanium White
- Venetian Red

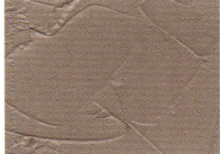

336. 6 white
1 burnt umber

337. 2 white
1 burnt umber
6 • cerulean blue

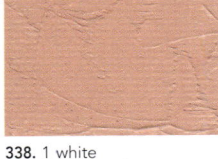

338. 1 white
2 • burnt sienna

339. 1 white
2 • cadmium orange
1 • cerulean blue

340. 3 white
1 raw sienna
1 • permanent blue

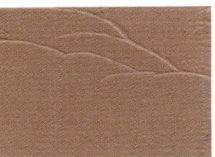

341. 1 #340
1 • burnt sienna
1 • permanent blue

342. 1 white
1 • cadmium orange
2 • Naples yellow

343. 1 white
3 • Naples yellow
1 • cobalt violet

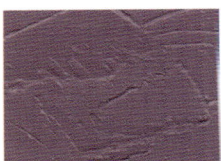

344. 3 white
1 alizarin crimson
1 permanent blue

345. 1 #344
2 white
2 • cadmium orange

346. 1 #344
2 • ivory black
2 • permanent blue

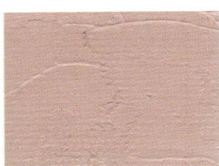

347. 3 white
1 #345
1 • cadmium orange

348. 2 cadmium yellow medium
2 cobalt violet
2 • permanent blue

349. 1 Venetian red
5 Naples yellow
1 permanent green light

350. 2 cerulean blue
1 cadmium orange

141

COLORS USED

- Burnt Sienna
- Cadmium Orange
- Cadmium Red Light
- Cadmium Vermilion
- Cadmium Yellow Light
- Cadmium Yellow Medium
- Naples Yellow
- Permanent Blue
- Raw Sienna
- Thalo® Green (Blue shade)
- Thalo® Red Rose
- Titanium White
- Viridian Green

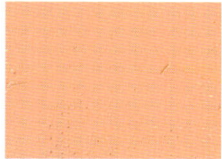

351. 16 white
1 • cadmium orange
1 Naples yellow

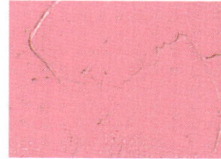

352. 1 white
3 • Thalo® red rose

353. 2 white
1 • cadmium vermilion

354. 3 white
1 • burnt sienna

355. 2 white
1 • cadmium yellow
med.

356. 2 white
2 • Naples yellow
1 • viridian green

357. 2 white
1 • Thalo® green
(blue shade)
3 • Naples yellow

358. 2 white
4 • Naples yellow
2 • viridian green

359. 1 #355
2 white
1 • permanent blue

360. 2 white
2 • cadmium yellow
med.
2 • Naples yellow

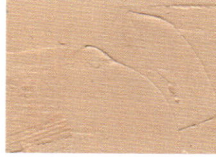

361. 2 white
2 • raw sienna

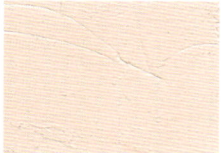

362. 4 white
1 • raw sienna

363. 1 white
2 Naples yellow
1 • cadmium red light

364. 1 #363
1 Naples yellow
1 • cadmium yellow
med.

365. 1 white
2 • Naples yellow
3 • cadmium yellow
light

COLORS USED

- Burnt Sienna
- Burnt Umber
- Cadmium Orange
- Ivory Black

- Naples Yellow
- Permanent Blue
- Raw Sienna
- Raw Umber

- Titanium White
- Venetian Red
- Yellow Ochre

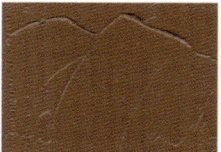

366. 2 white
1 raw umber
1 cadmium orange

367. 1 #366
1 white

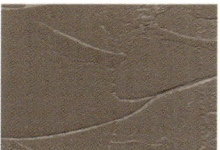

368. 3 white
1 raw umber

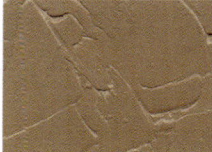

369. 2 #368
1 yellow ochre
1 white

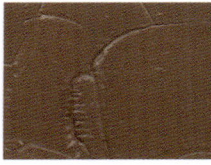

370. 2 white
1 burnt umber
1 • cadmium orange

371. 6 white
1 raw umber

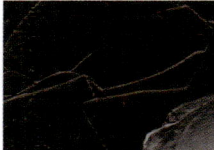

372. 2 ivory black
1 permanent blue

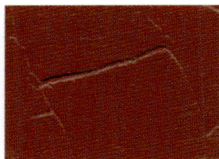

373. 2 burnt sienna
1 Venetian red
4 raw sienna

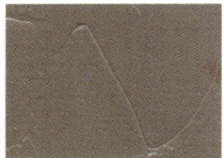

374. 3 white
1 burnt umber
1 • cadmium orange
4 • permanent blue

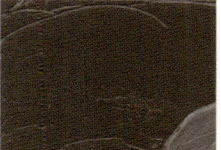

375. 2 ivory black
1 burnt umber
1 white

376. 1 #373
2 Naples yellow
1 white

377. 7 white
2 burnt umber
1 raw sienna

378. 3 white
1 burnt sienna
1 burnt umber

379. 1 #378
2 white
2 • permanent blue

380. 2 white
2 yellow ochre
1 • burnt umber

COLORS USED

- Alizarin Crimson
- Burnt Umber
- Cadmium Orange
- Cadmium Red Light
- Cadmium Yellow Medium
- Cobalt Blue
- Cobalt Violet
- Naples Yellow
- Permanent Blue
- Thalo® Blue
- Thalo® Green (Blue shade)
- Thalo® Red Rose
- Titanium White
- Viridian Green
- Yellow Ochre
- Zinc Yellow

381. 2 white
1 • Thalo® green (blue shade)

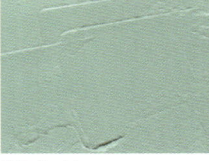

382. 2 white
1 • Thalo® green (blue shade)
3 • Naples yellow
1 • burnt umber

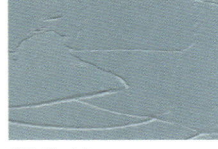

383. 2 white
1 • Thalo® blue
1 • burnt umber

384. 8 white
1 • Thalo® green (blue shade)

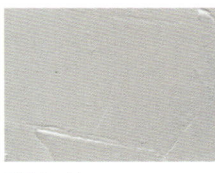

385. 3 white
1 • burnt umber
2 • permanent blue

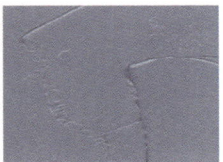

386. 1 white
2 • cobalt blue
1 • cadmium red light

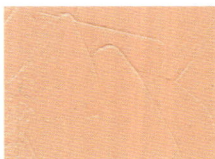

387. 12 white
1 cadmium orange
1 • Thalo® red rose

388. 4 white
1 • cadmium orange
1 • zinc yellow

389. 6 white
2 yellow ochre
1 permanent blue

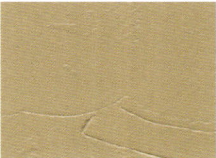

390. 2 white
1 #389
1 yellow ochre

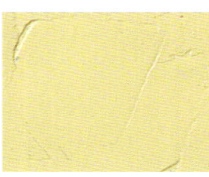

391. 8 white
1 cadmium yellow medium
1 • viridian green

392. 2 white
1 cadmium yellow medium
1 • cobalt violet

393. 1 white
4 Thalo® red rose
3 cobalt violet
1 permanent blue

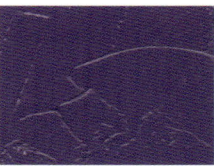

394. 1 white
6 cobalt violet
1 permanent blue

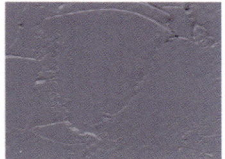

395. 2 white
1 permanent blue
3 • alizarin crimson
2 • burnt umber

COLORS USED

- Alizarin Crimson
- Burnt Sienna
- Burnt Umber
- Cadmium Orange
- Cadmium Red Light
- Cadmium Yellow Light
- Cerulean Blue
- Cobalt Violet
- Naples Yellow
- Permanent Blue
- Thalo® Red Rose
- Titanium White
- Viridian Green
- Yellow Ochre
- Zinc Yellow

356. 1 burnt umber
1 alizarin crimson
2 white

397. 2 #396
2 yellow ochre
1 white

398. 2 #396
1 permanent blue

399. 2 white
1 permanent blue
2 • cadmium red light

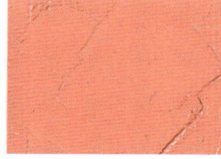

400. 2 white
1 • cadmium red light
2 • Naples yellow

401. 2 white
1 • cadmium red light
1 • permanent blue

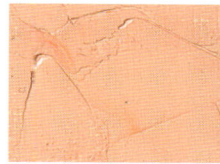

402. 1 white
1 • cadmium orange

403. 2 zinc yellow
4 cobalt violet

404. 8 cerulean blue
12 Naples yellow
1 cadmium orange

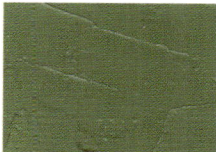

405. 2 Naples yellow
1 • cerulean blue
1 • cadmium orange

406. 5 white
1 cadmium yellow light
2 • cerulean blue

407. 4 white
6 cadmium yellow light
2 cerulean blue
1 viridian green

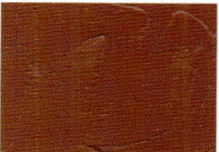

408. 2 Naples yellow
2 burnt sienna
1 • cadmium red light

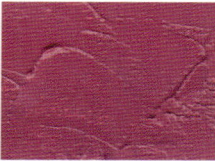

409. 4 white
6 Thalo® red rose
4 cobalt violet

410. 1 white
5 Thalo® red rose
4 cobalt violet

145

COLORS USED

- Alizarin Crimson
- Cadmium Orange
- Cadmium Red Light
- Cadmium Vermilion
- Cadmium Yellow Light
- Cobalt Violet
- Ivory Black
- Magenta
- Raw Sienna
- Thalo® Red Rose
- Titanium White
- Venetian Red
- Zinc Yellow

411. 4 white
5 cobalt violet
1 • Thalo® red rose

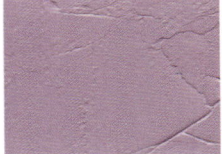

412. 15 white
1 magenta

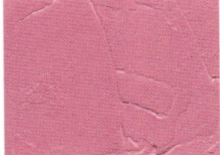

413. 5 white
1 Thalo® red rose
3 • cobalt violet

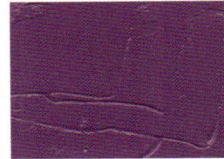

414. 4 cobalt violet
1 white
1 • Thalo® red rose

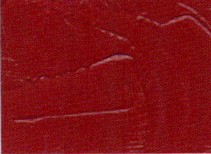

415. 1 white
3 alizarin crimson

416. 3 white
1 Venetian red

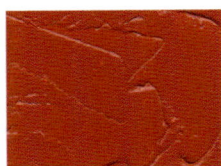

417. 1 cadmium red light
1 raw sienna

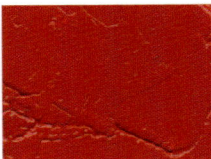

418. 2 cadmium vermilion
1 alizarin crimson

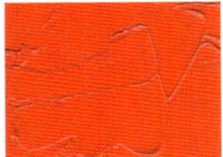

419. 2 white
4 cadmium red light

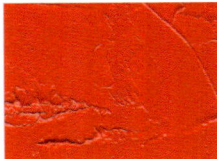

420. 2 cadmium red light
1 cadmium vermilion

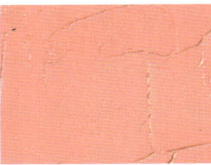

421. 2 white
1 • cadmium red light
1 • cadmium orange

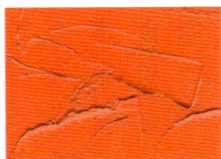

422. 2 white
4 cadmium red light
6 zinc yellow

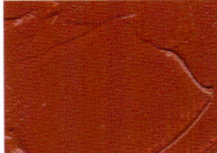

423. 7 alizarin crimson
9 cadmium yellow light
1 white

424. 3 cadmium red light
1 ivory black

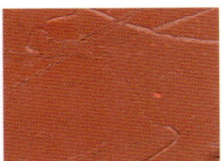

425. 1 cadmium red light
1 white
2 • ivory black

COLORS USED

- Alizarin Crimson
- Burnt Umber
- Cadmium Orange
- Cadmium Red Light
- Cadmium Yellow Light
- Cadmium Yellow Medium
- Naples Yellow
- Permanent Blue
- Thalo® Red Rose
- Titanium White
- Yellow Ochre
- Zinc Yellow

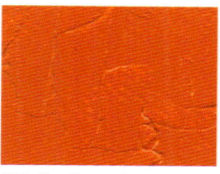

426. 2 yellow ochre
1 cadmium red light
3 cadmium yellow light

427. 2 cadmium orange
2 • alizarin crimson

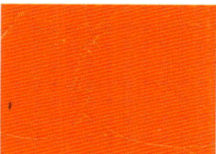

428. 1 cadmium orange
2 • cadmium yellow light

429. 4 white
3 cadmium orange

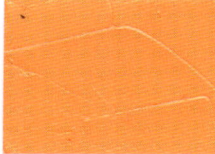

430. 10 white
2 cadmium orange
1 zinc yellow

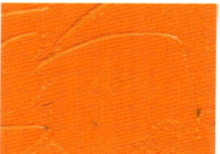

431. 5 cadmium yellow light
1 cadmium orange

432. 1 cadmium orange
1 Naples yellow

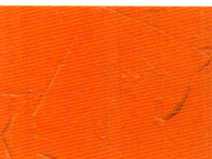

433. 1 cadmium orange
1 Naples yellow
1 cadmium yellow light

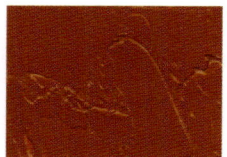

434. 1 cadmium orange
2 • burnt umber

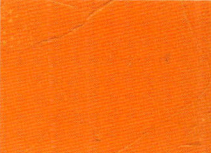

435. 9 zinc yellow
2 cadmium orange

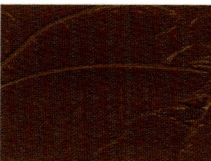

436. 3 cadmium orange
1 permanent blue

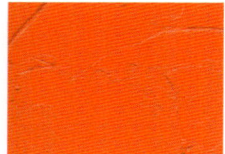

437. 8 white
2 cadmium red light
14 zinc yellow

438. 1 #437
2 • cadmium red light

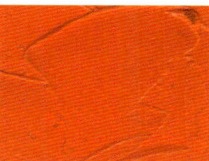

439. 2 cadmium orange
2 • Thalo® red rose

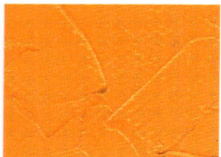

440. 2 cadmium yellow medium
1 • cadmium orange

LANDSCAPE RECIPES

COLORS USED

- Alizarin Crimson
- Burnt Sienna
- Burnt Umber
- Cadmium Orange
- Cadmium Red Light
- Cadmium Vermilion
- Cadmium Yellow Light
- Cerulean Blue
- Cobalt Violet
- Ivory Black
- Naples Yellow
- Permanent Blue
- Titanium White
- Venetian Red
- Zinc Yellow

441. 2 zinc yellow
1 cerulean blue
1 cadmium orange

442. 8 cerulean blue
12 Naples yellow
1 cadmium orange

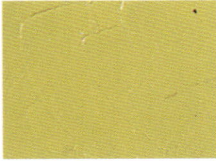

443. 1 white
1 cadmium yellow light
1 • ivory black

444. 3 white
1 permanent blue
5 cobalt violet

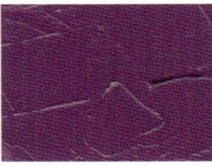

445. 6 cobalt violet
1 white

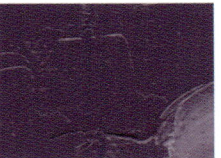

446. 1 burnt umber
1 alizarin crimson
4 permanent blue
3 white

447. 2 white
1 ivory black
1 • cadmium vermilion

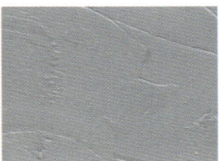

448. 1 white
3 • permanent blue
1 • burnt umber

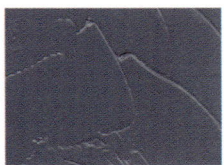

449. 5 permanent blue
3 white
1 burnt umber

450. 1 #447
2 • cerulean blue

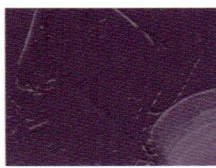

451. 2 white
2 permanent blue
1 alizarin crimson

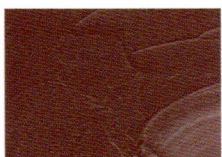

452. 1 white
1 Venetian red
3 permanent blue

453. 1 cadmium orange
2 cerulean blue

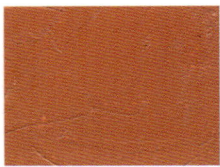

454. 2 white
12 Naples yellow
1 cadmium red light
2 burnt sienna

455. 1 burnt umber
1 alizarin crimson
2 permanent blue
6 white

COLORS USED

- Alizarin Crimson
- Cadmium Orange
- Cadmium Red Light
- Cadmium Yellow Light
- Cadmium Yellow Medium
- Cerulean Blue
- Naples Yellow
- Titanium White
- Zinc Yellow

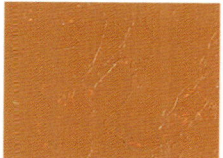

456. 3 Naples yellow
1 • cadmium orange
1 • cerulean blue

457. 4 white
4 Naples yellow
1 cadmium yellow light

458. 4 white
1 Naples yellow
2 • cadmium yellow light

459. 6 white
1 Naples yellow
1 • cadmium yellow light

460. 4 white
3 Naples yellow
1 • cerulean blue

461. 1 white
1 cadmium yellow light

462. 1 white
1 zinc yellow

463. 5 white
1 cadmium yellow medium

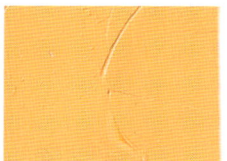

464. 3 white
1 cadmium yellow medium

465. 7 zinc yellow
2 cadmium orange

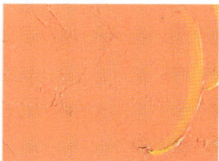

466. 4 white
1.5 cadmium orange

467. 1.5 white
2 cadmium yellow medium

468. 3 white
2 cadmium red light
4 zinc yellow

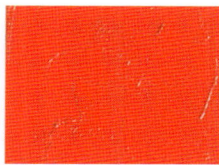

469. 2 #468
1 cadmium red light

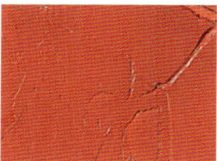

470. 11 white
3 alizarin crimson
5 cadmium yellow light

149

LANDSCAPERECIPES

COLORS USED

- Alizarin Crimson
- Burnt Umber
- Cadmium Orange
- Cadmium Red Light
- Cadmium Yellow Light
- Cadmium Yellow Medium
- Cadmium Vermilion
- Cerulean Blue
- Cobalt Violet
- Ivory Black
- Naples Yellow
- Permanent Blue
- Permanent Green Light
- Titanium White
- Yellow Ochre

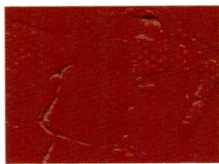

471. 2 alizarin crimson
1 cadmium red light

472. 5 cadmium orange
1 cerulean blue

473. 3 white
1 ivory black
2 cadmium vermilion
2 • cadmium orange

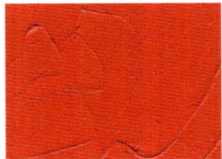

474. 1 white
1.5 cadmium vermilion
1 • cadmium red light

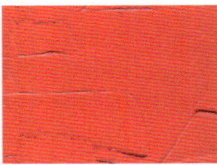

475. 3 white
1 cadmium vermilion
1 • cadmium red light

476. 2 cadmium red light
2 permanent green light
1 burnt umber

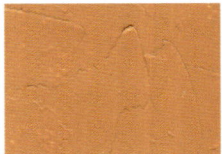

477. 1 Naples yellow
2 • #476
2 • white

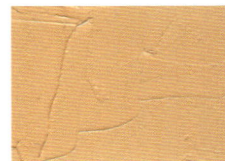

478. 1 #477
1.5 white

479. 1 cadmium yellow medium
3 cobalt violet

480. 2 ivory black
1 alizarin crimson
3 Naples yellow

481. 4 white
2 ivory black
1 cerulean blue

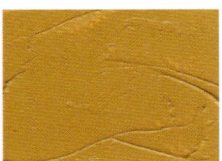

482. 2 cadmium yellow light
1 • ivory black

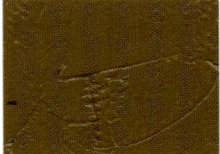

483. 4 cadmium yellow light
1 ivory black

484. 4 white
1 cadmium orange
3 permanent green light

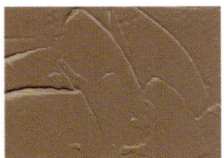

485. 6 white
3 yellow ochre
1 permanent blue

COLORS USED

- Alizarin Crimson
- Burnt Umber
- Cadmium Yellow Light
- Cerulean Blue
- Ivory Black
- Naples Yellow
- Permanent Blue
- Thalo® Blue
- Thalo® Red Rose
- Titanium White
- Viridian Green
- Zinc Yellow

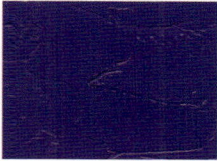

436. 1 white
3 permanent blue
1 • ivory black
1 • alizarin crimson

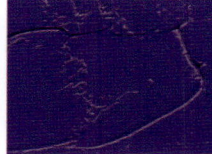

487. 1 white
4 permanent blue
2 Thalo® red rose

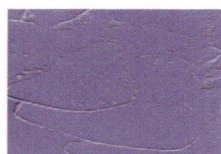

488. 2 white
1 #487

489. 1 white
2 Thalo® red rose
1 permanent blue

490. 1 cerulean blue
1 permanent blue

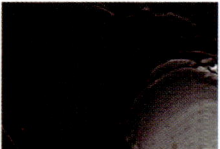

491. 2 cerulean blue
1 ivory black

492. 2 white
1 permanent blue
1 • burnt umber

493. 1 #492
1 white

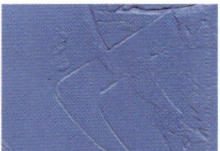

494. 1 cerulean blue
1 permanent blue
2 white

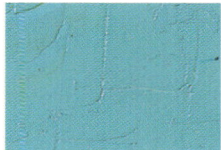

495. 1 white
1 • Thalo® blue
2 • Naples yellow

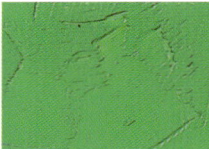

496. 2 #495
1 cadmium yellow light

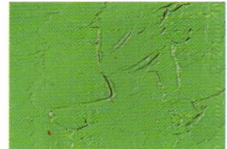

497. 1 white
1 cadmium yellow light
1 viridian green

498. 1 #497
2 white

499. 1 white
2 • viridian green

500. 1 #499
2 white
1 • zinc yellow

151

COLORS USED

- Alizarin Crimson
- Cadmium Red Light
- Cadmium Yellow Light
- Cadmium Yellow Medium
- Cerulean Blue
- Ivory Black
- Naples Yellow
- Titanium White
- Viridian Green
- Venetian Red
- Zinc Yellow

501. 1 white
3 • Naples yellow

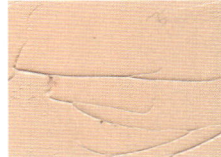

502. 5 #501
1 • Venetian red

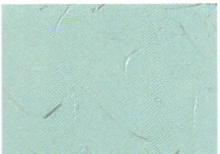

503. 1 white
1 #502
2 • cerulean blue

504. 1 white
3 #503
1 • cadmium red light
1 • ivory black

505. 2 white
1 • cadmium yellow
light

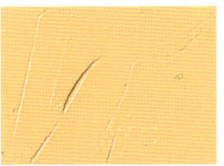

506. 1 #505
2 Naples yellow

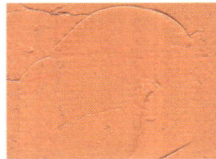

507. 1 #506
1 • alizarin crimson

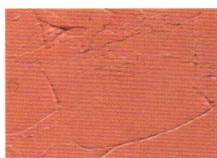

508. 1 #507
1 • alizarin crimson

509. 2 white
3 • cerulean blue
1 • viridian green

510. 1 white
4 • viridian green
2 • cadmium red light

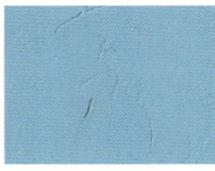

511. 1 white
3 • cerulean blue

512. 2 white
1 #511
1 • cadmium yellow
med.

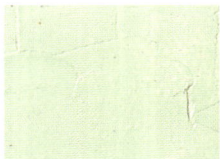

513. 1 white
1 #512
1 • zinc yellow

514. 2 white
1 cadmium yellow
medium

515. 1 #514
3 • cadmium red light
1 • alizarin crimson

COLORS USED

- Alizarin Crimson
- Burnt Sienna
- Burnt Umber
- Cadmium Orange
- Cadmium Yellow Light
- Cadmium Yellow Medium
- Naples Yellow
- Titanium White
- Yellow Ochre
- Zinc Yellow

516. 1 cadmium yellow light
2 • white

517. 1 zinc yellow
2 • white

518. 2 white
1 zinc yellow
1 • cadmium orange

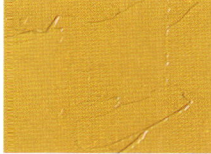

519. 2 cadmium yellow light
1 • burnt umber

520. 3 zinc yellow
1 • burnt umber

521. 2 cadmium yellow
medium
1 • burnt umber

522. 5 cadmium yellow
medium
1 • alizarin crimson

523. 2 cadmium yellow light
1 Naples yellow
1 white

524. 2 cadmium yellow light
1 • burnt sienna

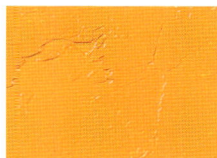

525. 2 cadmium yellow light
1 • cadmium orange

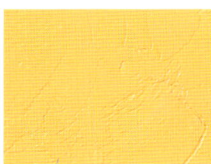

526. 2 white
1 #525

527. 1 #523
1 #525

528. 4 white
1 Naples yellow

529. 5 white
1 yellow ochre

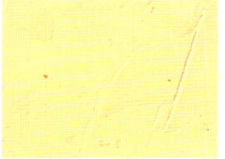

530. 14 white
1 cadmium yellow
medium
1 zinc yellow

LEGEND   Find the color or object you want to paint and its corresponding recipe number, and then turn to the Color Mixing sections (pages 12-70) for mixing ratios.

Colors are indexed by recipe number unless "page" is noted. Recipe numbers are identical in both the Oil & Acrylic and Watercolor sections. Watercolor-only recipes appear in italics. Oil & Acrylic-only recipes appear in bold.

LEGEND

○ Whiter: More white or water than color.

◐ Lighter: Lighten color a bit with white or water.

● Deeper: Deepen with darkest color in mix and use less water for watercolor.

LEGEND	Find the color or object you want to paint and its corresponding recipe number, and then turn to the Color Mixing sections (pages 12-70) for mixing ratios.

Colors are indexed by recipe number unless "page" is noted. Recipe numbers are identical in both the Oil & Acrylic and Watercolor sections. Watercolor-only recipes appear in italics. Oil & Acrylic-only recipes appear in bold.

LEGEND Find the color or object you want to paint and its corresponding recipe number, and then turn to the Color Mixing sections (pages 12-70) for mixing ratios.

Colors are indexed by recipe number unless "page" is noted. Recipe numbers are identical in both the Oil & Acrylic and Watercolor sections. Watercolor-only recipes appear in italics. Oil & Acrylic-only recipes appear in bold.

LEGEND

◯ Whiter: More white or water than color.

◔ Lighter: Lighten color a bit with white or water.

⬤ Deeper: Deepen with darkest color in mix and use less water for watercolor.

| LEGEND | Find the color or object you want to paint and its corresponding recipe number, and then turn to the Color Mixing sections (pages 12-70) for mixing ratios. |

Colors are indexed by recipe number unless "page" is noted. Recipe numbers are identical in both the Oil & Acrylic and Watercolor sections. Watercolor-only recipes appear in italics. Oil & Acrylic-only recipes appear in bold.

LEGEND

◯ Whiter: More white or water than color.

◔ Lighter: Lighten color a bit with white or water.

⬤ Deeper: Deepen with darkest color in mix and use less water for watercolor.

| **LEGEND** | Find the color or object you want to paint and its corresponding recipe number, and then turn to the Color Mixing sections (pages 12-70) for mixing ratios. |

Colors are indexed by recipe number unless "page" is noted. Recipe numbers are identical in both the Oil & Acrylic and Watercolor sections. Watercolor-only recipes appear in italics. Oil & Acrylic-only recipes appear in bold.

INDEX ENTRIES FOR THE PORTRAITS SECTION ARE LISTED BY PAGE NUMBERS.

LEGEND Find the color or object you want to paint and its corresponding recipe number, and then turn to the Color Mixing sections (pages 124-153) for mixing ratios.

Sky Color 106
Horizon Haze Color 64
Tan Granite Mountain
Mtn Base Color 340
Mtn Light Color 342 & 343
Mtn Shadow Color 341
Mtn Base Haze 343
Purplish Desert Mountain
Mtn Base Color 344
Mtn Light Color 345 & 347
Mtn Shadow Color 346
Mtn Base Haze 347
Ruddy, Dark Mountain
Mtn Base Color 396
Mtn Light Color 397
Mtn Highlight Color 400
Mtn Highlight Accent
Color 402
Mtn Shadow Color 398
Mtn Shadow Accent
Color 399
Mtn Base Haze 401
Mushroom
Gray 160, 241
Tan 340

N

Neutral Colors (See Beige, Ivory,
Black, Gray, and White)

O

Ocean (General)
Blue 333
Gray 334
Green 335
Green, Light 357
Ochre Earth, Reddish 50
Ochre Earth, Yellow 29
Orange Colors
Bright 428
Brownish 426
Burnt 427
Cadmium, Softened 432
Candy 424
Dull 436
Light 433
Muted 434
Pale 351
Peel 435
Reddish 438
Rich 437
Strong 439
Tinted 430
Yellow 431, 440
Orchid (Tints of purple for softening
light shadow colors)
Gray 411
Mist 412
Pink 413
Purple 414, 489

Rose 288
Tint 272

P

Pumpkin Yellow 304
Purples
Bright 410
Mauve Bluish 444
Reddish 445
Putty
Dark 104
Light 232

Q

Queen Anne's Lace 130

R

Red Colors (Can be used as is or to
gray green mixtures)
Bright Deep 420
Brownish 417
Cool 415
Dark 418
Dull 416
Medium Light 419
Pale Peach 421
Realgar Red 420, 42
Shaded 424
Toned 425
Violet 298
Warm 422
Reed Yellow Green 443
Rocks
Agate Rock
Black 42, 480
Brown 44, 46, 55
Gray 172
Green 242
Red 247
Yellow 246
Alabaster Rock Pink 248
Cinder Rocks
Gray 216
Red 19
Clay Rocks
Gray
Main Rock Color 207
Secondary Color 207 + 216
Light Color 208
Dark Color 216
Tan
Main Rock Color 7
Secondary Color 33
Light Color 6
Dark Color 39
Coal Rocks
Main Rock Color 42
Secondary Color 51
Chalk Rock
Blue 121

Pink 64
White 108
Conglomerate Rocks
(General, as colors
vary greatly)
Main Rock Color 39
Coral
Pink 248
Red 245, 54
Rose 244
Flint Rock Gray 217, 236
Garnet Rock
Brown 15
Green 228
Red 247
Granite Rocks
Gray
Main Rock Color 36
Secondary Color
36 + 35
Light Color 208
Dark Color 35
Tan
Main Rock Color 39
Secondary Color 7 + 38
Light Color 7
Dark Color 38
White
Main Rock Color 157
Secondary Color
155 + 157
Light Color 158
Dark Color 155
Graphite Rock Gray 216
Jasper Rock
Green 203, 163, 243
Pink 134
Red 16, 54, 245
Lava Rocks
Basalt
Reddish Rock Color 16,
235
Black Rock Color 42,
51, 216
Brownish Color 52, 220
Limestone Rocks
Light Gray
Main Rock Color 218
Secondary Color 215
Light Color 209
Dark Color 211
Tan
Main Rock Color 68
Secondary Color 72
Light Color 71
Dark Color 49
White
Main Rock Color 158
Secondary Color 157
Light Color 108

LEGEND Find the color or object you want to paint and its corresponding recipe number, and then turn to the Color Mixing sections (pages 124-153) for mixing ratios.

Main Color 111
Highlight Color 108
Shadow Color 112
Early Morning Warm Sky
Zenith 123
Secondary Color 124
Horizon Color 121, 123, 124
Early Morning Warm
Sky Clouds
Main Color 77
Highlight Color 108
Shadow Color 101
Morning Blue Sky
Zenith 106
Secondary Color 110
Horizon Color 111
Morning Blue Sky Clouds
Main Color 74
Highlight Color 108
Shadow Color 68
Afternoon Cumulus Sky
Zenith 125
Secondary Color 126
Horizon Color 127
Afternoon Cumulus Sky
Clouds
Main Color 129
Highlight Color 130
Shadow Color 128
Afternoon Warm Sky
Zenith 106
Secondary Color 114
Horizon Color 108, 111
Afternoon Warm Sky Clouds
Main Color 118
Highlight Color 108
Shadow Color 110, 117
Evening Sky, Clouds &
Light Rays
Zenith 114, 115
Secondary Color 114
Horizon Clouds 116
Evening Sky Clouds
Main Color 114
Highlight Color 108
Shadow Color 116
Light Rays Blended 108
Rising Sun, Reddish Clouds
Sky Zenith 511
Middle Sky 512
Lower Sky 513
Cloud Glow 515
Cloud Highlight 514
Cloud Shadow 510
Sunset Sky – Low Sun
Zenith 136
Sun Center 105
Sun Perimeter 131

Primary Glow 132
Secondary Glow 133
Sunset Sky – Low Sun Clouds
Bottom Glow 134
Middle Color 134, 135
Top Shadow Color 135
Sunset Sky – Dramatic Sky
Horizon Sun Zenith 124
Secondary Color 113+124
Horizon Color 113
Sunset Sky – Dramatic
Clouds
Main Color 146
Highlight Color 133 & 145
Shadow Color 147
Sunset Sky – Warm Orange
Zenith 143
Secondary Glow Color 142
Sun/Horizon Color 131
Sunset Sky – Warm Orange
Clouds
Main Color 141
Highlight Color 65
Shadow Color 144
Sunset Sky, Purplish
Zenith 138
Secondary Color 137
Sun/Horizon Color 139
Sunset Clouds, Purplish
Main Color 141
Highlight Color 129
Shadow Color 140
Sunset, Reddish Sky
Zenith 113 & 17
Secondary Color 5 & 117
Horizon Color 113 & 17
Sunset, Reddish Clouds
Main Color 17
Highlight Color 5, 113
Shadow Color 109, 17
Moonlight Sky
Moon 148
Moon Inner Glow 150
Moon Outer Glow 149
Outer Sky 151
Moonlight Sky Clouds
Main Color 152
Highlight Color 148 & 153
Stormy Gray Sky
Main Gray Color 154
Clouds Dark Color 155
Clouds Accent Dark 156
Light Glow Through Clouds
157 & 158
Mood Skies
Misty Sun
Sun 118
Glow 105

Sky 107
Grayish
Sun 5
Glow 117
Sky 68
Soft Greens
Sun 65
Glow 74
Outer Sky 111
Hot Yellow Orange
Sun 5
Glow 59
Sky 50
Low Setting Sun
Sun 505
Inner Glow 506
Outer Glow 507
Clouds 510
Pastel Dawn
Horizon 501
Middle Sky 502
Zenith 503
Clouds 504
Pink with Low Light
Horizon 65
Middle sky 117
Zenith 60
Sky Blues (General)
Afternoon Warm 105
Evening Dusk 75, 76, 115
Midday Bright 121, 122
Morning 110
Spring Fresh 114
Twilight Blue 110
Smog
Gray 389
Tannish 390
Smoke
Blackish Gray 288
Blue-Gray 280
Brownish Gray 223
Whitish 209, 212
Snow
Warm Light Source
Main Color 139
Shadow Color 125, 126
Highlight Color 130
Cool Light Source
Main Color 271
Shadow Color 75, 76
Highlight Color 108
Sunset Bright Snow
Main Color 130, 212
Shadow Color 106, 115
Highlight Color 249
Soils
Clay 36
Common Soils
Main Color 366

LEGEND

+ Mix listed recipe colors together for one resultant color
& Use all listed color mixes individually on the scene
, Multiple recipes separated by a comma indicates a variation of selections

Secondary Color 367
Northern Gray
  Main Color 368
  Secondary Color 369
Tropical Red
  Main Color 373
  Secondary Color 376
Mud
  Beige 368, 371
  Brown 370
  Gray 374
Soot Black 372
Steel Gray 447, 448
Stones & Pebbles (General)
  Brown 370
  Gray 218, 368, 371, 374
  Tan 206, 208, 369
  White 108, 168, 212, 249
Straw
  Brown 456
  Golden 457
  Green 460
  Old 459
  Yellow 458
Sunlight Source Colors
  (Colors for Time-of-Day Color
  Control)
  Early Evening
    Alizarin Crimson 470
    Cadmium Red Light 468
  Early Morning Cool 462
  Late Afternoon Warm
    Cadmium Orange 466
    Cadmium Yellow Medium
    464
  Mid Afternoon Warm
    Cadmium Yellow Light 461
    Cadmium Yellow Medium
    463
  Mid Morning Warm
    Cadmium Yellow Light 461
  Sunset Warm
    Alizarin Crimson 471
    Cadmium Orange 465
    Cadmium Red Light 469
    Cadmium Yellow Medium
    467

T

Teakwood 472
Terra Cotta 373
Thistle
  Gray 395
  Purple 394
Tomato
  Red 474
  Light Red 475
Trees
  Broadleaf Tree Underbark
  Colors
    Gray Green Underbark 278,
    279

Coniferous Tree Underbark
  Colors
    Reddish Brown 19, 23
Acacia Tree (Catclaw)
  Foliage Colors
    Dark 88
    Medium 89
    Light 90
  Trunk Colors
    Bark (Scaly)
    Basic 52
    Secondary 52 + 56
    Dark 26
    Light 34
Alder Tree (Red)
  Foliage Colors
    Dark 188
    Medium 189
    Light 190
  Trunk Colors
    Bark (Blotchy Scales)
    Basic 209
    Secondary 210
    Dark 211
    Light 212
Almond Tree
  Foliage Colors
    Dark 185
    Medium 186
    Light 187
  Trunk Colors
    Bark (Vertical furrows with
    horizontal cracks)
    Basic 213
    Secondary 213 + 215
    Dark 214
    Light 215
Apple Tree
  Foliage Colors
    Dark 185
    Medium 186
    Light 187
  Trunk Colors
    Bark (Scaly Older)
    Basic 210
    Secondary 210 + 216
    Dark 216
    Light 215
Apple Fruit
  Green 404, 405, 406, 407
  Red 471
  Yellow 365
  Apple Blossom (Pink) 137
Apricot Tree
  Foliage Colors
    Dark 169
    Medium 170
    Light 171
  Trunk Colors
    Bark (Ridged, Fissured)
    Basic 223

Secondary 222 + 223
  Dark 222
  Light 221
Ash Tree (White)
  Foliage Colors
    Dark 161
    Medium 162
    Light 163
  Trunk Colors
    Bark (Elongated diamond
    ridged pattern)
    Basic 166
    Secondary 166 & 167
    Dark 167
    Light 168
Aspen (Quaking)
  Foliage Colors
    Dark 161
    Medium 162
    Light 163
  Trunk Colors
    Bark (Smooth with black
    horizontal wart/scar marks)
    Basic 166
    Secondary 166 & 167
    Dark 167
    Light 168
Beech Tree (American)
  Foliage Colors
    Dark 194
    Medium 195
    Light 196
  Trunk Colors
    Bark (Smooth)
    Basic 155
    Secondary 155 + 156
    Dark 156
    Light 154
Birch Tree (Paper)
  Foliage Colors
    Dark 185
    Medium 186
    Light 187
  Trunk Colors
    Bark (Peeling in strips)
    Basic 168
    Secondary 166 + 168
    Dark 166
    Light 165
Blue Spruce Tree
  Foliage Colors
    Dark 173
    Medium 174
    Light 163
  Trunk Colors
    Bark (Scaly Dark Gray)
    Basic 38
    Secondary 38 + 26
    Dark 26
    Light 56

LEGEND Find the color or object you want to paint and its corresponding recipe number, and then turn to the Color Mixing sections (pages 124-153) for mixing ratios.

Buckeye Tree (Ohio)
  Foliage Colors
    Dark 226
    Medium 227
    Light 229
  Trunk Colors
  Bark (Fissured & Scaly)
    Basic 207
    Secondary 207 + 216
    Dark 216
    Light 208
Cedar Tree
  Foliage Colors
    Dark 81
    Medium 98
    Light 100
  Trunk Colors
  Bark (Ridged & Furrowed)
    Basic 44
    Secondary 44 + 26
    Dark 26
    Light 40
Cherry Tree (Black)
  Foliage Colors
    Dark 225
    Medium 226
    Light 227
  Trunk Colors
  Bark (Young, reddish
    brown with lenticels,
    Old,scaly lenticels
    brown/black)
    Basic 224
    Dark 222
    Light 223
  Blossom Pink 287
Chestnut Tree (American)
  Foliage Colors
    Dark 161
    Medium 162
    Light 163
  Trunk Colors
  Bark (Flat scaly ridges)
    Basic 217
    Secondary 217 + 216
    Dark 216
    Light 215
Cottonwood Tree
  Foliage Colors
    Dark 225
    Medium 228
    Light 229
  Trunk Colors
  Bark (Ridged, furrowed)
    Basic 217
    Secondary 217 + 218
    Dark 216
    Light 218
Cypress Tree
  Foliage Colors

Dark 193
    Medium 189
    Light 190
  Trunk Colors
  Bark (Fibrous/scaly)
    Basic 208
    Secondary 208 + 217
    Dark 217
    Light 215
Dogwood Tree (Flowering)
  Foliage Colors
    Dark 194
    Medium 195
    Light 190
  Trunk Colors
  Bark (Scaly bumps)
    Basic 220
    Secondary 220 + 219
    Dark 219
    Light 221
  Blossom, Pink 64
    White 108, 130
Elm Tree (American)
  Foliage Colors
    Dark 226
    Medium 227
    Light 229
  Trunk Colors
  Bark (Vertical ridges)
    Basic 210
    Secondary 210 + 216
    Dark 216
    Light 209
Eucalyptus Tree
  Foliage Colors (General)
    Dark 177
    Medium 176
    Light 179
    Bronze Green 233, 234
    Reddish Leaf Color 235
  Trunk Colors
  Bark (Peeling strips)
    Basic 180 & 184
    Secondary 180 + 181
    Dark 182 & 183
    Light Tan 181
Fir Tree (Douglas)
  Foliage Colors
    Dark 194
    Medium 195
    Light 196
  Trunk Colors
  Bark (Thick, furrowed)
    Basic 220
    Secondary 220 + 216
    Dark 216
    Light 208
Hemlock Tree
  Foliage Colors
    Dark 186

Medium 187
    Light 199
  Trunk Colors
  Bark (Deep furrowe scales)
    Basic 213
    Secondary 213 + 219
    Dark 219
    Light 218
Hickory Tree (Black)
  Foliage Colors
    Dark 188
    Medium 202
    Light 201
  Trunk Colors
  Bark (Deep furrows)
    Basic 211
    Secondary 211 + 222
    Dark 222
    Light Spots 209
Holly Tree (American)
  Foliage Colors
    Dark 225
    Medium 226
    Light 229
  Trunk Colors
  Bark (Thin, Gray, variety of
  bumps)
    Basic 211
    Secondary 211 + 216
    Dark 216
    Light 210
    Holly Berry 471
Juniper Tree (Western)
  Foliage Colors
    Dark 191
    Medium 192
    Light 189
  Trunk Colors
  Bark (Long Interlacing
  Ridges)
    Basic 23
    Secondary 23 + 39
    Dark 26
    Light 39
Joshua Tree
  Foliage Colors
    Dark 185
    Medium 187
    Light 190
  Trunk Colors
  Bark (Long Plates)
    Basic 213
    Secondary 213 + 208
    Dark 216
    Light 208
Laurel Tree (Sassafras)
  Foliage Colors
    Dark 226
    Medium 227
    Light 229

Trunk Colors
Bark (Bumpy, furrows)
Basic 52
Secondary 52 + 68
Dark 51
Light 68
Magnolia Tree
Foliage Colors
Dark 185
Medium 186
Light 187
Trunk Colors
Bark (Scaly)
Basic 213
Secondary 213 + 217
Dark 219
Light 217
Magnolia Flower White
212, 249
Maple Tree (Sugar)
Foliage Colors
Dark 226
Medium 227
Light 229
Flaming Red 416, 417
Flaming Yellow 461,
464, 467
Trunk Colors
Bark (Mature, scaly, slightly
furrowed)
Basic 236
Secondary 239
Dark 238
Light 237
Mesquite Tree (Velvet)
Foliage Colors
Dark 186
Medium 187
Light 190
Trunk Colors
Bark (Shaggy)
Basic 236
Secondary 236 + 218
Dark 216
Light 218
Mulberry Tree
Foliage Colors
Dark 185
Medium 186
Light 187
Trunk Colors
Bark (Mature, scaly)
Basic 38
Secondary 27 + 38
Dark 27
Light 36
Mulberry Fruit 393
Oak Tree (Black)
Foliage Colors
Dark 97
Medium 98

Light 99 & 100
Trunk Colors
Bark (Ridged, furrowed)
Basic 38
Secondary 27 + 38
Dark 27
Light 36
Brown Bark 44
White Bark 71
Oakwood Gray 164
Olive Tree
Foliage Colors
Dark 88
Medium 89
Light 90 & 91
Trunk Colors
Bark (Scaly)
Basic 206
Secondary 206 + 207
Dark 207
Light 208
Olive Fruit
Brownish 452
Drab 453
Greenish Dark 97 & 98
Palm Tree (Date)
Foliage Colors
Dark 93
Medium 94,
Light 95 & 96
Trunk Colors
Bark (rough from cut
dead fronds)
Basic 21
Secondary 21 + 27
Dark 27
Light 40
Palm Date Brown
Dark 452
Light 454
Palm Tree (Queen/King)
Foliage Colors
Dark 93
Medium 94,
Light 95 & 96
Trunk Colors
Bark (smooth, ringed at bot-
tom, rough from cut dead
fronds at top)
Basic 208
Secondary 208 + 217
Dark 217
Light 215
Peach Tree
Foliage Colors
Dark 225
Medium 226
Light 227
Trunk Colors
Bark (Scaly, Young has
Lenticels resembling lips)

Basic 237
Secondary 237 + 216
Dark 216
Light 215
Blossom Pink 288, 352
Cream 388
Pink 387
Pecan Tree
Foliage Colors
Dark 226
Medium 227
Light 229
Trunk Colors
Bark (Scaly Ridges)
Basic 207
Secondary 207 + 214
Dark 214
Light 208
Pinecone Brown 28, 30, 373
Pine Tree (Coniferous/
General)
Foliage Colors
Dark 81
Medium 98
Light 100
Trunk Colors
Bark (Scaly to plated)
Branches 398 & 26
Secondary 31
Dark 26
Light 40
Pine Tree (White)
Foliage Colors
Dark 169
Medium 170
Light 171
Trunk Colors
Bark (Wide verticals with
deep furrows)
Basic 162
Secondary 162 + 161
Dark 163
Light 161
Basic Pine Greens
Dark 81
Light 100
Middle 98
Plum Tree (Purple)
Foliage Colors
Dark 194
Medium 195
Light 196
Trunk Colors
Bark (Smooth to scaly with
some lentices)
Basic 224
Secondary Inner Bark
223 + 235
Dark 222
Light 223

OIL/ACRYLIC CONVERSION CHART

COLORS USED

OIL COLOR NAME	ACRYLIC COLOR NAME	EQUIVALENT MIXTURE
Alizarin crimson	Alizarin crimson	
Burnt sienna	Burnt sienna	
Burnt umber	Burnt umber	
Cadmium orange	Cadmium orange	
Cadmium red light	Cadmium red light	
Cadmium vermilion	Vermilion hue (or use mixture)	1 part Indo orange-red + 1 speck Naphthol crimson
Cadmium yellow light	Cadmium yellow light	
Cadmium yellow medium	Cadmium yellow medium	
Cerulean blue hue	not available (use mixture)	1 cerulean blue + 1 speck phthalo blue
Chrome oxide green	Chromium oxide green	
Cobalt blue	Cobalt blue	
Ivory black	Ivory black	
Naples yellow hue	Naples yellow hue permanent (or use mixture)	4 parts yellow ochre/oxide + 1 part white + 2 specks cadmium orange
Phthalo red	Naphthol crimson or phthalo crimson	
Raw sienna	Raw sienna	
Raw umber	Raw umber	
Titanium white	Titanium white	
Ultramarine blue	Ultramarine blue	
Venetian red	Venetian red or red oxide	
Viridian green	Viridian green or viridian hue permanent	
Yellow ochre	Yellow ochre or yellow oxide	
Zinc yellow	Yellow light hansa	

ABOUT THE AUTHOR

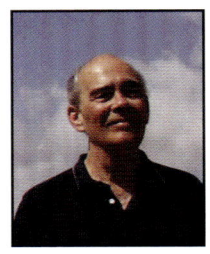

William F. Powell was an internationally recognized artist and one of America's foremost colorists. A native of Huntington, West Virginia, Bill studied at the Art Student's Career School in New York; Harrow Technical College in Harrow, England; and the Louvre Free School of Art in Paris, France.

He was professionally involved in fine art, commercial art, and technical illustrations for more than 45 years. His experience as an art instructor included oil, watercolor, acrylic, colored pencil, and pastel—with subjects ranging from landscapes to portraits and wildlife. He also authored a number of art instruction books, including several popular Walter Foster titles. As a renowned master of color, Bill conducted numerous "Color Mixing and Theory" workshops in various cities throughout the U.S. His expertise in color theory also led him to author and illustrate several articles and an educational series of 11 articles entitled "Color in Perspective" for a national art magazine. Additionally, he performed as an art consultant for national space programs and for several artist's paint manufacturers. His work also included the creation of background sets for films, model making, animated cartoons, and animated films for computer mockup programs. He also produced instructional painting, color mixing, and drawing art videos. William Powell passed away in 2019.

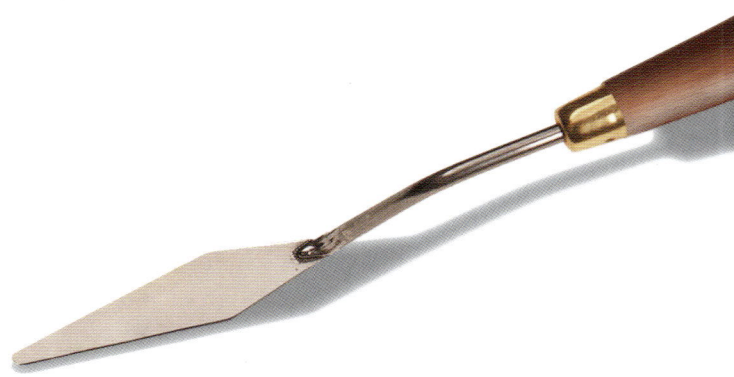